Writing Centers and Writing Across the Curriculum Programs

Recent Titles in
Contributions to the Study of Education

Writing Centers and Writing Across the Curriculum Programs

Building Interdisciplinary Partnerships

Edited by
Robert W. Barnett and
Jacob S Blumner

Contributions to the Study of Education, Number 73

Greenwood Press
Westport, Connecticut • London

Library of Congress Cataloging-in-Publication Data

Writing centers and writing across the curriculum programs : building
  interdisciplinary partnerships / edited by Robert W. Barnett and
  Jacob S Blumner.
      p.   cm.—(Contributions to the study of education, ISSN
  0196–707X ; no. 73)
    Includes bibliographical references and index.
    ISBN 0–313–30699–0 (alk. paper)
    1. English language—Rhetoric—Study and teaching.
  2. Interdisciplinary approach in education.   3. Writing centers.
  I. Barnett, Robert W., 1964– . II. Blumner, Jacob S, 1968–
  III. Series.
  PE1404.W69446   1999
  808′.042′0711—dc21   98–8236

British Library Cataloguing in Publication Data is available.

Library of Congress Catalog Card Number: 98–8236
ISBN: 0–313–30699–0
ISSN: 0196–707X

First published in 1999

Greenwood Press, 88 Post Road West, Westport, CT 06881
An imprint of Greenwood Publishing Group, Inc.

Printed in the United States of America

The paper used in this book complies with the
Permanent Paper Standard issued by the National
Information Standards Organization (Z39.48–1984).

10 9 8 7 6 5 4 3 2

In order to keep this title in print and available to the academic community, this edition
was produced using digital reprint technology in a relatively short print run. This would
not have been attainable using traditional methods. Although the cover has been changed
from its original appearance, the text remains the same and all materials and methods
used still conform to the highest book-making standards.

Contents

Acknowledgments

Many friends and colleagues have helped us through the process of creating this book. We wish thank those people who have contributed in many ways from the book's inception to its completion. Stephen N. Tchudi of the University of Nevada, Reno provided valuable advice on shaping our ideas for this text, and he guided us through the process of writing and marketing them. We would like to thank Stephen for the invaluable guidance he has provided.

Sharon Thomas of Michigan State University, Eric Hobson of Eastern Illinois University, Christina Murphy of University of Memphis, and Joe Law of Wright State University in Dayton, Ohio lent us their voices of experience in moving this project toward publication

Rebecca Ardwin of Greenwood Publishing Group, our production editor, answered our endless technical questions and gave us much needed support throughout the revision of this book.

We would especially like to thank our friend and colleague Janice Worth of the University of Michigan–Flint for proofreading the manuscript. She, along with Philip Greenfield, Monica Beck, Danny Rendleman, and Sidney and Helene Blumner, offered much encouragement and moral support throughout the past two years.

The publication of this book was made possible in part by a research initiative grant from the Office of Research at the University of Michigan–Flint.

Introduction

In 1994 Joan Mullin and Ray Wallace edited *Intersections: Theory-Practice in the Writing Center*, a collection of essays exploring Writing Center theory and practice. The volume presents powerful discussions central to Writing Center development. Since that time, more Writing Centers, voluntarily and involuntarily, have involved themselves in Writing Across the Curriculum (WAC) Programs. Mark Waldo's 1993 article "The Last Best Place for Writing Across the Curriculum: The Writing Center" in *WPA: Writing Program Administration* and Stephen North's 1984 article "The Idea of a Writing Center" in *College English* directly address the issue of the Writing Center/WAC relations, and both articles have spurred much debate. More recently, Michael Pemberton, in his *Writing Center Journal* article "Rethinking the WAC/Writing Center Connection," argues for a reexamination of the theoretical foundations that connect WAC Programs and Writing Centers, and cautions that they may not be the same (1995). This collection, *Writing Centers and Writing Across the Curriculum Programs: Building Interdisciplinary Partnerships*, addresses many issues raised in all three aforementioned texts by presenting a theory-into-practice examination of the evolving institutional relationships between Writing Centers and WAC Programs. Although the authors write about the concept of Writing Center/WAC partnerships from widely varying perspectives, they all begin from the same set of assumptions: (1) that Writing Centers have moved away from their previously marginalized status toward a more centralized institutional position with the potential to effect curricular change; and (2) that any discussion of Writing Center/WAC partnerships must include issues of student, faculty, and administrative involvement.

By exploring the possibilities and pitfalls of Writing Center/WAC partnerships that embrace disciplines across the curriculum, these essays open a unique dialogue that reveals the similarities and differences between the driving forces behind Writing Center theory and WAC theory and the institutional practices that unite or separate the two programs. More specifically, the aim of this collection is to acknowledge the inherent importance of Writing Centers and WAC Programs and to illustrate their impact on student writing at designated institutions at the secondary and post-secondary levels.

All of the articles speak to each other by engaging in research and sharing practices that accurately portray the true diversity of Writing Center and WAC Programs, as well as the compatibility of their missions with larger institutional missions, faculty involvement, and administrative support. What follows, then, is a variety of model approaches for Writing Center and WAC personnel to consider as they create or expand their own institutional programs.

Robert Barnett and Lois Rosen open the collection with an argument for the creation of a campus-wide "writing environment" through a partnership between the Writing Center and WAC Program. Using the University of Michigan–Flint as a site-specific example, they contend that the "housing" metaphor used in discussing where to situate a Writing Center/WAC partnership has become inadequate and that we must use the strengths of both Writing Centers and WAC Programs to create an all-inclusive writing environment across campus. Fundamental to their definition of a writing environment is the "campus-wide recognition that writing is central to students' intellectual development and to their success in the wider world." Creating a writing environment also implies "creating ongoing dialogue about writing and its relationship to thinking and learning among faculty as well as students." Barnett and Rosen believe that with their common goals the Writing Center and the WAC Program each contribute elements necessary to developing and sustaining an environment that establishes the value of writing in the larger university curriculum.

Scott Johnston and Bruce Speck take a slightly more cautious approach to the partnership concept, assigning the Writing Center a role as "ambassador plenipotentiary" for the WAC Program. When the Writing Center is "empowered to negotiate," it offers a realistic means for advancing the WAC agenda. Using the Writing Center/WAC partnership at the University of Memphis as a model, they offer a more global discussion of how their Writing Center is able to affect the WAC aim of advancing faculty's understanding of the relationship between writing and thinking. The discussion then turns to the Writing Center/WAC goal of helping initiate students into the discourse communities of their chosen disciplines.

Jacob Blumner uses the issues of disciplinarity and authority as keys to helping us understand "how best to help students enter discipline-specific communities and be productive citizens therein." Using the works of Michael Pemberton and David Russell as a starting point, Blumner proposes that Writing Centers and WAC Programs should "intimately integrate themselves" to address issues of specialization and student, teacher, and tutor authority. Using Writing Centers and WAC Programs as the catalyst, he argues that academic institutions can prepare students for what will face them beyond the university experience.

Using post-colonial and conflict theory, Carol Peterson Haviland, Sherry Green, Barbara Kime Shields, and Todd Harper also address issues of authority and how they manifest themselves in WAC Programs. When WAC Programs "create interdisciplinary partnerships with Writing Centers, the lessons learned from writing tutors can help shape future WAC projects." The authors focus on the tutor model of collaboration to help explain the joint inquiry that exists in tutoring sessions rather than the hierarchical structure of the teacher-student or expert-novice model.

Mark Waldo and Maria Madruga address some of the tensions created by Writing Center/WAC partnerships as they illustrate the often uneasy relationship between WAC-based Writing Center directors and English departments. They describe Madruga's situation as a Writing Center director and an English department faculty member when she began to have real success in instituting a WAC Program. Based on her example, they describe a theory of WAC which "lessens the importance of English departments to the campus-wide teaching of writing while increasing the importance of all other departments." Finally, Waldo and Madruga offers readers some practical and theoretical insights into a problem of importance to WAC related Writing Centers and English departments.

The Boise State University Writing Center, under the guidance of Richard Leahy, has developed a program named The Write Project as a way of advancing the Writing Center's role in the WAC effort. In this program, writing assistants are trained to accomplish two primary goals: "tutoring in one-on-one sessions and responding in writing to written drafts." The Write Project trains the Assistants in Classical rhetoric as a theoretical framework so they do not operate with a fragmented understanding of written discourse. Leahy's use of Classical rhetoric offers a systematic way of generating, thinking about, and responding to writing in all disciplines.

While a growing number of Writing Centers continue making important connections and contributions to WAC Programs, Muriel Harris examines what happens when a formal WAC Program does not exist. Lacking a formalized Writing Across the Curriculum program with which to coordinate, her Writing Center has become the de facto WAC Program and WAC Writing Center. Harris focuses on what such a center can or should do to meet the needs of a campus with a rapidly accelerating interest in WAC, addressing what a de facto WAC center "can do to meet such needs, which principles of WAC serve as guidelines, and how all this impacts on the center." She goes on to remind us that the de facto WAC Writing Center cannot be expected to duplicate what can be provided for in a structured WAC Program. It can, though, be the catalyst for initiating a WAC Program and for helping to determine its shape and structure.

Peshe Kuriloff, on the other hand, emphasizes the "potential gains to Writing Centers that provide a home for the interdisciplinary partnerships that often define Writing Across the Curriculum." Her argument is that WAC Programs, by nature, exist in fragments, and faculty seldom "acknowledge the dotted line that connects them to the writing program." Writing Centers, she contends, offer an important opportunity to overcome the weaknesses inherent in the nature of WAC. By taking the initiative, Writing Centers are poised to "promote a common mission, centralize resources, advocate for an approach to writing instruction that is reinforced consistently across the curriculum, and position themselves at the heart of the academic program."

Harris describes a WAC Program that has fallen into the Purdue Writing Center's lap and Kuriloff points to ways in which Writing Centers can take advantage of opportunities by positioning themselves at the heart of the academic program. Karen Vaught-Alexander contributes to this conversation by discussing her application of organizational development theory to improve and develop the Writing Center and WAC connection at the University of Portland. Using advisory committees to effect change in the writing programs, Vaught-Alexander demonstrates the power of effective communication between faculty, administrators, and the community at large without surrendering the integrity of the Writing Center/WAC connection to outside pressures.

The role of technology also has a place in advancing the work of Writing Centers and WAC Programs. As Irene Clark believes, the Writing Center can more effectively facilitate interdisciplinary dialogue in a WAC environment if it "adheres to the old saying about Mohammed and the mountain—that is, if the mountain will not come to Mohammed," then he should come to the mountain. In the context of the Writing Center/WAC partnership, this principle suggests that the Writing Center needs to assume a leading role in working with faculty, not just through contact and classroom involvement, but by creating "an interactive virtual space via the World Wide Web that faculty and students from a variety of disciplines can access and contribute to easily." Because it is not associated with a disciplinary agenda and has the potential for creating dialogue between writing and content experts, the Web may serve as a mediating mechanism for advancing both the Writing Center and WAC efforts.

The Saint Louis College of Pharmacy and the Massachusetts College of Pharmacy serve as the case studies for Eric Hobson and Neal Lerner's article which argues for a visible Writing Center/WAC role in forging curricular changes. They recount the rationale for and methods of accomplishing complete curricular restructuring which included the creation of writing coordinators at both colleges, whose responsibilities included creating a college Writing Center and helping plan and implement a Writing Across the Curriculum program for their pharmacy programs. Hobson and Lerner focus specifically on changes in "course content, delivery, and support services that offer myriad opportunities for Writing Center and WAC colleagues." They also provide suggestions for colleagues to consider when working with pharmacy faculty and curricula.

The concept of Writing Center/WAC partnerships is not limited to higher education. Though such collaborative ventures are less frequent at the secondary level, they offer the same potentials as post-secondary institutions, not only for Writing Center and WAC personnel but for students and teachers as well. And as Pamela Childers contends, though some high school Writing Centers function as developmental facilities, the Writing Center at The McCallie School in Chattanooga, Tennessee, like many others, functions as the hub of Writing Across the Curriculum. She reveals that the Writing Center director, rather than mostly working with students, has become more of a resource, guide, and facilitator for faculty research, discovery, and risk taking with writing, thinking, and learning across the disciplines. Her role focuses on how to encourage colleagues "to grow as both teachers and learners," and she models this belief by participating in their development to create a slightly different, yet necessary kind of partnership.

We end the collection not by looking back at what we have accomplished, but by looking ahead at the challenges that face Writing Centers and WAC Programs in the future. Christina Murphy and Joe Law predict that three dominant trends will affect the decentralizing of the traditional classroom and change the nature of Writing Centers and Writing Across the Curriculum Programs. "Those three trends are technology, demographics, and the available funding for education." Murphy and Law apply Futurist Theory to the changing nature of Writing Centers and WAC theory. Drawing on the work of Don Tapscott, they move beyond institutional walls and look at how processes of digitization, molecularization, virtualization, and other factors will affect the development of Writing Centers and WAC Programs. Using site-specific applications, they look at problems/opportunities that face these programs, and even question whether Writing Centers and WAC Programs will be housed within the traditional, physical academic institution.

When the notion of bringing Writing Center and WAC theory and practice together began to surface in the literature of our field, the major debate focused on where to house WAC and how to assign the Writing Center more than a minor, supportive role in carrying out the WAC agenda. As all of the contributors illustrate, Writing Centers and WAC Programs have largely moved beyond those initial concerns and have begun wrestling with the issues that move them closer to the heart of the institutional curriculum and force them to weigh their own joint missions with the missions of the larger community within which they function. Our hope is that these chapters offer an opening statement to the dialogue that must surely follow if Writing Centers and WAC Programs are to continue their crucial work with faculty and students as well as strengthen their push for long-term institutional stability.

─────────── 1 ───────────

The WAC/Writing Center Partnership: Creating a Campus-wide Writing Environment

Robert W. Barnett and Lois M. Rosen

INTRODUCTION

There has been much discussion in Writing Across the Curriculum circles about the best place to house a WAC Program. Louise Z. Smith contends that it should be housed in the English Department where faculty have "expertise in the study of the construction and reception of texts (both literary and nonliterary, written by professionals or students) and . . . in composition theory and pedagogy" (1988, 40). According to Catherine Blair, a true WAC Program "should be designed, administered, and taught equally by all departments," based on an interdisciplinary dialogue, with the English Department as only one of the voices (1988, 383), therefore, not housed at any specific site on campus. Mark Waldo argues that the most logical place for WAC is in a Writing Center which "reaches out to faculty through a well-designed consultancy and provides students with a comprehensive tutoring program," where cross-curricular writing support can be available to both students and faculty (1993, 16). At the University of Michigan–Flint, *where* to house WAC wasn't even a consideration—when the need for a WAC Program became apparent, the Director of Writing Programs initiated it with the support of administration and faculty across the disciplines.

Now several years into our program, we have come to the conclusion that a more crucial issue than housing in developing a WAC Program is the creation of a writing environment throughout campus no matter where the program might be situated. What do we mean by a "writing environment"? First of all, we believe it means campus-wide recognition that writing is central to students' intellectual development and to their success in the wider world. It also means that writing is visible, understood, and accepted as a valuable tool for teaching and learning across the disciplines. A campus-wide writing environment implies ongoing dialogue about writing and its relationship to thinking and learning among faculty as well as students, plus opportunities for faculty to exchange ideas and discuss issues in writing pedagogy. Finally, a writing environment necessitates a visible writing support system available for both faculty and students.

WAC/WRITING CENTER PHILOSOPHY AT THE UNIVERSITY OF MICHIGAN–FLINT

Writing Across the Curriculum at The University of Michigan–Flint works toward this ideal writing environment through a partnership between the WAC Program and the Writing Center, each adding crucial elements. Our WAC Program is based on the belief that writing should be embedded throughout the university curriculum, taking place in many courses and in all disciplines. Creating intradisciplinary environments that foster the development of critical thought through writing has also been central to our emerging WAC philosophy. And we do not separate writing-to-learn, with its many uses of informal writing to think on paper, from Writing in the Disciplines, with its emphasis on acculturating students into a discipline's discourse community. We believe both approaches are important and may, in fact, be used effectively in the same course by an instructor with a clear set of goals and an understanding of how writing can help achieve those goals. As Mark Waldo points out, "research shows that writing improves writing, writing about course content generates thinking about that content, and writing within a particular context strengthens understanding of that context" (1993, 18).

Despite the fact that we espouse writing-to-learn in all subject areas, we consider our program discipline-specific because we believe that the discourse community and established characteristics of writing in each discipline dictate the most appropriate means for using writing to help students learn course material and master the rhetoric of the field. A discipline-specific WAC Program such as ours works not only to empower the faculty in any given discipline to make informed choices about when, how, and why to use writing in their courses, but it also acknowledges that each discipline has its own set of practices, its own specialized discourse community, and its own set of rhetorical values supporting this discourse community. Working with and recognizing the value of writing within each discipline has allowed us to create a larger, interdisciplinary environment, where "multiple discourse communities," each with its own "socially-constructed conventions of language," can begin sharing how they incorporate writing into their respective curricula (Pemberton 1995, 117).

We have always favored this discipline-based yet inclusive approach to WAC over a WAC Program that becomes synonymous with designating certain courses in each discipline as writing-intensive courses and requiring a certain number of these courses for graduation. The idea of writing-intensive programs runs theoretically counter to the inclusive approach to WAC that we advocate, one in which we encourage every course to be writing-intensive based on the goals of the course and instructor. In fact, the tendency in writing-intensive programs is to relegate responsibility for writing in any particular discipline to junior faculty. One of the obvious problems with designating specific courses as writing-intensive is the implication that writing does not take place in any other courses within that discipline, which suggests that other faculty in the field don't have to take responsibility for students' writing because this is all handled in the writing-intensive course. A second, more serious problem, is that such an approach to WAC has the potential for ghettoizing writing within the disciplines, something composition theorists and practitioners have struggled against in their own field for years.

Another argument against a writing-intensive approach to WAC is that it takes responsibility for writing in the disciplines out of the hands of many and places it in the hands of a few, who rarely have little more than a peripheral voice in department policy. In his 1990 *College English* article, "Writing Across the Curriculum in Historical Perspective: Toward a Social Interpretation," David Russell argues that, "Writing intensives, sometimes supported by a remedial lab, are perhaps the most common curricular model for WAC. But writing-intensive courses . . . concentrate responsibility for initiating students into the discourse community in a few professors or teaching assistants, while freeing most faculty resources for activities which the community views as more important than initiating new members" (65). The University of Michigan–Flint's approach to WAC supports a much broader sharing of responsibility for using writing and writing assignments in class, promoting a campus-wide writing environment that involves every faculty member. Our role is largely that of facilitator, helping faculty negotiate the use of writing so that it supports the overall goals of their courses. When more than a few faculty across campus use writing in this manner, and when WAC consultants help faculty succeed at using writing as yet another tool for learning, then the initiation of new members into a discourse community becomes a widely and necessarily shared responsibility.

The partnership between our WAC Program and our Writing Center has always seemed like a natural one because of their common assumptions about writing. The Writing Center's philosophy of inquiry, collaboration, and negotiation—that is reading a student's paper, asking pointed questions that engage a student in conversation, and offering goal-specific suggestions for revising a paper—is an evolution of what Patrick Hartwell and Robert Bently initially created when our Center opened in 1972. This approach to tutoring works to empower students to make their own informed choices about developing and revising the writing assigned them by their instructors. They are active participants, negotiating the meaning of their text with the tutor and collaborating to make the writing as clear and concise as possible.

The notion of asking the right questions of students and of their writing represents perhaps the most central aspect of tutoring, and it melds us philosophically with our WAC Program. More specifically, two types of question-asking dominate our work with student writers and align us with the intentions of their instructors. The first type, discovery questions, is intended to help students see for themselves what they meant, what they said, and what they have yet to say in their writing. When a student's writing becomes vague or confusing, the cause is usually a lack of detail or description which prevents the reader from clearly grasping the meaning of the text. For example, a student comes to the Writing Center with a draft of a paper about his relationship with his father. The assignment sheet indicates that the essay must retell a personal experience, use vivid detail, and include a clear description of what happened. Early in the essay, the tutor comes across a sentence that reads: "My dad is a really nice guy and I think he is great." Asking questions like "What does your dad do that makes him a really nice guy?" or "Why do you think he is great, and how does that affect your relationship with him?" will help the student bring to the surface what is already inside of his head. The discovery comes when he makes the connections between what he has written and what he actually meant. When this line of questioning is done well, students are led back into their papers where they can wrestle with the questions posed to them by tutors and pull additional information from their own data banks rather than from a tutor's. To witness this interaction is to witness the process of critical thinking in action, the making of meaning that epitomizes the evolution of all writers.

The second type of question-asking that takes place in tutoring is what links the Writing Center most closely to individual instructors and to a larger extent to the WAC Program itself. One of the major functions of our WAC work is to help faculty create effective writing assignments that reflect the goals of their courses. Similar in nature to discovery questions, goal-oriented questions are always linked directly to the writing assignment itself. Whether students bring assignment sheets to the Center or not, tutors must determine the goals of any particular assignment and tie those goals to the questions and suggestions they offer students. For example, a philosophy professor has asked her students to read two articles that articulate opposing views on the egoist debate. In a three to five page paper, she has asked students to summarize each author's views, tie them to the main topic of egoism, and offer an evaluation of each author's points. The instructor's goals for this assignment necessarily become the tutor's agenda when these philosophy students come to the Center for help. Therefore, the need to address goal-oriented questions in tutoring becomes paramount, considering the fact that students will be evaluated on how appropriately they have met the instructor's goals. Based on these shared philosophical values, the WAC Program and the Writing Center have worked both independently and cooperatively to create the university-wide writing program described below.

THE WAC PROGRAM

Our WAC Program began in fall 1992 with the distribution of a Faculty Writing Survey designed to find out how much and what kinds of writing were being done throughout the university. Its hidden agenda was to raise the visibility of writing on campus and to get a dialogue started that would lead to the development of a WAC Program. Designed by a committee of composition instructors, the survey was responded to by approximately a third of the faculty, yielding information similar to data reported in writing surveys done at other universities: students wrote a lot in freshman composition classes, very little during their sophomore year, and then were asked to produce increasingly longer papers that had increasingly more weight toward their course grade as they moved into their junior and senior years. The research paper and essay forms predominated with little or no use of informal writing to learn strategies reported outside of English.

Faculty complaints about students' writing ranged from poor critical thinking and organizational skills to problems with grammar and mechanics. Many faculty seemed to expect the one-year freshman composition sequence to provide students with all the writing skills they would need for the rest of their undergraduate years, an assumption made more problematic when one considered that over half our students are transfer students who took their freshman composition courses at community colleges and universities all over Michigan and the United States, programs with varying expectations that often differed dramatically from ours. Although we can safely expect our own freshmen to have been exposed to a specific set of academic writing and research skills, we have no control over the kinds of training over half our students bring with them to our campus. Examining the results of the survey, we were also concerned over the lack of informal writing to encourage thinking on paper, fluency, and development of ideas. We were especially concerned about the one to two year writing hiatus that many students had between freshman composition and the upper level courses in their major, which so often required an extended essay or research project as a culminating activity.

The Director of Writing Programs presented the results of the survey to faculty directly after the annual fall Convocation for the 1993–1994 academic year to insure a reasonably large audience from all units of the university. The ensuing discussion revealed many of the faculty's frustrations about our students' writing and some ideas about what might be done about it. The presentation was followed by a written report of the survey's results distributed to all faculty. The faculty dialogue about writing had been launched.

In February 1994, all units of the university sponsored a two day "WAC Kickoff" with Dr. Patricia Stock from Michigan State University. Dr. Stock gave two half-day faculty workshops on the relationship between writing and thinking, one on Thursday and the same presentation on Friday, to insure that as many faculty as possible could attend. Over 50 faculty members participated in one of these workshops, many of them still active in our WAC activities today. She also gave a public lecture on writing in the disciplines followed by a reception, attended by over 100 faculty, education students, and teachers in local schools. In addition, the Office of Multicultural Initiatives sponsored a seminar attended by over 100 students in which Dr. Stock demonstrated techniques for using writing as a study tool to help students learn course material more effectively. The success of this initial series of programs led to further administrative support, and a committee of interested faculty was formed to plan ongoing programs and activities chaired by the Director of Writing Programs.

Since the initiation of our WAC Program in 1994, several components have remained ongoing. Each semester, we give at least one faculty workshop on such topics as assignment-making, grading writing, and using informal writing to learn assignments. We have formed panels of successful WAC faculty to share why and how they use writing in their classes and have asked individual faculty members to lead a workshop on a particular topic such as assignment design. Each year we invite a well-known person in WAC circles to present a full-day workshop for faculty, usually on a day right after classes end when faculty members are not constrained by class schedules.

These workshops and panels keep writing visible throughout campus, offer new ideas about ways to use writing in a wide variety of contexts, and permit those faculty members who strongly believe in the writing/thinking connection to share their insights, enthusiasms, and successful practices with colleagues. Perhaps the most important benefit of these activities is the opportunity for faculty to come together to talk about their teaching, something not offered in any other way on campus except informally in corridors or over lunch. Evaluations of our workshops often mention the opportunity for faculty dialogue as a significant benefit over and above the new material they learned. Another way in which we share ideas about writing is by publishing a WAC newsletter once or twice a year with articles written by faculty members.

The success of a campus-wide writing program depends to a large extent on the support system available for faculty to draw on as they begin to use writing in their teaching or look for ways to improve what they have already been doing. To this end, we offer a large collection of articles and books on teaching with writing, including copies of general handbooks about writing and samples of the many student handbooks designed to supply information about writing in specific subjects such as the social sciences, psychology, history, literature, and the sciences. Faculty often do not know about these handbooks to teach students how to write in their own fields. Participants frequently leave our workshops with articles about writing in their own discipline, and the other resources are available for browsing or borrowing. In addition to this, we offer consulting to individual faculty members, departments, and programs throughout campus. During the past few years the WAC Program has worked with numerous faculty members on assignment design and evaluation, and has consulted with departments across campus about such issues as writing assessment for program evaluation and effective use of portfolio evaluation processes. We have watched participation in our WAC Programs and consulting climb over the years and feel we have made steady progress in our goal of creating a writing environment at the University of Michigan–Flint.

In addition to these ongoing activities sponsored by the WAC Program, the Writing Center contributes a considerable amount toward achieving our goals. Because we recognize the crucial need for student as well as faculty support in any WAC endeavor, we have taken steps to combine these two writing functions in visible ways. The most important of these is our annual WAC/Writing Center Open House, held in mid-September in the Writing Center. We open the Center to faculty and staff for an afternoon, provide abundant refreshments, and load the Center's worktables with multiple copies of articles about such general aspects of writing as responding, grading, portfolios, and assignment-making. We also have articles on writing for each discipline on campus. We advertise the Open House as a way for faculty to engage in dialogue about teaching with writing, to gather materials, and to meet the composition staff and tour the Writing Center to learn about the support available for students.

THE WRITING CENTER COMPONENT

Though widespread agreement exists that Writing Centers and WAC Programs function exceptionally well as partners, the opinions are less unified when it comes to who sets the partnership agenda and whose perspective is the main catalyst for initiating the work with faculty and/or students. Some conceptualize the partnership from a clearly WAC perspective (Walvoord 1996), while others propose a connection sanctioned entirely by the Writing Center (Waldo 1993). We believe that to remain true to the idea of a partnership and to create a well-defined writing environment, the decisions should not be made only from a Writing Center perspective or only from a WAC perspective, nor do we believe one person should be left to forge the partnership and carry out the Writing Center/WAC agenda. The Writing Center has become integral in the WAC program at University of Michigan–Flint not as a secondary element, but rather as an element necessary to accomplish what we see as a common goal between WAC and the Writing Center: to offer faculty and students the support they need for thinking, learning, and individual growth through writing.

The resources and services provided by the Writing Center are intended to help sustain and encourage the campus-wide environment for writing initiated by the WAC/Writing Center partnership. To help accomplish this goal, the Writing Center provides specific components directed at narrowing the communication gap that traditionally hinders teacher expectations and student comprehension of those expectations. Because we are in a position to work so closely with everyone involved with writing assignments (from those who create, assign, and evaluate them to those who interpret, complete, and learn from them), we can use the knowledge that we gain from working with teachers and students in order to help them begin finding some common ground and speaking the same language. The result is, and we have seen this happen many times, students write more focused papers that better reflect their understanding of the instructors' material, and instructors write more focused assignments that better reflect the goals of the course.

Our Writing Center, housed in the English Department, funded by the Dean of the College of Arts and Sciences via the department budget and to a much lesser extent by the provost, is open to all 6,500 undergraduate and graduate students on campus. Much like the Writing Lab that Muriel Harris describes in Chapter 7, "A Writing Center without a WAC Program: The De Facto WAC Center/Writing Center," our Center sees a large number of students from our own Freshman Composition Program. The developmental writing course is also run, in part, through the Writing Center. Students who place into the developmental course spend from two to four hours each week in the Center working with tutors on assignments for that class. Since all but a handful of freshman writers who come to the Writing Center eventually choose majors in fields outside of English, we see the experience created by the Composition Program and the Writing Center as the starting point for our student-centered WAC efforts. Many students who pass through the Composition Program return to the Writing Center as business majors looking for help writing corporate summaries or as philosophy majors who need someone to read their papers on the teachings of

Kant or, and these are some of our favorites, math majors who have been asked to write a paper on the theory of derivatives. These students who come back to the Center have more than likely realized the value of their early writing experiences and carried that with them as they became immersed in their new discourse communities.

Beyond the freshman writing courses, we help students from virtually every department on campus in the form of one-on-one tutoring. On average in any given semester we see students from 25–30 departments represented by 120–130 different classes. Our work with these students is crucial in helping us create a campus-wide writing environment that really is campus-wide. And as the writing across campus continues to grow, the Writing Center's role become even more ingrained in the WAC effort.

With our WAC-based approach, the Writing Center has been able to reach out to our students in other ways as well. We have recently initiated a group tutoring service for students who are completing collaborative projects or group lab and research projects. Students find this form of tutoring more helpful because they are able to talk through the issues of the project with each other, using the tutor as a mediator and consultant. We find the concept of group tutoring to be a more consistent support system for assignments that are collaborative in nature. The Writing Center also provides in-class tutoring, where students work in small groups with a tutor to facilitate the task at hand. This service is usually offered to faculty in the disciplines who are willing to devote one class period to peer response of the writing they assign. Once an instructor sees the value of this kind of intervention, we are usually invited back again and again. For instance, the Writing Center/WAC partnership has developed an ongoing relationship with a philosophy professor (she has attended several WAC workshops on grading criteria, assignment design, and evaluation) who because of student performance on her recent assignments has decided to completely change the nature of the writing she assigns. Her desire is to write assignments that more clearly reflect the overall goals of her course and of the specific assignments she gives to her students.

Finally, the Writing Center helps students with resources on anything from revision to documentation to resume/cover letter samples to citing sources on the Internet. We make hard copy handouts available to anyone who comes to the Center, and we are in the process of putting them all on our recently constructed Web page so that students will have access to our resources even if they are not on campus. Ours is a commuter campus, and students tend to appreciate any service that makes life easier for them. While we have developed numerous ways of reaching our students, the most effective way has always been through the faculty. Students usually listen to their instructors' advice, so if we can convince faculty that the Writing Center is a useful aspect of the WAC effort, then students will surely take advantage. Several faculty outreach initiatives are described below, but the one that helps us best to bring students to the Center is our beginning of the semester letter campaign. We go through the previous semester's statistics to find out which departments have used the Center, and we send letters to all department chairs. In the letters, we thank them for encouraging students to use the Writing Center and invite them to remind their faculty at the first department meeting to mention the Center and its services to their students. We follow this correspondence up by inviting all faculty on campus to let us come to any of their classes early in the semester for a brief ten-minute introduction of the Center for their students.

A fully functional and successful writing environment cannot be created and sustained without the active participation of faculty. In addition to the many WAC activities that cater specifically to faculty in the disciplines, the Writing Center supports faculty in several ways. In addition to the faculty-oriented services already described, the Writing Center has developed a two-part approach to educating faculty on the Writing Center's role in WAC (and its larger institutional role) and to offering them ongoing support once they have committed to make writing a part of their teaching: a statement of Writing Center goals and objectives and a Faculty Assignment Drawer (FAD). The statement of goals and objectives is an eight-page document created as a way to specifically define the Writing Center's role on campus for faculty and administrators, who have access to it via our Writing Center Internet site. (For a detailed discussion of the statement and a list of its major goals, see Robert Barnett's "Redefining Our Existence: An Argument for Short- and Long-Term Goals and Objectives" in *The Writing Center Journal*, Spring 1997).

The second faculty component, the FAD, was designed to both encourage faculty involvement in the WAC/Writing Center partnership and to increase the visibility of the growing culture of discipline-specific writing at our University. As faculty consult with the WAC directors to created, revise, or otherwise improve their writing assignments, we invite them each semester to submit copies of their assignments to the Writing Center, where we keep them on file, one for every instructor on campus. We also put out an open call for assignments at the beginning of each semester. As their students bring papers to the Center for tutorial assistance, the tutoring staff is able to pull any instructor's file, find the assignment, and become more aware of what the professor is asking of the student. This practice allows for more focused, goal-oriented tutoring, and the tutors are able to maintain more consistency in helping students complete the given writing tasks. The FAD is perhaps one of the strongest arguments for moving away from the idea of housing the WAC agenda and bringing together the participants who will ultimately be responsible for developing and nurturing the environment that helps us find a proper place for writing in our University curriculum.

HOW THE PARTNERSHIP SUPPORTS THE ENVIRONMENT

An examination of our university-wide WAC Program shows that three major elements form the basis for creating and sustaining a writing environment in which WAC and the Writing Center contribute substantially and in unique ways: (1) building faculty knowledge and establishing the value of writing, (2) providing a support system for faculty and students, and (3) supplying resources for faculty and students.

Building Faculty Knowledge and Establishing the Value of Writing

Our WAC/Writing Center partnership works in multiple ways to build faculty understanding of how writing can be used to enhance learning and practical methods that lead to more successful student products. In this, we view ourselves as well informed and experienced colleagues sharing what we know with other faculty members. But faculty across the disciplines also know a lot about their own discourse communities and about the writing they have used to improve students' critical thinking and learning in their courses. Our ongoing program of presentations and panels has worked well to keep WAC visible, to develop increased faculty understanding of the role writing can play in students' learning, and to offer a vehicle for faculty to share what they do as teachers. In a recent WAC newsletter article written by a faculty member after attending a WAC panel of four presenters from four different disciplines, she was struck by how little we know about "what goes on behind closed classroom doors," and "how enriching it can be to spend time 'exposing' to each other the selves our students know and the selves we wish to become as teachers" (Faires 1998, 10). To continue this sharing and keep WAC visibility high, the WAC Program sponsors the following activities:

- Workshops on such informational topics as writing-to-learn, assignment-making, responding to writing, grading writing, computers and writing
- Panels of experienced faculty sharing what they do with writing
- Presentations by individual faculty on successful techniques
- Giving free books on teaching writing to each faculty member participating in the annual spring WAC workshop
- Publishing a WAC newsletter for and by faculty once or twice a year

Providing a Support System for Faculty and Students

The environmental partnership created by the Writing Center and WAC program at the University of Michigan–Flint continuously works to build a firm support system for both faculty and students. By offering them appropriate tools for making their own best, informed decisions about writing, we are empowering students and faculty with the ability to help sustain the environment that they themselves have helped to create.

Faculty Support

- One-on-one consultation with individuals, departments, programs
- Informational visits to classrooms
- Writing Center/WAC Open House
- Faculty Assignment Drawer (FAD)
- Flyer listing writing resources and help available for faculty and their students

Student Support

- One-on-one collaboration with trained peer tutors
- Small group tutoring
- In-class tutoring for large and small classes
- Annual undergraduate paper competition
- Flyers, handouts, e-mail
- Writing Center newsletter for students
- Writing Center Web site

Supplying Resources for Faculty and Students

Both faculty and students benefit from the ready availability of hand-outs and materials on writing and teaching writing when they need them. To this end, we have gathered and created a wide variety of support materials available through the Writing Center and the WAC Program.

- Articles on using writing in individual disciplines gathered from disciplinary journals and writing journals
- Handbooks on the mechanical/grammatical aspects of writing
- Student handbooks for writing in individual disciplines
- Articles and handouts on topics in writing: portfolios, peer response groups, writing-to-learn techniques, grading writing
- Writing Center materials on such topics as citation formats in various disciplines, proofreading skills, generating ideas

CONCLUSION

The writing environment that we are working to sustain on the University of Michigan–Flint's campus is the product of a mutual partnership between WAC and the Writing Center that has developed over time. When the WAC Program began on this campus, we did not intentionally set out to create a partnership. However, it soon became apparent that we shared similar goals and that many of our roles were overlapping, such as consulting, which exists through the Writing Center's Faculty Assignment Drawer and also through individual WAC consultations. The WAC and writing center directors easily fell into a pattern of working together to plan the WAC agenda each semester.

Because our vision for a campus-wide writing environment has grown out of the philosophy that writing is central to learning in every discipline, this partnership seems ideal for our purposes. It has permitted us to draw on the strengths of the Center as well as on the facilities of the WAC Program, keeping writing visible through a continuous flow of programs, flyers, announcements, and offers of support. A prime advantage of our partnership is that we do not compartmentalize our efforts but instead work in tandem. No matter where WAC is situated, this kind of partnership becomes a highly effective way of increasing the value of writing as a tool for teaching and learning throughout the curriculum.

WORKS CITED

Barnett, Robert W. "Redefining Our Existence: An Argument for Short- and Long-term Goals and Objectives." *Writing Center Journal* 17.2 (1997): 123–133.

Blair, Catherine Pastore. "Only One of the Voices: Dialogic Writing Across the Curriculum." *College English* 50 (1988): 383–389.

Faires, Nora. "What Goes on Behind Closed Classroom Doors?" *UM–Flint WAC Newsletter* 5.1 (1998): 4.

Hartwell, Patrick. "A Writing Laboratory Model." *Basic Writing: Essays for Teachers, Researchers, and Administrators,* eds. Lawrence N. Kasden and Daniel R. Hoeber. Urbana, IL: National Council of Teachers of English, 1980: 63–73.

Pemberton, Michael A. "Rethinking the WAC/Writing Center Connection." *Writing Center Journal* 15.2 (1995): 116–133.

Russell, David R. "Writing Across the Curriculum in Historical Perspective: Toward a Social Interpretation." *College English* 52 (1990): 52–73.

Smith, Louise Z. "Why English Departments Should 'House' Writing Across the Curriculum." *College English* 50 (1988): 390–395.

Waldo, Mark L. "The Last Best Place for Writing Across the Curriculum: The Writing Center." *WPA: Writing Program Administration* 16.3 (1993): 15–26.

Walvoord, Barbara E. "The Future of WAC." *College English* 58 (1996): 58–79.

----------- 2 -----------

The Writing Center as
Ambassador Plenipotentiary in
a Developing WAC Program

Scott Johnston and Bruce W. Speck

In a recent article, Mark Waldo argues that his inquiry-based approach to WAC has had, after seven years of fairly general WAC workshops that deal with assignment-making, a significant impact on the ways faculty at his university think about and use writing. So significant, in fact, that the general workshops are no longer sufficient because the faculty "know their disciplines have individual frames for thinking and writing, and that the English Department or any one department cannot teach their students to write. Their concerns become, then, how best to link writing to thinking expertly in their own fields" (1996, 12). Though Waldo presents a persuasive case, our similar WAC workshops, offered for the past nine years, have not produced nearly the same results. We suspect our experience is true for many, if not most, WAC Programs across the country.

In this chapter, we first consider why our faculty have historically assailed the principles discussed during our general WAC workshops. After that, we propose an approach to WAC that deals effectively with such resistance. In this arrangement, the Writing Center becomes an ambassador plenipotentiary for the WAC Program which requires two general tasks: 1) working alongside the WAC director during general WAC workshops, and 2) working independently to establish relationships with faculty who may or may not have attended the workshops. Our experiences have convinced us that this can (and has) also lead faculty to consider how to link writing to thinking expertly in their own fields. Though it may not produce such large-scale results as quickly as those Waldo describes, it may well be more easily implemented and realistic for beginning or struggling WAC Programs.

BELIEFS COMMON AMONG WAC FACULTY PARTICIPANTS

From our perspective, faculty at our university have not recognized and discarded the "myth of transcience" (Rose 1989; Russell 1991), the belief that writing is a skill independent of any content learning and that once mastered can be transferred equally well from one class to another, at any level, in any discipline. In other words, a student should be able to learn to write proficiently in a writing course and then should be able to write equally as proficiently in any geography or physics or biology course. What discipline requires the writing and what subject the student writes about are immaterial. In fact, in a recent series of WAC workshops, a number of professors from a variety of humanities and natural science disciplines maintained throughout that "good writing is good writing."

We consider the myth of transcience to be a general and somewhat abstract notion, so in working with faculty we have tried to identify specific characteristics that reflect one's belief in the larger myth. It is not surprising that the five most common characteristics seem at odds with the process-oriented philosophy that we promote. Moreover, we believe that though many of these beliefs will sound familiar, a brief review of each will serve as a reminder of the sometimes overwhelming resistance that WAC Programs generally face from many well-intentioned faculty. Indeed, David Russell has documented numerous cases where WAC Programs have succumbed to the pressure of that resistance and gradually faded away to become one more entry on the long list of failed educational initiatives (1991, 296). Quickly recognizing and addressing the ideological sources of friction from faculty, however, may well turn potential adversaries into supporters and increase WAC's chances of not just survival but growth.

1. Many faculty believe that content is more important than sentence-level issues such as grammar, usage, spelling, or stylistic conventions. What is really important, faculty often assert, is the students' ability to regurgitate content when writing. Somehow, the relationship between content and the language used to express that content is bifurcated.

2. The same faculty appear to contradict themselves, often in the same breath, with the claim that grammar is more important than content in evaluating writing. Probably the most revealing comment a faculty member made at one of the WAC seminars was this: "I am not sure how to mark students' papers because I have forgotten the grammar I was taught." The faculty member does not realize that even if he used the technical language of grammar to mark students' papers, his students would neither understand what he was saying nor learn to avoid the same errors in future writing. They, too, do not know that technical language, and even if they did it would not guarantee that they would be able to apply the formal terms and rules to their own writing (Harris 1977).

3. Closely related to faculty placing undue importance on grammar and other sentence-level issues is their tendency to evaluate them at inappropriate times (Braddock, Lloyd-Jones, and Schoer 1963; Hillocks 1986). According to what our faculty have told us, this manifests itself in two ways: 1) faculty may correct grammar on every draft they read, regardless of whether it is a first or final draft, and 2) faculty may correct grammar on essays the students will not be allowed to revise.

4. Faculty from every discipline, including English, often claim that there simply is not enough time to have students write frequently in large undergraduate classes. The implication here is that writing does not offer enough benefits for the amount of time necessary to incorporate it into a course.

5. Faculty have not distinguished between writing to learn and learning to write. When faculty do see the distinction between teaching students to use writing to learn course

content and teaching students what constitutes acceptable writing in a discipline, they also may continue to cling to various arguments about why they will have difficulty implementing a writing process in their classes.

Perhaps the reason faculty hold to such beliefs is the poor quality of the WAC seminars, yet we do have evidence that the seminars have had a positive impact on faculty participants (Pitts, Sigsbee, and Speck 1996). Nevertheless, when compared with the achievements Waldo describes, our results seem quite meager. Faculty on our campus, for instance, often wonder aloud why the English Department is not preparing students to write effectively in business, science, and engineering courses. In fact, we address this problem at the outset of the WAC workshops, and, as yet, faculty have not told us we are beating a dead horse. Instead, they nod their heads, affirming the validity of the problem we raise.

Another reason faculty persist in their affirmation of the myth of transience could be the quality of our faculty. For instance, it may be the case that faculty members who are entrenched in the university and in the logical-positivistic paradigm simply are unwilling to consider the validity of our arguments exposing the myth of transience as a myth. We have encountered some of this, but participants in the WAC workshops are more often than not new faculty members who seem to want genuinely to learn more about being effective teachers of writing.

In rejecting any answers that focus on either the poor quality of the WAC workshops or the poor quality of our faculty, we think the complex answer to our question of why faculty believe in the myth of transcience has something to do with the faculty's own education, our institutional leadership, and the university's allocation of economic resources.

For example, part of the answer may well be the training in pedagogy that the faculty did not receive. Having become teachers, and having little if any training in effective teaching, faculty model their teaching on the classroom pedagogy they experienced as students. Given their own educational experiences in which writing was taught from a logical-positivist viewpoint, faculty members use writing in their classes most often as a measure of recall rather than a means of extending information or learning new concepts.

At the same time, we think that institutional leadership and the allocation of funds at the university complete the answer. On the one hand, we must praise the leaders who provide funding for the WAC Program, enabling it to be a major source of faculty development on our campus. On the other hand, we question the lack of funding for the Writing Center that has kept it in the developmental stages typical of Writing Centers in their infancy. In short, faculty attitudes supporting the myth of transience and other logical-positivistic beliefs are probably confirmed by administrative funding that has limited faculty development initiatives designed to unveil these beliefs for what they are: a stubborn resistance to the findings of composition research. Even when researchers demonstrate empirically that "'good writing' is a culturally defined phenomenon, and that good academic writing has a particular definition within the academic circles of a culture" (Purves and Hawisher 1990, 183), or that "data cast doubt on the assumption that 'a good writer is a good writer' regardless of the assignment" (Quellmalz, Capell, and Chou 1982, 255), faculty members may not be moved to renounce the myth of transience.

Clearly, the roots of the challenges from faculty and administration to our WAC principles are varied and often seemingly resistant to change. However, identifying why faculty and administration believe what they do is ultimately less important than finding ways to persuade them of the benefits WAC offers them and their students. So far, our best success has come as a result of the Writing Center functioning as an ambassador plenipotentiary for the WAC Program. Among other reasons, this configuration allows for a significant amount of personalized one-on-one interaction with faculty concerning writing. It has been primarily in these cases that faculty have come to recognize and reject the myth of transcience and the practices it leads to.

AMBASSADOR RELATIONSHIP BETWEEN THE WAC PROGRAM AND THE WRITING CENTER

The *American Heritage College Dictionary* defines ambassador plenipotentiary rather simply: An ambassador empowered to negotiate treaties (41). Considering other kinds of ambassadors allows a better understanding. The common ambassador is the highest diplomatic representative that one sovereign power sends officially to another. An ambassador-at-large is not assigned to any one foreign state, and an ambassador extraordinary is sent on a special diplomatic mission. Each type of ambassador has one common element: a "sovereign power" to which each ambassador is subordinate. This is and is not true in our case. It is true because the Writing Center, in its capacity as ambassador plenipotentiary for the WAC Program, works to advance WAC principles across the university by participating in the WAC seminars and by establishing relationships with faculty who are interested in using writing more effectively in their classes. In other words, the Writing Center work overtly supports the WAC Program. It is not true because the WAC Program does not hold any real power over the Writing Center. The programs are funded by and answer to different departments. Moreover, the Writing Center has as much to gain from the relationship as the WAC Program. Simply put, ambassador plenipotentiary offers a useful metaphor for understanding the relationship between the Writing Center and the WAC Program; it is not meant to be taken literally.

Metaphorically speaking then, the Writing Center as ambassador plenipotentiary "negotiates treaties" with faculty interested in understanding and using writing. Negotiations revolve around WAC principles of discipline-specific process writing including discussions about designing and revising writing assignments, identifying discipline-specific writing values, assessing student writing, and using peer response groups. The professors involved may have been part of the WAC workshops but most often they have not. Generally, after students meet with a tutor at the Writing Center they are asked to pass a Writing Center pamphlet along to their professors. The pamphlet explains the services the Writing Center offers for faculty as well as students, and several faculty have contacted the Writing Center as a result, requesting assistance with one or more of the writing-related areas mentioned in the pamphlet. One of the primary differences in the two programs is that the Writing Center is able to work individually over long periods of time with professors while the WAC Program meets with large groups of professors for five two-and-a-half hour workshops over a semester.

Another noteworthy difference between the ways the two programs work is that the Writing Center's work as ambassador plenipotentiary has been slower in many regards than the WAC Program's. While the WAC seminars drew over thirty professors last year, the Writing Center worked with only three professors. Though we would have liked to have begun negotiations with more professors, given the newness of the Writing Center in this role, three seems to represent a good start. Moreover, the relationships that evolved and the work that was accomplished with the three professors were especially encouraging and will be detailed later in this Chapter.

HISTORY OF THE WAC PROGRAM

We mentioned earlier that our WAC Program has existed for nine years. It began as a result of the university-wide and nation-wide thrust toward recognizing the importance of writing in any career and toward using writing to facilitate understanding, problem-solving, and retention of information in the specific disciplines (Mortimer et al. 1982). "The WAC Program was developed to support a new general education program for undergraduates which requires that all freshman and sophomore courses include writing as an integral component. In addition, the program requires baccalaureate students to take at least one junior or senior course labeled 'writing intensive'" (Pitts, Sigsbee, and Speck 1996, 56).

WAC was housed in the general education program and was designed to assist faculty in teaching required courses that integrated writing into the courses' content. Toward this end, a number of courses required in the general education program were designated as writing intensive, and a series of workshops were offered both to those faculty who would be teaching the writing-intensive courses and the faculty at large who were interested in learning more about using writing in their own classes. While we are aware of the debates regarding the problems associated with writing-intensive courses such as the possibility of ghettoizing rather than cultivating writing in the disciplines, we can only say that at our university writing-intensive course at least represent the administration's recognition of the need to support more writing on campus.

Four to six WAC workshops, each lasting two-and-a-half hours, were offered each semester until 1994. The workshops were highly interactive and topics discussed included the writing process, writing assessment, syllabus modification, journaling, and critical thinking. Although a 1994 review found the WAC workshops had been somewhat successful in introducing participants to WAC concepts and that some "participants used those concepts introduced in the workshops to change classroom practices" (Pitts, Sigsbee, and Speck 1996, 62), it was clear that better results were desirable.

One note of interest from the data Pitts et al. collected was that the faculty turnover of those who participated in the WAC workshops was approximately 10 percent after three years. This means that one out of every ten faculty members who participated in the WAC Program was no longer working as a professor on the campus after five years. We will discuss the implications of this later.

HISTORY OF THE WRITING CENTER

Before 1996, the Writing Center was directed by a full-time instructor who received a course release for her efforts. Viewed by most faculty, students, and even the tutors as an English remediation service, the center assisted approximately 450 students each semester, most of whom were undergraduates and came from remedial English courses with instructions to correct their problems with grammar, usage, punctuation, and spelling. In many ways the center fit Andrea Lunsford's description of Writing Center "storehouses" that "operate as information stations prescribing and handing out skills and strategies to individual learners" (1995, 110).

In 1996, Scott Johnston was hired to refashion the center based on the latest research in composition and rhetoric. Almost immediately a number of significant changes were made. Tutoring services were offered to students and faculty across campus; clients were seen by appointment rather than as drop-ins; sessions lasted from thirty to sixty minutes, depending on the length of the paper; and tutors were required to attend weekly training meetings. In addition, the Writing Center became active in promoting itself as a university-wide service that incorporated collaborative tutoring strategies and was sensitive to discipline-specific rhetorical values, strategies, and styles. The tutors, mostly the same instructors as before who continued to receive course releases, were trained to use an inquiry- and criteria-based approach in which global issues (elements related to overall success of an essay including assignment directions, purpose, meaning, intent, organization, and thesis) were addressed first; mid-global issues (elements at the paragraph level including relationship to thesis, details, and explanation) were addressed second; and local issues (sentence-level) were addressed last. Tutors were also prepared to engage students in conversations about these issues through question asking rather than supplying answers or directions for the student. The rationale for this approach was fourfold: 1) essays with global and mid-global problems could not improve significantly from tutoring sessions that focused almost exclusively on local errors; 2) students remember information longer and better when they generate information themselves rather than receive it from another source (Slamecka and Graf 1978); 3) students who engage regularly in this type of tutoring for one semester learn to consider global issues as more important to their writing than local issues and address global issues appropriately in revisions (Johnston 1996); and 4) students eventually learn to ask themselves the same kinds of questions their tutors do and become capable of doing more advanced writing and thinking on their own (Vygotsky 1979).

Significantly, the tutors understood that they would begin to work with professors and would be expected to draw on the same strategies they used with students. In other words, the tutors would be expected to function not only as tutors but as WAC ambassadors. The tutors were also encouraged to speak with professors they knew who might be interested in developing ties with the Writing Center that would lead to WAC-related work.

By the end of the fall semester, the Writing Center had an increase of over 300 percent in students seen; the tutors had worked with a number of graduate students and faculty members; and the new tutoring method had produced such dramatic improvements in students' writing that the tutors were reinvigorated.

DEVELOPMENT OF THE WRITING CENTER/WAC PARTNERSHIP

When the fall semester began, we met to discuss the specific nature of the Writing Center/WAC collaboration. We began by first reviewing the goals, procedures, and expectations of the WAC Program. It became clear that given the limited amount of money and time allocated to WAC, the Writing Center could serve an important role in advancing WAC principles across the campus if it became an ambassador plenipotentiary. For instance, as discussed earlier, the WAC Program at the University of Memphis consists of a total of only ten hours of large-group meetings and there simply is not enough time to fully address a number of important issues. For instance, there is never enough time for faculty to thoroughly discuss, design, and revise their writing assignments. In addition, the WAC seminars only present an introduction to the complex topic of assessing students' writing. As a result, though the faculty participants may become somewhat more knowledgeable about the nature of writing in their classrooms and disciplines, there remains much that could be done.

We saw immediately the potential the Writing Center had for covering and supplementing issues related to writing, particularly writing-assignment design and writing assessment, because these issues are understood more thoroughly when working closely with individual faculty. Moreover, working closely with individuals to improve their writing is the Writing Center's primary function and working with faculty as ambassador plenipotentiary would be an extension of the type of work that the Writing Center already did. Such a division of labor under the aegis of both WAC and the Writing Center also was designed to make a statement to the faculty that though the Writing Center and the WAC Program were separate entities, they shared several goals. For example, both programs emphasize teaching students the writing process. Also, much like the method Mark Waldo describes, both of our programs rely on inquiry to determine faculty and student writing goals and how best to achieve those goals (1996). Since this partnership was an idea very much in the developing stage, we decided to experiment gradually over the first year. We did not know if faculty would even be interested in continuing WAC work after the initial seminars concluded.

We also decided that since one of the ways the Writing Center would function as ambassador plenipotentiary would be to overtly support the WAC

Program, Johnston should participate in the WAC seminars throughout that semester. At the first seminar Johnston explained to the faculty participants what the Writing Center's functions and goals were and how the Writing Center could support and advance the WAC principles that were discussed during the seminars. The faculty participants seemed genuinely interested and asked many insightful questions. More than a few participants made assurances that their students would soon be making frequent use of the Writing Center. Interestingly, more than one participant also remarked that they were unaware that something like the Writing Center even existed at the University. By participating in the WAC seminars, Johnston was able to speak directly to faculty (presumably those already interested in supporting writing development programs given their participation in the seminars) who he may not normally have had contact with had the Writing Center remained separate from WAC.

THE FALL 1996 WORKSHOPS: A WAC/WRITING CENTER COLLABORATION

Earlier in the chapter, we outlined five attitudes that usually indicate an underlying belief in the myth of transience. Often, these attitudes have caused faculty to oppose concepts they are introduced to during the WAC seminars. Such attitudes also may have inhibited large numbers of faculty from participating in WAC at all. Though many of the faculty we have worked with have softened their attitudes as a result of the WAC seminars, others have not. We found during the most recent fall seminars and throughout the spring semester, however, that when the Writing Center became an ambassador plenipotentiary, we were able to persuade more faculty of the value of writing than usual, and Bruce Speck was relieved from a little bit of the pressure of the past when he alone worked with the faculty.

More specifically, during the fall 1997 workshops, the Writing Center fulfilled part of its role as ambassador by working alongside the WAC Program to address the five often contentious beliefs shared by faculty participants. During the five fall seminars, we presented the Writing Center and the WAC Program as a united front while we introduced the following topics: the writing process, collaborative writing, grading writing, and ESL students' writing. Speck presented materials and addressed questions designed to lead the participants to endorse the claims that "writing is the greatest tool for thinking ever invented by man" (Mellon 1976, 73) and that writing is context specific (Bizzell 1987). Johnston gave a presentation on Writing Centers and writing assignments which reinforced the principles Speck advocated. In addition, Johnston initiated the second element of the Writing Center's ambassadorship by cultivating relationships among the participants that lead to meetings outside the seminars. These meetings will be discussed more thoroughly in the next section.

When many of the faculty at the seminars told us that "good writing was good writing" and that content was more important than sentence-level issues in their students' writing—the first characteristic that reflects a belief in the myth of transience—we raised the issue of the relationship between content and delivery, thereby circling back to the myth of transience. "What constitutes 'good writing' in your discipline?" was an appropriate question. "Is it the case that how something is stated has nothing whatsoever to do with what is being stated?" was another. Although we did not quote them directly, we introduced concepts from noted experts in composition theory and practice. For instance, we drew on Odell and Cooper's assertion that "different tasks—even different expository tasks—have to be judged by different criteria" (1980, 40), and Quellmalz's statement that, "The hierarchical, logical relationships common to exposition and persuasion call on reasoning and writing techniques that are different from the coordinate, chronological connections used to relate a sequence of events" (1984, 29). In other words, asking faculty members to think critically about the types of writing in their own discipline served as one point of entry for discussing the myth of transience and the bifurcation of content and delivery.

We found another point of entry was to discuss research about how faculty evaluate writing. For instance, faculty often claim they evaluate one aspect of students' writing, such as content, but they actually evaluate using criteria other than content (Harris 1977). In addition, faculty evaluation may not match their classroom pedagogy. More specifically, teachers might say that spelling is a high priority when they evaluate students' writing but they devote little or no time to helping students become better spellers (Kline 1976). Such research allows us to raise the issue of how readers read texts and opens up the possibility of discussing theories of reading that point to a construction of text on the part of the writer and the reader (Ruth and Murphy 1984). Thus, students' writing is not static. It is not something that inherently contains set meanings. Rather, through interaction with a text, a reader develops meaning and that meaning may not be what the author intended. In other words, meaning—the content many faculty claim to judge—is not entirely separate from the teacher who reads the writing. To suggest that content is something intact in a piece of writing seems like a common-sense approach to reading, but it certainly has been questioned vigorously (Ede 1989; Gabriel 1990; Greenhalgh 1992; Lawson and Ryan 1989; Miller 1984; Murray 1991; Schwegler 1991), and faculty members need to consider objections that have been raised about the common-sense notion of reading that they espouse uncritically.

When faculty participants claimed that grammar was more important than content in evaluating writing—the second characteristic that reflects a belief in the myth of transience—we agreed that grammar was indeed important, but we asked whether the participants could specify what they meant by the term. Even a brief lesson on how language is acquired begins to open the door for faculty to examine what they mean when they say "grammar." Instead of appealing to the technical language of grammar, faculty members need to state in their own words what the problem is with a student's prose. Models of such teacher response to student writing can help faculty members learn how to respond in helpful ways to students' writing without resorting to the technical language of grammar.

But the more pressing question concerning grammar relates to the writing process. When should the teacher evaluate grammar and mechanics? Typically, faculty who believe in the myth of transience feel that they need to correct grammar on every draft they see, whether revisions will follow or not—

the third characteristic we described earlier. Unless faculty understand the role grammar plays in the writing process, they will talk at cross purposes with those in the WAC and Writing Center Programs. And, if faculty in the disciplines do not understand the need to foster writing as a process in their classrooms, they will evaluate writing in first-draft form as though it were finished writing. On their own, most students will not produce a series of drafts which include peer review before submitting a final draft for a grade. Indeed, faculty may not have made the connection between their own writing process and the need for students to use a writing process in completing writing assignments. If faculty did pause to consider the process they use and then question the assumptions they make when assigning and evaluating writing assignments, they might recognize the need to make the process explicit for students. Perhaps, however, faculty have never made the process explicit for themselves. Perhaps they have not thought about their process, only practiced it. Perhaps a faculty member's process is counterproductive, so he or she has abandoned much of his or her publishing responsibilities. The WAC seminar is a good place to discuss the writing process and challenge faculty to consider using an explicit writing process in the classroom to help students learn more about writing.

In addition, Johnston explained to the participants how students are tutored at the Writing Center, giving faculty insight into productive ways to help students write and to deal with issues of grammar. Moreover, when faculty participants did define what they meant by grammar, Johnston reminded them of the differences between grammar, usage, spelling, and punctuation. Faculty seemed surprised (and somewhat dubious) when they learned that many of the writing errors their students made were not grammatical errors at all but rather usage errors.

When faculty participants claimed that there simply was not enough time to use writing in large undergraduate classes—the fourth characteristic that reflects one's belief in the myth of transcience—we were sympathetic to the need for students to learn content. However, we suggested that writing is the premier way of thinking and that, while the content students learn may become obsolete within five years, the process of learning and thinking about that content has lasting value.

These two points, however, do not appear as axioms when first presented to faculty. The pressure to present content—to get through the lecture notes—is so great that faculty have difficulty envisioning a classroom in which some content is replaced by more critical thinking. The problem here is that faculty perpetuate the methods their teachers have used without critically analyzing the outcomes of those methods. Critical analysis may seem superfluous because, after all, the faculty members received a Ph.D. in a content area by jumping through hoops. Why, then, shouldn't others jump through the same hoops?

The solution to this self-perpetuating myth is not easy, but we used time during the seminars to show the faculty the advantages of learning through writing and of thinking about ways to replace dull textbook exercises with writing opportunities that allow students to think about the material the professor presents. Part of the problem, too, may be one of authority. Giving students a discipline's "official line" is much easier than answering pesky questions students may ask, questions that raise issues about that official line.

Much has been written about the need for teachers to share authority in classrooms so that students can take responsibility for their learning (e.g., Calabrese 1982; Duke 1975; Olsen 1975; Throop and Jameson 1976), but convincing faculty of the value of restructuring their classrooms so that students become active learners can be a tough sell. None of this is an attempt to deny the need for students to learn content. That is not the issue. The issue is how best to learn that content and what is the essential content to learn. Again, faculty may not have thought critically about what content is essential—really essential—and what content is a notch below essential. Perhaps inviting faculty to play a bit of triage with their course content would be helpful in getting them to consider ways they can loosen up space in their courses to make room for active learning activities involving writing.

Interestingly, many of the WAC seminar participants have never been introduced to the difference between teaching students to use writing in order to better learn course content and teaching students how to write prose that meets a discipline's rhetorical values. In fact, most of the faculty we meet with feel that it is not their job to teach their students to write, and this reflects the fifth characteristic of those who believe in the myth of transcience. One way that we introduce them to the concepts during the seminars has been to read aloud a column from Ann Landers in which a woman asks Ann whether she should marry a particular fellow. The woman then recites the pros and cons of her relationship with the fellow and dramatically ends with these words, "'Don't bother to answer this, you have helped me more than you know'" (Lindemann 1986). The woman provides an excellent example of writing to learn. She starts with a problem and through the process of writing about the problem, she comes to a solution. Were she to write a letter to someone and explain why she was terminating her relationship with the fellow, she would probably write to inform, and her focus on a particular audience would help her to make (subconsciously perhaps) rhetorical choices. Her decision, which was at the conclusion of a process of discovery, would most likely come first: "I've decided not to marry Fred, so I'm writing to let you know why."

The woman's letter is not unlike students' rough drafts, and faculty often nod their heads in agreement when they are asked to see the relationship between the letter and a student paper in which the thesis is at the end. In the WAC seminars, we stress the importance of the writing process—an umbrella term for various ways students can learn through writing and learn to write for specific disciplines. We find that to the extent faculty are willing to accept the need for using the writing process in their classes, they are willing to change their classes to promote better student learning. To the extent that they are unwilling to use the writing process, to that extent they perpetuate the myth of transience and its sundry arguments. Unfortunately, the myth of transience is so powerful that it has become gospel for many. To suggest that "good writing is not always and everywhere good writing," and that writing functions in a context which defines what is good about writing, is perceived as heresy by those who have uncritically accepted much of the training they have received from

English departments and their discipline. The problem of evaluating writing by paying undo attention "to surface features, and appearance," though of little comfort to WAC and Writing Center programs, is seemingly an international problem (Purves 1990, 114).

THE WRITING CENTER ON ITS OWN

As mentioned earlier, one of the Writing Center's roles as ambassador plenipotentiary was to work closely with the WAC Program during the fall seminars. While it seemed that the faculty participants were more likely to be persuaded of the benefits of the WAC principles because we each addressed them using different approaches, we do not know for sure to what extent the faculty changed their uses of writing in their classes as a result. However, such is not the case with the WAC work the Writing Center did outside of the WAC seminars, the second responsibility of its ambassadorship. In these instances, the Writing Center acted more truly as an ambassador plenipotentiary because it worked independently to initiate contact with other professors around campus who may not have participated in the WAC seminars. Specifically, Johnston established "treaties" with two sociology professors and refined a third with an English professor. Neither of the sociology professors had attended the WAC seminars; the first contacted the Writing Center after receiving pamphlets from several of her students who had met with tutors at the Writing Center, and the second contacted the Writing Center after hearing the first professor speak enthusiastically about the positive impact her new Writing Center alliance had on her students' writing and on her writing assignment design. The English professor had participated in the WAC seminars and wanted to continue to develop the writing assignment and writing assessment ideas mentioned during the seminars and supplemented by the Writing Center.

Both of the sociology professors were dissatisfied with the students' writing in previous years and were interested in finding ways to help their current students write more effectively in response to the writing assignments that would be given during the semester. The first professor, Dr. U., was teaching two sections of the Sociology of Gender, and was very specific about what she wanted from the Writing Center. She requested that Johnston make three classroom visits during which her students should first be lectured about how to do a peer review, then how to write a position paper, and last how to write a library research paper. She also sent a copy of her course description and paper assignments to help Writing Center personnel prepare for the lectures.

After reading the paper assignments, it became clearer why her students were having such problems completing them successfully. If Reiff and Middleton are correct that writing assignments are an act of communication between the teacher and the students (1983, 264), it appeared to us that Dr. U.'s communication with her students was somewhat garbled. The first paper assignment read in its entirety:

Before coming to class, think about your life at work, at school, at home, at church or temple, or some other place where you spend time. Identify gender patterns and gender differences. Write about the patterns. Describe how men and women (or girls and boys) experience the same setting or organization differently.

Length: 3 pages.

After reading the assignment, Johnston scheduled a meeting with Dr. U. so that she could explain more specifically what she expected from the assignment and from the students. For instance, Johnston asked her how many places should be written about? How many of the gender patterns and differences should be explained? How should they be explained? Should examples be used and, if so, what constituted well-written examples? Should students use description, dialogue, or something else? Should students do more than think about differences and perhaps do an observation and take notes? And, stylistically, could the students use the first person? What kind of introduction would be appropriate? What other rhetorical values were common to sociology and would the students be aware of them? After considering the questions Johnston asked, Dr. U. was able to articulate concise answers.

Then Johnston met with Dr. U.'s class and explained what he understood the assignment to mean based on his conversations with Dr. U. Since Johnston had asked Dr. U. to remain in the room, she was able to confirm or amend his ideas. Judging from the looks on the students' faces and the questions they began raising, it became clear that the students had not understood the assignment very well. If Johnston had not convinced Dr. U. in the meeting prior to the class that the assignment was confusing, the students made her painfully aware of that fact with their questions.

The next step was to have several student volunteers read sections from their drafts out loud. This proved not to be overly difficult with some coaxing, and once the students realized that they would get immediate (and mostly encouraging) feedback from Dr. U. For example, several students read their introductions and Dr. U. explained why they were or were not what she expected. She also gave students suggestions for revising what they had read. The process was repeated until examples of all of the sections of the assignment were covered. Unfortunately, by this time the class only had a few minutes left to do peer response so Dr. U. decided to use half of the next class to complete the process.

When Dr. U. eventually assessed the students' papers, she contacted the Writing Center to inform Johnston that the improvements over previous groups of students was significant. Of course, it may be that she simply had more talented writers than usual in that class. However, based on several of Dr. U.'s classes in which Johnston conducted similar workshops and on the course evaluations the students wrote about the effectiveness of the workshops, we feel confident that the students' writing improved, and not because the students were highly talented writers. In fact, the primary reason for student improvement was the changes Dr. U. made in the way she approached writing assignments. Those changes were made possible because Johnston as a WAC ambassador was able to spend time working closely with Dr. U. Though the process Johnston used to help Dr. U. reevaluate her writing assignments may seem obvious to teachers experienced with the intricacies of using writing in their classes, to faculty like Dr. U., the Writing Center as WAC ambassador provides the best chance for showing professors how and why to incorporate these steps whenever writing is assigned.

Johnston's work with the other sociology professor, Dr. H., was nearly identical with one exception. Dr. H. was so impressed with her students' writing after Johnston met with her once and conducted just one workshop for the students that she decided to increase the amount that her students would write during the rest of the semester. However, based on continuing conversations with Johnston, Dr. H. decided that rather than assign additional formal assignments she would use informal writing tasks to teach her students to understand course content.

One interesting note: both Dr. U. and Dr. H. had several usage and grammatical mistakes on each of their writing assignments. When Johnston asked if they were intentional, both professors were embarrassed to admit they were not. In both cases, this opened the door for useful discussion about the importance of sentence-level issues, including conversations about the difference between errors and mistakes (errors signal a gap in the student's understanding while mistakes reflect poor proofreading, carelessness, or typos); how sentence-level issues are best taught rather than corrected during the drafting stages (Hillocks 1986); and how much importance should be placed on sentence-level issues during final copy assessment.

We believe that the significant amount of personal attention and classroom modeling Dr. H. and Dr. U. received from the Writing Center enabled them to think critically about the ways they used writing and to recognize the need for and benefits of change. In addition, we suspect that the work the Writing Center did as ambassador plenipotentiary was in many ways more authentic than what most professors experience during the WAC seminars. That is, the professors Johnston met with were currently experiencing difficulty and frustration and wanted immediate assistance. During the discussions Johnston provided that assistance but was also able to engage the professors in discussions about larger, more theoretical issues that informed or explained why the professors were experiencing what they were. In these cases, practice (how to fix the professors' problems) preceded theory (why the professors were experiencing difficulty), and as the problems were solved, the professors became quite interested in the theoretical aspects of the writing process. In the WAC seminars, on the other hand, the professors often are not experiencing difficulties with writing in their classes. As such, they often have no real motivation to try something new. Discussions tend to be more abstract, more theoretical—detached from the professor's actual current classroom experiences.

We feel that this is perhaps what the Writing Center as ambassador plenipotentiary offers to the WAC Program: the chance to reach professors who are experiencing real difficulties with writing in their classes. It may be in these cases that the professors are truly ready to understand, and reject, the myth of transcience and its impact on the way they think about and teach writing.

RESULTS OF WAC/WRITING CENTER RELATIONSHIP

Given our experiences, what possibilities do we see for this type of WAC/Writing Center partnership? We are presenting a model that has not been fully implemented and tested but based on our modest success thus far, we believe that this partnership has the potential to help faculty implement WAC principles in their classes more effectively than WAC alone might. We also see that the WAC seminars alone are not adequate in promoting WAC principles, even when faculty buy into those principles. In many ways, the WAC seminars offer an introduction to principles of discipline-specific rhetorical theory. The application of those principles can be aided by Writing Center personnel when they meet with faculty to discuss specific and current assignments and reasons and ways to use writing in their classes. In addition, the WAC Program promotes the role of the Writing Center as ambassador plenipotentiary by recognizing that WAC workshops alone are insufficient in changing the way faculty *use* writing in their classes. WAC workshops, as we have conceived them, break ground and sow some seeds so that the Writing Center can cultivate and water the soil.

Our experience also adds to the debate about the location of WAC and the Writing Center. While Waldo supports housing WAC in the Writing Center (1993) and others lobby for housing WAC either in the English department (Smith 1988) or in the disciplines (Blair 1988), we believe that where WAC and the Writing Center are housed should depend on theoretical and economic support. That is, the best place for WAC and the Writing Center is where their joint mission is supported by those who adhere to the theoretical advances on rhetorical theory and have adequate resources. In our situation, WAC has worked well under the auspices of the General Education Program because its director is in full sympathy with WAC principles. The director, by the way, is a classicist who learned about WAC as a part of his administrative duties. We wonder whether many faculty in the English Department at Memphis are either aware of WAC principles or practitioners of those principles in their classrooms. Housing WAC in the English Department in our institution, therefore, might not be beneficial to the WAC Program.

A CAUTIONARY CONCLUSION

While we have argued the merits of the Writing Center becoming an ambassador plenipotentiary of the WAC Program and have provided evidence of the need and success of such a relationship, we end on a cautionary note by reviewing the problems we experienced and by noting, unhappily, that changes in the conditions at Memphis cast doubt on the continuing development of the relationship.

First, only one professor in the fall workshops asked for additional writing assignment assistance from the Writing Center. This means that none of the other workshop participants contacted Johnston to ask for help in implementing writing changes in their classrooms, though many indicated that they would. We do not have data to help explain why the professors did not follow up, so any attempt to explain their silence would be speculative. We do see, however, that the burden for assisting professors to implement WAC principles lies with the WAC-Writing Center alliance. Unfortunately, as we will explain momentarily, that alliance has become tenuous.

Second, the Writing Center was underfunded. Administrative support promised to Johnston when he interviewed for the directorship of the Writing Center was not available when it was needed. When minimal support was provided, it was too little and too late. We are not blaming anyone in particular for this problem. We simply note that without adequate support to hire tutors and to conduct the day-to-day business of the Writing Center, it will have difficulty surviving, much less acting as ambassador for the WAC Program.

Now, what is the future? Johnston has taken a position at another institution, primarily because he saw the long-term problems associated with lack of funding for the Writing Center. Indeed, faculty in various departments are reconsidering their commitment to staying at the University because of the funding crisis. The statistics we cited earlier, the average turnover of one WAC participant each year, may well increase. Dr. U., by the way, has taken a position at another institution in another state. The professor in English who worked with Johnston is also leaving because of cuts in the English Department's budget. Are the professors who attend WAC workshops and/or work with the Writing Center the ones who will move to universities where they will be rewarded for their initiative?

Because of the University's economic crisis, Johnston's position will be filled by an English Department instructor, someone who does not have training in Writing Center theory and practice. Will the Writing Center revert to its former method of operation? What will become of the tutoring method Johnston instituted? The new director will receive one course release per semester to administer the Writing Center, so the incentives and rewards for continuing the WAC-Writing Center relationship are quite slim. In addition, Speck has taken a new position within the University, Acting Director of the Center for Academic Excellence. Although he will continue conducting the WAC workshops, the relationship he and Johnston developed between WAC and the Writing Center is probably a historical concern rather than a hope for the future.

Whatever gains we made may become smaller, indeed, as the University strives to tread water during difficult economic times. We hope that Russell's (1991) prediction about WAC Programs becoming failed educational initiatives will not be true for Memphis. Moreover, we are extremely cautious about hoping for a WAC-Writing Center relationship in which the Writing Center continues to function as ambassador plenipotentiary.

The good news is that a Writing Center can be an ambassador plenipotentiary for a modest cost. Certainly, a Writing Center could benefit from substantial expenditures on its behalf, but even the Writing Center at Memphis can move from infancy to adolescence with a modest budget to cover the costs of the director's and the tutors' time. The focus need not be on equipment, such as computers, but on spending time working with students and professors. In addition, both the WAC coordinator and Writing Center director need to be willing to work together to meet students' and professors' needs, not to get in turf wars or ego conflicts. Longevity is also critical. Building a WAC-Writing Center alliance takes time. Both Writing Center and WAC work are slow, requiring years of effort to reach a significant part of the faculty. Building long-term relationships requires a commitment on the part of the University, so ultimately, administrative philosophy and policy are critical in helping faculty develop as teachers, learning how to use writing effectively in their classes.

We began this chapter with the recognition that the myth of transience is alive and kicking in the academy and that the reasons this myth thrives are complex. We end on the same note, believing, though, that the model we have sketched has the potential to eradicate the myth. This can happen only if the other element of the complex organization called the university (an in our case, the state legislature) lend their support to promote enlightened practice based on wise theoretical premises.

WORKS CITED

American Heritage College Dictionary, 3d ed., (1993) s.v. "ambassador."

Bizzell, Patricia. "What Can We Know, What Must We Do, What May We Hope: Writing Assessment." *College English* 49 (1987): 575–584.

Blair, Catherine Pastore. "Only One of the Voices: Dialogic Writing Across the Curriculum." *College English* 50 (1988): 383–389.

Braddock, R., R. Lloyd-Jones, and L. Schoer. *Research in Written Composition*. Champaign, IL: NCTE, 1963.

Calabrese, Marylyn E. "I Don't Grade Papers Anymore." *English Journal* 71.1 (1982): 28–31.

Duke, Charles R. "The Student-Centered Conference and the Writing Process." *English Journal* 64.9 (1975): 44–47.

Ede, Lisa. "On Writing Reading and Reading Writing." *Encountering Student Texts: Interpretive Issues in Reading Student Writing*, eds. Bruce Lawson, Susan Steer Ryan, and W. Ross Winterowd. Urbana, IL: NCTE, 1989. 147–157.

Gabriel, Susan L. "Gender, Reading, and Writing: Assignments, Expectations, and Responses." *Gender in the Classroom: Power and Pedagogy*, eds. Susan L. Gabriel and Isaiah Smithson. Urbana, IL: University of Illinois Press, 1990. 129–139.

Greenhalgh, Anne M. "Voice in Response: A Postmodern Reading of Teacher Response." *College Composition and Communication* 43 (1992): 401–410.

Harris, Winifred Hall. "Teacher Response to Student Writing: A Study of the Response Patterns of High School English Teachers to Determine the Basis for Teacher Judgment of Student Writing." *Research in the Teaching of English* 11 (1977): 175–185.

Hillocks, George, Jr. *Research on Written Composition*. Urbana, IL: NCRE, 1986.

Johnston, Scott. "Basic Writers and Peer Tutoring." Dissertation, University of Nevada, Reno, 1996.

Kline, Charles R., Jr. "I Know You Think You Know What I Said." *College English* 37 (1976): 661-662.

Lawson, Bruce, and Susan Steer Ryan. "Introduction: Interpretive Issues in Student Writing." *Encountering Student Texts: Interpretive Issues in Reading Student Writing*, eds. Bruce Lawson, Susan Steer Ryan, and W. Ross Winterowd. Urbana, IL: NCTE, 1989. vii–xvii.

Lindemann, Erika. *A Rhetoric for Writing Teachers*. 2nd ed. New York: Oxford University Press, 1987. 6.

Lunsford, Andrea. "Collaboration, Control, and the Idea of a Writing Center." *Landmark Essays on Writing Centers*, eds. Christina Murphy and Joe Law. Davis, CA: Hermagoras Press, 1995. 109–116.

Mellon, John C. "Round Two of the National Writing Assessment—Interpreting the Apparent Decline of Writing Ability: A Review." *Research in the Teaching of English* 10.1 (1976): 66–74.

Miller, Susan. "The Student's Reader Is Always a Fiction." *Journal of Advanced Composition* 5 (1984): 15–29.

Mortimer, K. P., A. W. Austin, J. H. Blake, H. R. Bowen, Z. F. Gamson, H. L. Hodgkinson, and B. Lee. "Text of a New Report on Excellence in Undergraduate Education." *The Chronicle of Higher Education.* (24 Oct. 1984): 35–39.

Murray, Heather. "Close Reading, Closed Writing." *College English* 53 (1991): 195–208.

Odell, Lee, and Charles R. Cooper. "Procedures for Evaluating Writing: Assumptions and Needed Research." *College English* 42 (1980): 35–43.

Olsen, Turee. "Grading Alternatives." *English Journal* 64 (1975): 106–108.

Pitts, Mary Ellen, David Sigsbee, and Bruce Speck. "The Vital Role of Writing Across the Curriculum Programs in Faculty Development." *Perspectives* 26.1 (1996): 53–80.

Purves, Alan C. "Reflections on Research and Assessment in Written Composition." *Research in the Teaching of English* 26.1 (1992): 108–122.

———, and Gail Hawisher. "Writers, Judges, and the Text Models." *Developing Discourse Patterns in Adolescence and Adulthood*, eds. Richard Beach and Susan Hynds. Norwood, NJ: Ablex, 1990. 183–199.

Quellmalz, Edys S. "Toward Successful Large-Scale Writing Assessment: Where Are We Now? Where Do We Go From Here?" *Educational Measurement: Issues and Practice* 3.1 (1984): 29–32, 35.

———, Frank J. Capell, and Chih-Ping Chou. "Effects of Discourse and Response Mode on the Measurement of Writing Competence." *Journal of Educational Measurement* 19.4 (1982): 241–258.

Reiff, John D., and James E. Middleton. "A Model for Designing and Revising Assignments." *Fforum*, ed. Patricia L. Stock. Montclair, NJ: Boynton/Cook, 1983. 263–268.

Rose, Mike. *Lives on the Boundary.* New York: Free Press, 1989.

Russell, David R. *Writing in the Academic Disciplines, 1870-1990: A Curricular History.* Carbondale IL: Southern Illinois University Press, 1991.

Ruth, Leo, and Sandra Murphy. "Designing Topics for Writing Assessment: Problems of Meaning." *College Composition and Communication* 35 (1984): 410–422.

Schwegler, Robert A. "The Politics of Reading Student Papers." *The Politics of Writing Instruction: Postsecondary*, eds. Richard Bullock and John Trimbur, Portsmouth, NH: Heinemann, 1991. 203–205.

Sigsbee, David L., Bruce W. Speck, and Bruce Maylath, eds. *Approaches to Teaching Non-native English Speakers Across the Curriculum.* No. 70, *New Directions for Teaching and Learning.* San Francisco: Jossey-Bass, 1997.

Slamecka, N. J., and P. Graf. "The Generation Effect: Delineation of a Phenomenon." *Journal of Experimental Psychology, Human Learning and Memory* 4 (1978): 592–604.

Smith, Louise Z. "Why English Departments Should 'House' Writing Across the Curriculum." *College English* 50 (1988): 390–395.

Throop, David P., and Daphne A. Jameson. "Behavioral Grading: An Approach Worth Trying." *The ABCA Bulletin* 39.3 (1976): 3–5.

Vygotsky, L. S. *Mind in Society*, eds. Michael Cole et al. Cambridge: Harvard University Press, 1979.

Waldo, Mark L. "The Last Best Place for Writing Across the Curriculum: The Writing Center." *WPA: Writing Program Administration* 16.3 (1993): 15–26.
————. "Inquiry as a Non-invasive Approach to Cross-curricular Writing Consultancy." *Language and Learning Across the Disciplines* 1.3 (1996): 7–19.

3

Authority and Initiation:
Preparing Students for Discipline-specific Language Conventions

Jacob S Blumner

Michael Pemberton's article "Rethinking the WAC/Writing Center Connection" asks pointed questions about the success of Writing Across the Curriculum (WAC) Programs and their relationship to Writing Centers. He addresses what he calls the "myth of disciplinarity" in undergraduate education in which students supposedly learn discursive practices specific to each discipline (1995, 120). Pemberton points to shortcomings in the practice, noting that students might simply relay information rather than create knowledge as social constructionists intend, and that students simply may be unaware that they must master discipline-specific conventions (122). In short, according to Pemberton, WAC often fails to provide adequate learning opportunities for students. Compounding the WAC concerns, Pemberton questions the role of the Writing Center, specifically in relation to power structures imbedded in academic institutions. Authority appears in the student-teacher relationship as well as the student-tutor relationship, and Pemberton praises the possible "parity" that can develop between student and tutor.

Pemberton's concerns force WAC coordinators and Writing Center directors to question their practices and relationships. How do WAC Programs function on campuses, and how do they interact with Writing Centers? Issues of disciplinarity and authority are keys to understanding how best to help students enter discipline-specific communities and be productive citizens therein. As Pemberton shies away from the WAC/Writing Center relationship, calling for more examination of both programs, I forward that the two necessarily work together or deprive the students of institution-wide language learning opportunities. David Russell's book (1991), *Writing in the Academic Disciplines, 1870–1990*, chronicles the glacial movement toward and into academic, discipline-specific communities, broadly broken up into departments and further compartmentalized into specializations. Though crossover exists, the nature of discourse has become necessarily specialized, and teaching students how to communicate within disciplinary communities has become a requirement. In addition, some fields, like electrical engineering, have become so complex that the four-year undergraduate degree is extinct, so universities must work to introduce students into a discipline effectively and efficiently.

Instead of working independently or in a loosely connected fashion, I propose Writing Centers and WAC Programs intimately integrate themselves to address issues of specialization and student/teacher, student/tutor, and tutor/teacher authority. With active communication and organization, preferably headed by a single entity, academic institutions can prepare students for the tasks that face them beyond the university.

DISCIPLINE-SPECIFIC LANGUAGE AND STUDENT PREPARATION

Academic institutions train students in particular discipline-specific subject matter, and the primary catalyst, or source, for that learning is the instructor, the closest contact the institution has with the student. There is much debate as to how that instruction should take place and where it should take place, but few debate the importance or primary role of the instructor. In a sense, the instructor is a student advocate, helping the student learn what is necessary to perform certain types of tasks or think in particular ways. The instructor provides activities like reading, lectures, and projects that facilitate that learning. Charles Bazerman, for example, describes how students learn language used in chemistry:

Language use in the communal enterprise of chemistry is taught and learned in textbook diagrams and charts to be memorized, in classroom discussion of the previous night's reading, in pencil problems to be solved, in the teacher's commentary on demonstration experiments, in getting particular bottles down from the shelf, in student groups with lab book on the table attempting to set up an experiment, in the teacher's comment on the experiment's write-up. (1988, 305)

The practices Bazerman lists reflect those of many academic disciplines. Though students may not be taking bottles down from shelves, most will learn from readings, teacher commentary, and practicing what they learn. This is how students "determine whether their results fit in the standard description, how to answer questions" (305). Without these practices and guidance, students struggle unnecessarily to enter a discipline. Each class the student takes within a department or major builds upon knowledge learned in previous courses until the student becomes proficient in the chosen field. For example, the English Department at Kent State University has revised the English major and has incorporated many new courses, required and elective. In a recent discussion at a departmental retreat about the content of those classes, many faculty debated what knowledge students should gain from the three courses, Literature in English I and II, which are sophomore-level courses, and English Studies, a junior-level course, and what expectations faculty members should have of the students passing those courses. Both knowledge and skills were discussed, as well as levels of proficiency. These discussions, formal and informal, are not uncommon in universities, and they are intended to prepare students to do work in later courses and the field at large. Much of the discussion focused on what terms students should learn about literature studies and what writing techniques they should learn and be introduced to. Everyone agreed that certain aspects of writing about literature should be learned. For instance, some faculty believe students must know what a genre is and be familiar with many of them.

Requirements, like the ones considered by my department, point toward the need for students to learn the language of their chosen discipline. One primary requirement of learning a discipline is to master the language of that discipline. In fact, it is a requirement before acceptance into the academic community. David Russell describes writing in the disciplines as "a complex and continually developing response to specialized text-based discourse communities, highly embedded in the differentiated practices of those communities" (1991, 5). Learning the language, the text-based discourse, is vital because, as Tony Becher describes in *Academic Tribes and Territories*, each discipline is a distinct "community, a network of communication, a tradition, a particular set of values and beliefs, a domain, a mode of enquiry, and a conceptual structure" (1993, 20). Thus, the language necessary to talk about the discipline-specific set of values and beliefs, the conceptual structure, and the mode of inquiry is necessary for successful entry into the field of study. Without it, the gates of the discipline are closed. Richard Rorty adapts Thomas Kuhn's concept of normal science to discourse, calling it "normal discourse." He defines it as "that which is conducted within an agreed-upon set of conventions about what counts as a relevant contribution, what counts as answering a question, what counts as having a good argument for that answer or a good criticism of it" (1979, 320). Normal discourse is what people within a discipline participate in daily. As we speak with colleagues, as we speak with students, we use normal discourse. When we venture outside of the accepted discourse, we risk being dismissed by our colleagues or sounding absurd. Students run the same risks, though the ground they stand on is far more tenuous. Rorty labels this as "abnormal discourse," or discourse that does not follow convention. It can be considered nonsense or intellectual revolution. Breaking from the normal discourse, Galileo believed and argued that the earth was not the center of the universe, and he was considered mad, nearly losing his life. Of course we know that his work did result in intellectual revolution. Students, unfortunately, seldom provide intellectual revolution, but often struggle to create normal discourse that will be accepted by the community and more immediately, an instructor. Therefore, it is important to examine how students learn the needed discourse conventions.

The keys to normal discourse taught in the introduction to literature courses at Kent State University, then, develop a greater importance. What will those classes look like, and what guarantee do students have that the conventions and practices introduced to them will help them succeed in future classes and begin their journey into a disciplinary community? During the retreat, I considered the ramifications of students not learning particular discipline-specific conventions, like simply indenting block quotes properly, and I thought about what my colleagues might say in the faculty workroom about student writing inability. The importance of disciplinary conventions is clear. How they are taught and who teaches them, though, is another matter.

AUTHORITY IN EDUCATION

In a discussion of authority, Michel Foucault, in *The Archeology of Knowledge and the Discourse on Language*, ties discipline-specific conventions to authority when he asks, "who is speaking? Who, among the totality of speaking individuals, is accorded the right to use this sort of language (langage)? Who is qualified to do so?" (1972, 50). I ask these questions to begin examining the authority faculty members possess in their respective disciplines and classrooms. Education provides entry into many disciplines—it is the gatekeeping devise. To earn an education means entry into a community of other educated people in a specific discipline. Additional degrees beyond a bachelors degree implies entry into more exclusive communities, and a doctorate can provide entry into the most exclusive of groups.

Foucault uses a medical example to elucidate his point. Our society expects doctors to have earned a college degree, a medical degree, and to excel in rigorous internships. Without those credentials, we, as a society, do not allow people to practice medicine or publish in medical journals. Would you allow an untrained, unlicensed person to perform surgery on you? Most likely not. Still, licensing does not guarantee acceptance or a voice within a disciplinary community. Community members who use abnormal discourse may be considered mad, just like Galileo. For example, the mainstream medical profession often shuns or ghettoizes homeopathic medicine because it is not an accepted part of the profession and discussions of it are frequently considered abnormal discourse. The use of marijuana to help chemotherapy patients long fell into the realm of abnormal discourse. Contribution to the medical conversation about treating cancer patients with marijuana, even from a doctor with the proper credentials, was rejected. Foucault's commentary in this book points to problems people have when not using the "common discourse" stretching back to the Middle Ages. People speaking outside the norm were considered mad, and the potential penalty was death. Today, in the United States, the common discourse is much broader and the penalty is much less severe, but the invisible barriers within disciplines can still be sinister. The common discourse, or normal discourse, of a discipline does not have such clearly defined guidelines, but the cost of not using the proper language or not using the language properly is still exclusion. A simple example is the use of first-person pronouns in hard science writing. Though a scientist may find exemplary results, presenting the information in a first-year composition narrative essay would inevitably result in rejection.

I frequently see this when students struggle to use language new to them. Again in the faculty workroom, instructors lament or mock student misuse of language rather than considering why and how the students use new language. Near the end of the spring term, a faculty member showed me a sophomore's paper about surrealism. First, I was amazed that a student would tackle such a difficult topic on her own. Then I was amazed at her knowledge of surrealism, but it was clear that the student misunderstood some of the ideas Andre Breton presents in *Manifestos of Surrealism*. The faculty member's complaint stemmed from the student's mislabeling of things surreal. Given Breton's affinity for kicking people out of the movement (if that is possible), I understand why anyone would have difficulty defining surreal literature and art. This student stretched the definition to include fantasy, which is probably too great a stretch. I discussed with the instructor how and where the student apparently struggled with the concept. This seems a battle between a cup half full or half empty; I admire the risk the student took, and I sympathize with the student trying to find a place to practice the language of a discipline and having that place of practice (an essay) evaluated. The faculty member in this case, given Foucault's commentary, considered this student mad because she failed to use the normal discourse properly, and he is correct in his evaluation; her definition was unacceptably broad. This example presents problems with learning discipline-specific language. Just as a basketball player may practice free throws for hours in a relatively encouraging environment before needing to shoot them in a game, the student needs to practice specialized language without punitive results before performing in a "game" situation.

Charles Bazerman discusses the learning of academic language in *Shaping Written Knowledge: The Genre and Activity of the Experimental Article in Science* and applies Vygotsky's language development theory for children to students learning the language of a discipline. Teachers socialize students to associate specific meanings with specific "concrete operations on concrete objects" when they enter a discipline, and that association informs not only their use of language, but also the ways in which they think (1988, 305). Thus, the literature student most likely will find different meaning for the green light in *The Great Gatsby* than will the chemistry student. After learning this specialized language, according to Bazerman, community members work to solve problems and to do this they must share more than just the meaning of words; they must understand, "how those generalized words apply in this situation and how they are to be realized in action" (302). More specifically, David Russell claims individuals must be able to operate within the disciplinary matrix of a field in order to write within it (1990, 53). The student writing about surrealism and Breton had not fully developed language and associations to address the problems about which she was writing. Instead, she used words she had just enough knowledge about to get her into trouble. The student's misuse of specific terms set off her instructor's alarm bells. In fact, this type of mistake with language can raise more questions than avoidance of important discipline-specific concepts and terms. So it seems a penalty for the student to try to use the language which she is required to learn. How then can students practice using the language of the discipline in a situation that is conducive to learning and that does not penalize them?

Traditionally, classroom instruction seldom addressed language use and rhetorical strategies directly. And each discipline has its own strategies to teach its students. Within the classroom, there are some drawbacks to learning related to two issues: authority and gatekeeping responsibilities. The two are closely related. The instructor has authority within a number of arenas. First is within the discipline itself. Disciplinary membership is assumed with the education and experience required of academics. With membership comes the authority and expectation to participate in discussions within the field. They may take place in academic journals, at conferences, or among colleagues in the hall. The education also guarantees (for better or worse) the authority to teach within the field. Once in the classroom, other authority issues surface. The teacher-student relationship adds complexity to the situation. Not only does the instructor have membership and authority within the discipline, but also within the classroom at the most basic level because she grades student work. Grading is the primary gatekeeping devise for academic disciplines. If a student cannot succeed within college courses, the institution, with authority to grant entry into a discipline, denies him membership. Herein lies the problem. The instructor is both advocate and evaluator.

Having a student advocate and evaluator in the same classroom, in fact in the same person, can stifle potential learning opportunities. Writing assists learning, as Judith Langer and Arthur Applebee found in their study *How Writing Shapes Thinking* (1987), And in most classes, writing, a primary tool in learning discipline-specific language, serves an evaluative purpose. Classes which use writing traditionally consist of papers or essay exams. It is the exceptional class that uses journal writing or ungraded writing. Papers and essay exams allow students the opportunity to perform the language discussed in class, and they will most likely receive feedback from an authority in the subject, the instructor, in the form of written comments. Those comments, when content based, can serve as a form of conversation within a disciplinary community, thus practice for students to learn how to discuss ideas within a particular discipline. Ultimately, though, the evaluated writing does not allow students to practice in a setting that allows for error and correction, the writing can have punitive results (e.g., a poor grade). Rather, in-class essays and term papers usually serve as tools for the gatekeeper; they provide the instructor the opportunity to determine the success level of each applicant for admission as they should. Sometimes instructors allow students to revise their papers and respond to comments provided. This extends the conversation within the discipline and introduces students to the kind of interactive conversations that take place. The instructor must constantly struggle with which role is primary, advocate or evaluator, and students usually assume the latter.

Disciplinary conversations also take place in the classroom. The instructor may lecture, in what Paulo Freire calls the "banking" model. The instructor simply "pours" information into the students' heads, they take notes and learn the material presented and the language in which it is presented, and the "transaction" is complete (1970). This conversation is one-sided, the authority imparting knowledge to the student. In this model, which George Hillocks (1986) calls the Presentational Mode, the student seldom gets to participate in the conversation, often restricted to question asking at the end of a class session.

A second method of conversation in the classroom is through class discussion, in which students interact with each other, covering the material for the class. It allows students to participate in the conversation and have a valuable input, and the presence of the instructor can guide the students to stay within the bounds of normal discourse. Class discussion can be a double-edged sword because students can practice with guidance, but students also know that their conversation is evaluated and can influence their grades. So, the students get immediate feedback regarding their level of conversational success, but, just like an essay, the opportunity to practice is evaluated and can have punitive results. Also, those not participating, for various reasons, can suffer because they fail to demonstrate knowledge of the material. The constant evaluation can inhibit students, effectively silencing them and denying them valuable opportunities to practice disciplinary conversation. Another drawback of class discussion that Kenneth Bruffee points to is faculty's propensity to turn class discussions into monologues so students "get it" (1984, 10). This, too, can quickly inhibit students from commenting in class. In fact, it doesn't take a monologue to silence students. A simple dismissal or disagreement with a student comment can essentially end a fruitful class discussion.

The faculty member faces a dilemma. As an instructor in an educational institution, her primary role is to prepare students to enter their chosen fields. That means she must serve as a student advocate by designing courses and assignments that facilitate learning and allow students to practice discipline-specific language. She must prepare students to work in the chemistry lab, as Bazerman describes, or deconstruct a piece of literature, and then, more importantly, allow them to do it. Relying on the banking method of education only handicaps students, slowing their preparation for professional activity. She must participate in the discourse of her discipline, remaining an active member who understands changing disciplinary conventions so she may successfully guide students. She must also act as disciplinary gatekeeper, the judge who determines successful preparation for entry into a field and denies underprepared students entry into the disciplinary conversation. Foucault's questions remind us of society's expectations and trust that educational institutions will not grant degrees to the unworthy. If that trust is undermined, then the system fails and the disciplinary conversation becomes meaningless.

How, then, does the faculty member serve as student advocate while simultaneously serving as gatekeeper? Even if she designs assignments and discussions that develop discipline-specific skills without evaluative consequences, students will still view the work in this manner, and rightfully so. The faculty member inevitably makes value judgments about student work and class comments, whether it is graded or not. This is one of her roles. How, then, can educational institutions continue to gatekeep and assist students to enter their chosen academic communities?

Faculty already serve as gatekeepers quite well. They know when a student is ready to advance in or fully enter a disciplinary conversation. They know what is required of normal discourse and they know what it looks like. Sometimes they are less successful conveying requirements to students as other contributors in this book describe, but few question a student's successful entry into a field. What students and faculty do need help with is providing nonpunitive advocacy.

LANGUAGE PRACTICE AND THE WRITING CENTER

Students need the opportunity to practice the language conventions of their discipline, to make their own associations used for knowledge-making and disciplinary communication. Again, though this happens in the classroom, development can be hampered by the desire to perform for the instructor. Instead, a place like the Writing Center allows students to work on their writing and discuss their material without concern for sounding brilliant.

Many have debated the use of the Writing Center as a space for disciplinary conversation. Kenneth Bruffee, in "Peer Tutoring and the 'Conversation of Mankind,'" offers the Writing Center as an alternative to the traditional classroom and a place where "students can experience and practice the kinds of conversations that academics most value" (7). Students can bring writing assignments into a Writing Center and share their ideas and objectives with someone other than their instructor. This allows them to struggle through ideas, explaining and reexplaining concepts and rhetorical decisions to a captive audience that has no grade-giving authority over them. This conversational approach in student/tutor discussion provides different opportunities than the student/teacher conversation. Alice Gillam notes that students "'speak the same language,' they offer more suitable conversation partners than do classroom teachers" (1994, 43). I am not claiming this to be a pure collaboration in what might be considered Andrea Lunsford's "Burkean Parlor" Writing Center, though I think Lunsford's model often proves true in practice. Instead, conversation, in which students speak the same language, affords an opportunity for practice in a different situation that cannot be replicated in the classroom.

Critics of this opportunity and approach first question the meaning of the term "peer" and wonder, first, if it really is a conversation between peers, and, second, if the conversational practice truly benefits the student. John Trimbur questions the juxtaposition of the terms peer and tutor and calls it "a contradiction in terms" (1987, 23). His concerns are valid; a tutor is not an equal to most students entering the Writing Center. Tutors typically have more experience with writing and talking about writing than the students coming for sessions, and the students are typically more experienced in the disciplinary conventions than the tutor.

Still, Bruffee defines students and tutors as peers because they share a common institutional status, that of student. This, too, can be questioned because tutors have an institutional obligation due to their employment in the Writing Center, an extension of the school. I agree that the relationship of peer strains under the obligation of the tutor to the Writing Center, but the boundaries for the tutor are broad and guided by respect for faculty and general Western ethics. For example, no one, tutor or otherwise, should advocate lying or plagiarism, as Alice Gillam discusses in "Collaborative Learning Theory and Peer Tutoring Practice." This is disrespectful of the instructor who assigns writing tasks designed to assist learning and it violates social conventions of lying or stealing ideas. Even with the different knowledge base and the skewed student relationship, the student/tutor discussion offers students the chance to practice disciplinary conventions in a meaningful way.

Some form of inquiry and collaboration is common practice in Writing Centers today. Numerous programs described in this volume rely on it (Barnett and Rosen, Johnston and Speck, Kuriloff, Haviland et al.). It provides opportunities unavailable in the classroom while guarding against the colonization that

Mark Waldo warns against in his article, "Inquiry as a Non-invasive Approach to Cross-curricular Writing Consultancy." Faculty cannot participate in the discussion the same way students do because of the authority and gatekeeping issues. The student will not react the same way to questioning by a faculty member, and the faculty member has a different responsibility to the student when responding to a text. It becomes an ethical gray area when a faculty member considers how much guidance to give a student. Should she tell the student everything he needs to improve, even when inquiry fails? This question magnifies in value when we remember that the instructor will eventually evaluate the student's work. Tutors do not have this conflict when tutoring, so inquiry and collaboration provides another means for students to practice language use (This is not to imply the instructor is not the primary and necessary source of practice as well, only that tutoring provides an additional facet).

Few question the power of the Writing Center to assist students with their writing, and most Writing Center directors would claim that their centers are designed to help students become better writers through the vehicle of the work they bring into a tutoring session. And that writing represents practice for the disciplinary conversation in which students strive to participate. Peer tutoring, with the debates surrounding the terms and approaches, provides students the opportunity to work with the language of their classes and field in non-evaluative settings. Students know when they enter a Writing Center that they will get the undivided attention of a person interested in ideas, writing, and the success of fellow students.

COLLABORATIVE WRITING CENTER AND WAC EFFORTS

The authors in the collection present varied view of how Writing Centers and WAC Programs should collaborate or coordinate, or cautiously advance. Based on the successes discussed here, philosophically, administratively, and practically, more attention should be paid to the possibility for curricular improvement university-wide. Even within potentially disparaging cases like Purdue University's de facto-WAC Center or Mark Waldo's cases of English department colonization, successes can be found, and coordination appears a necessity. Michael Pemberton notes that the Writing Center/WAC connection partly depends "upon certain kinds of instructional failure in WAC Programs," and as he suggests (tentatively and with qualification), the Writing Center staff should address disciplinary discourse in tutoring sessions (1995, 14). Not only should Writing Centers address disciplinary discourse concerns in tutoring sessions, but Writing Center administration should work with WAC administrators and faculty to improve the program failures. In many cases, as discussed in this collection, Writing Center administrators also direct or are intimately involved with WAC programming by serving as WAC committee members or ambassadors to other departments. Interaction benefits Writing Centers and WAC Programs and is vital to each for success.

Writing Centers and WAC Programs play important roles in student learning of discipline-specific language conventions. Faculty represent the primary connection and pathfinders for students wishing to enter discipline-specific communities. They assist students in learning and using language necessary for successful entry into their chosen fields through the earning of a degree, and they are the best prepared to show students the requirements because they understand most intimately what knowledge students need and how they must apply it.

The privileged position of disciplinary community members that faculty maintain also thrusts them into the responsible role of gatekeeping, an inescapable authoritative position. And, in this position of power, faculty must balance precariously the role of student advocate and protector of disciplinary, and academic, standards. As Pemberton points out, sometimes the "WAC courses and their modes-based writing assignments fail" to prepare students for work within the discipline (1995, 14), and I believe this is in part due to faculty's difficulty in this balance. Most faculty using writing in their courses do not have time to work extensively with all of their students, so most faculty only see in the students' final products. In some cases, the so-called "good" students talk with the professor during office hours, but this is only a distorted perspective of how well students interpret and work on a writing assignment. Students often seem intimidated of even the most student-friendly faculty on campus, and seldom ask questions that provide the necessary insight for an instructor to be successful. I certainly know the student-evaluation bubble sheets my students fill out provide little insight into why an assignment was successful or not.

The Writing Center is a place in which students will discuss (uncensored) how well they interpret their writing assignments. Students seem more comfortable in a setting of fellow students, without the faculty member watching and evaluating. In the Writing Center setting, tutors help students solve their own problems with an assignment. Obviously tutors can take the information they gather about student success and difficulty, relay it to a Writing Center administrator, who works with the instructor to refine the writing task. Robert Barnett and Lois Rosen use the Faculty Assignment Drawer (FAD) as one place for coordination. Carol Haviland and Rick Leahy use tutors as liaisons across campus. Tutors, as a resource, should not be foolishly wasted. I am not implying that tutors must be familiar with all disciplinary conventions, as we know that to be impossible, but they can interpret, through direct conversation or body language, how well students understand and react to an assignment. That information, alone, can benefit faculty. Last term a faculty member at my institution decided to rearrange the formats of his assignment, streamlining them with bullets, based on comments students made to my tutors concerning the difficulty they had gleaning specific requirements from the assignment's paragraph form.

As a Writing Center director who coordinates a WAC effort, I am often asked by faculty from different disciplines how much and what kind of structure should be provided to the students; how, and to what degree, they might weigh the assignment for a class; and what methods might be most efficient for grading. I do not claim to have simple answers or all-purpose solutions, as Pemberton warns against. Instead, having worked with students and faculty from many disciplines, I can discuss success stories and failures I have seen. I can coordinate faculty discussions in which faculty with similar goals can share their experiences.

Teaching lore, helpful as it can be, must be supported by theory and reproducible results. Programs, like the one developed at University of Nevada, use Participatory Action Research to work with faculty from various departments like criminal justice, electrical engineering, political science, and accounting to begin to identify and concretize disciplinary conventions in specific writing situations. In this program, faculty designed assignments, used them, and evaluated their success in assisting students to learn discipline-specific knowledge and rhetorical structures. From their results, they improved the assignments and their teaching strategies. I then took the data gathered in meetings and used them as models for others interested in pursuing the same kind of development (Waldo, Blumner, and Webb 1995). This approach succeeded in helping the faculty improve the teaching of writing department-wide and provided the Writing Center with valuable information about what kinds of tasks faculty ask students to perform. In Writing Center meetings, I conveyed faculty goals and assignments to the tutors so they may better assist students, and the tutors relayed information the students told them. I took this information, in a generalized form to protect individual students, back to the faculty so they could use the feedback for improved assignment design. The coordinated efforts of the Writing Center and the WAC Program improved the learning conditions for students because the communication allowed the instructors to better understand their students' writing and their assignments and the Writing Center reached more students with information previously unavailable. Ultimately, the students' potential learning environment improves because of strong assignments and varied locations in which the student can get assistance: the professor representing an authority within a discipline and a center of fellow students providing nonjudgmental opportunities for discussion and discovery.

The University of Nevada program developed practices, using Bazerman, Vygotsky, Russell, Kuhn, Rorty, Lunsford, Harris, White, and others that supported the understanding that students need proficiency in the language conventions of their chosen discipline and that the WAC faculty and the Writing Center must work together to effectively prepare students to participate in normal discourse. Each institution has its own concerns and circumstances ranging from philosophic perspectives on the goals of educational programs to the simple pragmatics of the size of student populations, and schools must develop a programs that supports their needs. As disciplines continue to specialize, (an apparent inevitability), Writing Centers and WAC faculty need to find solutions to issues of student preparation while maintaining disciplinary standards. And I believe the best way to assist students, given the advantages of both WAC Programs and Writing Centers is to partner the efforts of the two, creating a highly efficient, well-coordinated program that services student needs and expedites student progress toward participation in a discipline's normal discourse.

WORKS CITED

Bazerman, Charles. *Shaping Written Knowledge: The Genre and Activity of the Experimental Article in Science.* Madison: The University of Wisconsin Press, 1988.

Becher, Tony. *Academic Tribes and Territories: Intellectual Enquiry and the Cultures of Disciplines*. Buckingham, England: The Society for Research into Education & Open University Press, 1993.

Bruffee, Kenneth. " Peer Tutoring and the 'Conversation of Mankind.'" *Writing Centers: Theory and Administration*. Ed. Gary A. Olson, Urbana, IL: NCTE, 1984.

Foucault, Michel. *The Archeology of Knowledge & the Discourse on Language*. trans. A. M. Sheridan Smith. New York: Pantheon Books, 1972.

Freire, Paulo. *Pedagogy of the Oppressed*. New York: Continuum, 1970.

Gillam, Alice M. "Collaborative Learning Theory and Peer Tutoring Practice." *Intersections: Theory-Practice in the Writing Center*, eds. Joan A. Mullin and Ray Wallace. Urbana, IL: NCTE, 1994. 39–53.

Hillocks, George, Jr. *Research on Written Composition*. Urbana, IL: NCTE, 1986.

Langer, Judith A., and Arthur N. Applebee. *How Writing Shapes Thinking: A Study of Teaching and Learning*. Urbana, IL: NCTE, 1987.

Lunsford, Andrea. "Collaboration, Control, and the Idea of a Writing Center." *Landmark Essays on Writing Centers*, eds. Christina Murphy and Joe Law. Davis, CA: Hermagoras Press, 1995. 109–116.

Pemberton, Michael A. "Rethinking the WAC/Writing Center Connection." *Writing Center Journal* 15.2 (1995): 116–133.

Rorty, Richard. *Philosophy and the Mirror of Nature*. Princeton: Princeton UP, 1979.

Russell, David R. "Writing Across the Curriculum in Historical Perspective: Toward a Social Interpretation." *College English* 52 (1990): 52–71.

———. *Writing in the Academic Disciplines, 1870-1990: A Curricular History*, Carbondale: Southern Illinois UP, 1991.

Trimbur, John. "Peer Tutoring: A Contradiction in Terms." *Writing Center Journal* 7.2 (1987): 21–28.

Waldo, Mark. "Inquiry as a Non-invasive Approach to Cross-curricular Writing Consultancy." *Language and Learning Across the Disciplines* 1.3 (1996): 7–19.

———, Jacob Blumner, and Mary Webb. "Writing Centers and Writing Assessment: A Discipline-based Approach." *Writing Center Perspectives*, eds. Byron L. Stay, Christina Murphy, and Eric H. Hobson. Emmitsburgh, MD: NWCA Press, 1995. 38–47.

4

Neither Missionaries Nor Colonists Nor Handmaidens: What Writing Tutors Can Teach WAC Faculty about Inquiry

Carol Peterson Haviland, Sherry Green,
Barbara Kime Shields, and M. Todd Harper

Many WAC/WID (Writing in the Disciplines) compositionists feel themselves facing two competing and limiting roles: that of expert knowledge transmitter and that of support service provider. On the one hand, because of their affiliations with English departments, cross-disciplinary colleagues and administrators see WAC compositionists as the writing experts who will dispense their expertise to eager faculty members and students, perfecting campuses' WAC projects and thereby eliminating student writing problems. On the other hand, because of the "service status" of composition, WAC compositionists are perceived as handmaidens, relegated to merely supporting the writing programs of other faculty members; in this role, scholarly compositionists chafe at their limited roles and disparage the knowledge they do contribute to avoid imposing on the their disciplinary colleagues' classrooms. In either case, WAC compositionists exist within a "subject-other" relationship with their disciplinary counterparts: either they are the subjects willingly defining and imposing correct writing and ideology upon their disciplinary "others," or they become the others, allowing the institution and their colleagues to define them and their subservient roles. In neither case do they negotiate collaborative and intersubjective relationships with the other. One way of mitigating these hierarchical relationships is for WAC Programs to create interdisciplinary partnerships with Writing Centers, using lessons learned from Writing Center tutors to shape WAC projects. Because tutors work within small groups or one-on-one, they become adept at breaking down barriers and role distinctions between experts and novices, between skills-based partitions and content-based instructors.

Many chapters in this text note the particular contributions writing tutors make to WAC, most often focusing on the work tutors do in improving writers and their writing. This chapter, however, emphasizes the contributions tutors make to faculty WAC participants and to the restructuring of teaching-learning relationships as it foregrounds the tutor-tutee relationship as a rich model of non-hierarchical collaboration. To do so, it describes and theorizes two enactments of this model: 1) a series of in-class draft workshops conducted in an introduction to philosophy course and guided chiefly by Writing Center tutors and 2) a graduate WAC course paired with a faculty WAC seminar. In the draft workshops, faculty members study tutor interactions as tutors and students draft and revise a philosophy instructor's assignments; in the graduate WAC course/faculty WAC seminar, students are paired with disciplinary faculty and Writing Center tutors to pool their expertise as they reimagine the relationships between the disciplines, genres, and pedagogies. In both cases, WAC staff and disciplinary participants begin to transcend the hierarchical roles of subject/other, constructing roles that are more collaborative and intersubjective.

POST-COLONIAL CRITICISM OF WAC

To contextualize this third possibility, we begin by elucidating the subject-other hierarchy that has plagued many WAC compositionists who have found themselves in one or both roles. This hierarchy is at the forefront of the post-colonial critiques of WAC posed by Catherine Blair, Susan McLeod, Christine Farris, Donna LeCourt, Richard Young, and David Kaufer.

In a 1988 article, Blair outlines WAC scholars' struggles against WAC's "missionary seeking to convert the natives" persona. She argues that WAC must leave English departments and be governed by an interdisciplinary committee because of the historical and institutional traditions that place English faculty as "experts presumed to know" about writing and writing-based pedagogies. She insists that when WAC Programs are based in English departments, the faculty are tempted to dominate what should be a heteroglossic and collaborative conversation.

McLeod and Farris refine Blair's critique by extending her model and its rationale. McLeod notes that WAC's roles as "conqueror," "Peace Corps volunteer," "missionary," or "diplomat" position it either as its own agent or as the agent of others, such as university administrations or English departments, thus imposing ideology rather than facilitating change through interdisciplinary collaboration. While Farris does not develop a model, she captures this gap between WAC's rhetoric and practices as she argues that the "us/them" power relationships based in WAC's colonialism are a result of WAC's representation of the disciplines and itself. She notes that WAC constructs the disciplines as idealized or inferior others who lack what only WAC can provide. This position suggests that only WAC conversion can make the disciplines whole. Or as Farris puts it:

Writing Across the Curriculum, in theory, assumes (1) fields not unlike our own are already inviting initiates to join interesting disciplinary conversations and engaging in the sorts of practices we hope to foster; or (2) after colleagues are converted in Writing Across the Curriculum, writing in their courses will function in the ways we want it to:

as a mode of social behavior characteristic of a particular discourse community. (1992, 113)

The latter, in particular, is revealing in that Farris suggests that WAC is attempting to control disciplinary pedagogies by creating identifiable and recognizable others.

All three, Blair, McLeod, and Farris, argue for an interdisciplinary model of WAC, Blair for WAC to be overseen by an interdisciplinary committee; McLeod for WAC to remain an autonomous agent, accountable only to itself; and Farris for WAC to rethink its representations to go beyond a simple us/them dichotomy. However, Farris only hints at Elaine Maimon's Beaver College experience as something along these lines. Indeed, even inquiry that appears less colonial—efforts to understand "how sociologists (or chemists or accountants) write"—often is chiefly focused on helping WID compositions become the disciplinary writing experts who then can tell sociologists how to improve their own or their students' writing. Less often, it constructs learning exchanges that reshape the writing and the teaching of both compositionists and sociologists. George Dillon, in fact, criticizes Elaine Maimon's work in his article "Maps and Genres: Exploring Connections in the Arts and Sciences" for trying to secure disciplinary ideology and culture by mapping out genre conventions. He writes that "her basic metaphor is thus exploration and mapping of discursive space, populated by helpful natives, and filled mainly with rules clustered around genres." Dillon adds, "had she considered instead the equally common metaphor of disciplines as cultures, however, she might have been less sanguine about the ease with which English teachers could 'become conversant' in other disciplines, much less penetrate to the tacit knowledge of participants, package it, and convey it to the students in a required composition course" (1991, 3).

At some level, all of these positions place WAC/WID compositionists as colonists or missionaries, representing the disciplines as wholly "other" than itself and tacitly characterizing them as "heathen" or "novices" and, thus, at once reducing difference yet radicalizing it. Like many pedagogical reforms that precede it, WAC initiates change by projecting onto the other a lack or void for which only WAC can fill. WAC then attempts to replicate itself through the convert who is a disciplinary native yet ideologically whitewashed with WAC pedagogies. These converts—sociologists in WAC clothing—WAC compositionists hope will be able to slip WAC further into unfriendly disciplinary territories while policing existing disciplinary practices.

On the other hand, both Louise Smith and Donna LeCourt have cautioned WAC directors not to become complacent with the other role of "other"—with what we have termed the "handmaiden" in service to her disciplinary others. In this role, rather than as contributors of significant knowledge, WAC compositionists are perceived as simply giving the disciplines the language they need to talk about what they already know.

Smith, who wrote the original response to Blair, argues that WAC should not give up what it does know about writing, and she insists that WAC should remain housed within English departments because English faculty, in particular composition specialists, have invested a great deal of time into research into writing. However, she also notes that WAC should not be dominated by English faculty. LeCourt is even more direct, stating: "What I fail to realize when we express concern about foisting our agenda on our colleagues is that any WAC work involves initiating both pedagogical and theoretical change. If change is not included as part of WAC work, we effectively silence ourselves as much as the missionary model silences our colleagues" (1996, 402). LeCourt's contention should not be taken lightly. Many WAC compositionists do silence themselves in fear that they will not silence the other. LeCourt's contention also shifts the debate by considering how we might theorize a model that silences neither WAC compositionists nor their disciplinary partners—how WAC participants can enact and interrogate ideologies of change without either dominating or being dominated in their conversations.

In theorizing this model (this third possibility), it is important to note something about these critiques. First, the representations that Farris, in particular, speaks of require a certain amount of distance between WAC and its disciplinary counterparts in order to theorize one as "subject" and the other as "other." Indeed, many WAC compositionists are loathe to know their disciplinary colleagues beyond workshop presentations or telephone consultations about how to gain WAC status within the university. Where there is more contact, often it is as WAC compositionists assess disciplinary classrooms. Yet, too rarely, WAC administrators actually have a great deal of close one-on-one contact with their disciplinary colleagues because of time, size of the university, or budgetary constraints. Second, post-colonial theories open particularly fruitful critiques of WAC scholarship and practices as they interrogate the ways WAC has colonized the disciplines by imposing writing practices from English departments or rhetoric and composition scholarship. Indeed the teaching culture that promotes gaining authority through knowledge and visible expertise undergirds much of faculty members' experience (the ways that they have acquired degrees, their acceptance into university discourse communities, and their progress through promotion and tenure reviews), so it is difficult for them to discard these strategies as they move into cross-disciplinary discourses.

David Kaufer and Richard Young offer quite possibly the best solution to these problems, suggesting "reflective practices" as a model that encourages faculty to begin using writing-based pedagogies by reflecting on their own writing experiences, their class goals, and their students. Within this model, WAC directors work intimately with one or two disciplinary practitioners rather than large groups of faculty members to facilitate reflection. While it is true that colonizing can occur within any relationship, these more intimate pairings in which the distinctions between experts and novices, between skills-based practitioners and content-based instructors begin to blur, help disciplinary practitioners realize that they too can build theory (lore) from their practices. Kaufer and

Young cite Donald Schon's work on reflective practices in education: "A clear implication of Schon's theory is to blur the boundaries between insider and outsider since a reflective practitioner must constantly 'get outside' his or her context in order to understand it better. Consequently, Schon argues that a reflective practitioner should have an entirely different relationship to a client than a professional committed to the notion of the technical expert [which we see critiqued in the post-colonial criticisms]" (1993, 98). In short, the reflective practices create an intersubjective and interdisciplinary space where the distinctions between the participants begin to blur as they interchange roles, skills, and knowledge.

Unfortunately, many would point out, most WAC Programs do not have the time to work one-on-one with faculty. In fact, many programs rely on large workshops and seminars as their only contact between faculty. However, the writing tutor model offers a way out of these problems because tutors work in a different arena. A central characteristic of tutoring writing is that it is conducted on an interpersonal and collaborative level. Tutors are not removed from day-to-day contact with others as so often WAC directors can become. Instead, they are transients, daily learning and negotiating meanings with others, less conditioned to exert claims of expertise and to dominate their arenas because their educational goals usually are different from those of the student writers they tutor. As they model this movement between the roles of teacher and learner, tutors can bring faculty members more into these same fluid roles. Thus, writing tutors often engage in the very type of reflective practices encouraged by Kaufer and Young. For example, students may find dealing with the academic communities' new ideas and genres both frustrating and intimidating. Teachers trying to engage these newcomers also may feel overwhelmed not only by the sheer number of students by also by their various backgrounds and learning styles. Writing tutors can help bridge these gaps as they guide both students and faculty members through the complex negotiations the discourse community boundaries present. Tutors can help students and faculty members communicate with each other and locate themselves within their shared communities.

Certainly, there is no guarantee that tutors will not intentionally or unintentionally colonize; just like faculty members, some tutors crave control and dominance even when they do not possess it, and others may colonize as they attempt to be helpful. However, several of tutors' characteristics help distance them from the role of colonizer and the possibility of colonization.

First, because tutors are students and not saturated with professorial authority, they lean toward learner rather than teacher roles. Because they are less frequently treated with deference, they are more likely to negotiate than to impose. Second, tutors have little to gain by colonizing; each day they move between colonies, so they regularly see their own colony as but one of many. Third, even if tutors do try to colonize, students are more likely to resist them than they are professors. Unlike professors, tutors do not give grades, so they exert less tangible pressure, and they do not have disciplinary authority, so students bring essential authority to the tutoring tables.

COLLABORATIONS GUIDED BY WRITING CENTER TUTORS

Being in the middle often is seen as undesirable, as losing no matter which way one turns. Tutors occupy this middle position in almost every writing conference they conduct, for they are situated between student writers and faculty members or other assignors/readers of that writing. However, rather than letting themselves be battered by the opposing forces, tutors quickly learn to construct their middleness positively so that they can connect writers and readers without providing themselves as bloodied battlefields. As they participate in WAC work, then, writing tutors can show faculty members how they too can reimagine the novice-expert roles that often construct faculty WAC participants: composition faculty as writing experts and philosophy novices; philosophy faculty as philosophy experts and writing novices. Rather, tutors can show both how moving to the middle helps them collaborate more fully, and how they can become more than a compositionist and a chemist duct-taped together.

An example of this middleness arose out of our discussions with a philosophy faculty member on the ways faculty members and students negotiate assignments. We had begun our collaboration with him when he called, despairing of his students' "inability or unwillingness to write coherent and properly edited" papers. He had asked students to read two classical philosophical arguments, the Eurthyphro and the Crito, to summarize one of them, and then to argue a position, using the text's argumentation model. Students struggled to read the texts and then struggled harder to write their own arguments, often because they neither understood nor valued the project. They certainly could not imagine why anyone other than their philosophy professor would care whether piety was pious because it was loved by the gods or was loved by the gods because it was pious. Indeed, their summary comment to the writing tutors was that they were very tired of the pious and their piety. Likewise, even though they did care a great deal about whether U.S. citizens had a moral obligation to support U.S. laws, they became hopelessly tangled in Socrates' Crito argument and saw it as an obstacle rather than an aid to charting their own decisions as citizens. And, because they felt so disinterested and hopeless about the assignment to summarize philosophical arguments and use them in their own decision-making, they paid even less attention to editing their papers in the academic English their instructor desired.

Initially, the philosophy professor saw negotiation as students' efforts to chip away at assignments, to make them easier, to earn higher grades with less effort. Thus, he felt on guard when students questioned their assignments, resolving that next time he would write the assignment even more carefully so that it could not be misinterpreted and left little to question. He saw his students' view of negotiation as a way to make an assignment easier: requiring fewer resources or less time, due on a more convenient (later) date, or graded more flexibly. His sense was that both he and they saw negotiation as a win-lose situation, one that the philosophy professor tried to avoid and students tried to make more subtle and thus successful.

Opening several class sessions to tutor-led draft workshops showed all of us—philosophy and WAC faculty, WAC tutors, and philosophy students—that all assignments *are* negotiated, whether faculty members or students are aware of the processes. We could see that even when faculty members stonewall, students negotiate collectively or individually through resistance. More often, however, some visible negotiation occurs, but with both negotiators working toward not losing too much rather than imagining that both could win.

Also, tutors helped all of us see how the win-win could occur. For example, when the philosophy professor saw that his students were indeed struggling both to understand the reading and to compose their writing, he began to listen to their comments, and, as he listened, their comments became questions rather than complaints. As he watched tutors work through the assignments with students, he could see that just "reading it again" produced little gain, and he could see that although he had been inspired by Socrates and Plato, his students were befuddled or angered. He then began to watch tutors create logic bridges, asking what kinds of decisions students made that resembled the piety or citizenship issues of the Eurthyphro and the Crito. He began to see that simply trying to foist his enthusiasm for Socrates off on his students was enacting a dream rather than teaching. And so, he began to read with his students rather than exhort them to "read more carefully." He showed them what careful reading means in philosophy, but he also showed them how that same kind of careful reading might be useful in advertising or chemistry.

Then, as students began to write, he listened as tutors drew out their questions. A second feature of this middleness is that when tutors work with students, roles often are reversed as students become teachers. For example, when tutors tried to help students untangle their philosophy arguments, students first had to explain the philosophy to their tutors, which helped the students understand the arguments they were trying to make. Tutors, as interested, intelligent, but uninformed audiences, could encourage students to organize philosophical arguments that would make sense to other readers. This interaction also is valuable because it reinforces students' positions as members of the philosophy discourse community and it enacts composition theories about reader-writer relationships.

As he heard them ask students why they took the positions they selected, he was able to help students craft those positions into Socratic logic—and finally to see how Socratic logic might help them argue with California's governor about affirmative action or with an employer about workplace ethics. When he could see students' negotiating as trying to situate themselves within discourses, and when students could see negotiating not merely as reducing their work loads but as creating more productive interactions with both their professor and their writing projects, both could see the newly-negotiated writing assignment as a more worthwhile project.

Thus, rather than the WAC director hierarchically moving in to reshape the philosophy culture with her beliefs about student-centered learning, tutors occupied their "in the middle" roles that illuminated the philosophy and compo-

sition stages. Rather than any of the actors—philosophy professor, WAC director, tutors, or students—being missionaries, colonizers, or handmaidens, all engaged in trying to understand and construct the arena. However, tutors were
central to this understanding and constructing because they were best positioned
to see common interests and beliefs as well as differences and could thus open
forums where participants could suspend belief and learn from their differences.
We believe that because only tutors can enact this in the middle position, they
may be the best suited to model non-hierarchical collaboration and, therefore,
are critical models for Writing Center/WAC collaborations. We are not arguing
that either WAC directors or disciplinary faculty are expendable—indeed their
knowledge and positions make their leadership essential to the existence and
continuity of WAC Programs. However, again we want to reject the either/or in
favor of a richer choice—the WAC director/writing tutor/interdisciplinary faculty orchestration that allows WAC directors and faculty to learn from tutors as
well as for tutors and students to learn from and produce for directors and faculty members.

TUTORS ENACTING COLLABORATION IN A FACULTY WAC SEMINAR

A second example of tutors modeling non-hierarchical collaboration
occurred in a graduate composition and rhetoric course in WAC offered in conjunction with a faculty WAC seminar. Graduate students met twice weekly in a
regular class configuration to read, discuss, and write about WAC theory and
practice. In addition, several class members attended the weekly faculty WAC
seminar, pairing themselves with a faculty member from a discipline other than
English. Barbara Kime Shields, who was linked with a sociology faculty member, describes their collaboration: "What was most striking is that in one sense
we both were experts, but in another sense neither of us was. She was a professor and I was a student, but I wasn't her student, so our relationship was unfamiliar enough to both of us that neither had preconceived plans for it—we just
both worked along. I was trying to learn what I could from her about sociology
and writing, and she was trying to learn from me about writing and sociology,
so we didn't worry too much about who knew what. For both of us, it was easier
to forget about expertise than it had been in any other academic setting."

Similarly, the sociologist described an unusual freedom working with
Barbara, noting Barbara's fluid movements from teacher to student to teacher in
the sociology office, the Writing Center, or the WAC seminar room. Her students also observed their professor in a new role as she interacted with Barbara
in the sociology classroom. Again Barbara was in the middle: she could ask the
sociologist when she was confused about a piece of writing, and she could ask
students about the ways they were understanding the class, modeling an openness of inquiry that had not existed before she joined the class.

How then can this partnership model become more than just a good
idea? We conclude then, by offering suggestions in these areas: work for the

WAC compositionist/WC director, work for tutors, and work for disciplinary WAC faculty.

WAC Compositionist/Writing Center Director

The ideology and practices of the WAC compositionist/WC director are central. In some settings, this involves a single person, in others two or more, but in any case, this position(s) is key. Unless these leaders invite and model non-hierarchical collaboration, tutors will not challenge the visible hierarchies and disciplinary faculty are likely to follow established norms: tutors working under faculty members' direction. However, our work on this chapter confronted us with a provocative example of how quickly we let these roles shape us.

When Sherry, Barbara, and Carol began discussing the chapter's conclusion, they agreed quickly that it should provide a "so what?" And, they easily settled on describing the contributions that these new WAC collaborations needed from WAC director, tutors, and disciplinary faculty. Equally quickly, they agreed that Carol should describe how WAC directors could best help tutors emerge from their handmaiden positions—and here we stepped into the same trap we had been critiquing. Sherry and Barbara, not Carol, knew best what they needed from Carol to insert more fully into the collaboration. To enact our own model, then, Sherry and Barbara describe ways WAC directors and disciplinary faculty can foreground the knowledge that tutors bring from their middle positions.

Tutors

Although it takes real effort for professors to listen rather than speak, tutors actually have harder work to do. Not only do we have to recognize what we can contribute, we also have to make those contributions heard by people who aren't trained to listen to us. So, first we need WAC directors and disciplinary faculty who recognize our value as more than handmaidens, and they have to take the lead in this.

We go into WAC classrooms or student conferences expecting to help students wrestle with the writing others have assigned; we are in the middle but closer to the students, and we are working with professors from whom we expect to learn more than teach. We ask more questions than they do! For example, when Sherry began working with the philosophy project, she began by helping with class workshops that Carol orchestrated with a philosophy professor (Chris). As Sherry describes it:

The first shift came says Sherry when Carol asked me to join Chris and her in planning the workshops. I began to understand what we were doing before we did it; however, the biggest change came when Carol referred one of Chris' questions to me. Rather than answering his question about why students were confused about their exegeses, she asked me, commenting that I'd worked with more of his students than she had and probably had better insight. At first this shocked me; I didn't expect this role, but then it made a lot of sense because I knew exactly why they were stuck. However, I would not have spoken up if Carol hadn't asked me. Her move was essential, both to get me to talk and to get Chris to take me seriously. From that point on, we worked more like a team of three—or four or five or six, depending upon how many tutors were involved.

Something similar occurred in the WAC seminar, says Barbara:

The first day we came, we students just naturally took seats around the room's periphery, not at the seminar table with the faculty, and no one questioned our choice. However, as we sat there, we were observers, even when we knew we could have asked some useful questions. The following week, we were invited to move to the table, and later we were officially paired with faculty members. These two moves the directors made changed our relationships. Sitting at the table made us speak up and be heard like all of the other participants, and having a designated pairing helped both us and the faculty see that the directors knew we could do more than watch.

Also, there is a second element, says Barbara:

In addition to creating these relationships within existing collaborations, WAC directors also could promote tutor legitimacy by arranging other tutor-disciplinary faculty interactions. For example, tutors often know best why students can't write professors' assignments because they hear the students' questions directly and so are ideal consultants on writing assignment design. When I worked with a group of sociology students, I functioned as an ear, listening for where they were struggling to produce their papers. I think that students were more willing to show their confusion to me than to their professor because they didn't see me as having the same power over them; it didn't matter whether I thought they were brilliant or not. In fact, they saw me as a struggling student writer too. Later, when I met with their professor, I could relay the students' concerns with the assignment, and then we worked together to revamp her writing assignments so that students could better understand and then produce them. Thus, if WAC/WC directors advertised assignment consultations with tutors as part of Writing Center/WAC services, tutors would be positioned as collaborators rather than as handmaidens.

So, from WAC directors, tutors need two things, say Sherry and Barbara: they need to help us recognize in our own minds what we know, and they need to legitimate us in the eyes of disciplinary faculty. But they can't do everything, Sherry and Barbara add:

Clearly, tutors need WC/WAC directors to help them connect as professionals with faculty members. But, they have to do some of the work themselves. We need to step up—to take the risks of being fuller participants, which means we need to risk thinking aloud along with our professors and occasionally to be wrong, just as they are, say Sherry and Barbara. One way for tutors to do this with faculty members is use the same kind of thoughtful questioning with professors that we use with students. Here again our middleness helps. We don't just tell students what's wrong with their writing and how to fix it, and this is productive with professors too. Rather than saying that their assignments are lousy, from hell, or not likely to generate the responses they are hoping for, we can ask for their intended responses or for the assignments' goals. Just as we do with students, we can help professors discover their own answers to their questions, and it keeps us from colonizing. We aren't trying to sell them our answers to their questions but to help both of us understand the complexity of both the questions and the answers.

Disciplinary WAC Faculty

Again, although our first response was to ask a disciplinary faculty member such as Chris to write this section, we turn to Sherry and Barbara to help us see how disciplinary faculty can make these collaborations work.

Says Sherry, Chris did something in his class last term that reshaped our relationship with us and with his students. At first, he asked us to be the philosophy grammar police, to go over his students' papers and list the areas where they violated written academic English. When we resisted this role, arguing that we could and should do more with writing, together we revised his plan so that students came to us for more global assessments both of their own writing and of the writing assignments. Our discussions with Chris repositioned all of us: the tutors became co-inquirers with the professor, the tutors and students became collaborators, and the students and professor worked together on philosophy papers rather than have students writing and professor grading.

Likewise, the sociologist I worked with made some moves that shaped my relationship with her positively, reports Barbara. After we were paired in the WAC seminar, she invited me to attend some of her classes and then to meet with her to talk about sociology, her students, and their writing. This made me believe that she was taking me seriously, that we were meeting not just for me to learn from her but for us to learn about the intersections of sociology and writing together. Also, as I began to tutor some of her students in the Writing Center, I began to see myself as part of the sociology discourse community, as did an increasing number of sociology students who began to seek me out for writing conferences.

So, tutors need disciplinary faculty to reimagine the tutor-professor relationship as that of co-inquirers, to expect to learn as well as to teach, to risk not knowing everything in front of a student, even a graduate student. Also, tutors need disciplinary faculty to model this regard to students; when they show students that they see tutors not as handmaidens but as collaborators, students will be more likely to follow their lead.

In sum, the writing tutor model offers a rich third possibility that transcends the troublesome otherness of the colonial and the handmaiden models. Unlike WAC missionaries or handmaidens, writing tutors are in the middle, and their responses to this middleness are significant for WC/WAC partnerships. Both missionaries and handmaidens use the unequal leverage of competing ideologies to play off one another rather than to negotiate shared meaning. Missionaries use the ideology of the English department, composition studies, or university administrators to convert the disciplinary practitioners who have been constructed as the unenlightened and who thus are not valued for the knowledge they do have. Within such situations, for example, science faculty teaching WAC courses are pressed to adhere to discourse conventions that reflect the essay writing of the humanities and not the report writing of the sciences. For handmaidens, the situation is reversed so that the ideology of the disciplinary participant is all that counts. Handmaidens thus are placed within service roles in which they cannot offer any of the pedagogical reform that might shape disciplines constructively.

In contrast, successful writing tutors negotiate different ideological positions rather than resist one in order to impose another. In the case of the philosophy classroom, writing tutors worked with the WAC director, the philosophy professor, and the philosophy students to generate a solution that helped guide the students through a shared construction of the Eurthyphro and the Crito. Similarly, as Barbara collaborated with the sociologist, she negotiated in a manner that reminded both tutor and sociologist that meaning was constructed rather than already determined. Indeed, both post-colonial theory and WAC pedagogy suggest that this interdisciplinary partnership of WC and WAC is fertile and that the writing tutor model is pivotal in challenging the existing missionary/handmaiden roles.

More importantly, though, writing tutors reduce the distance between the goals of WAC Programs and disciplinary practitioners by establishing one-on-one relationships. These close contacts are especially important when WAC Programs are too large for directors to meet with faculty members individually. By orchestrating contact between a number of tutors and faculty members, directors are freed to direct WAC Programs. Moreover, as Kaufer and Young point out, such contact accompanied by active reflection from both tutors and disciplinary practitioners will begin to break down the barriers that objectify disciplinary practitioners as potential converts or WAC administrators/tutors as handmaidens. Rather, through these contacts, both groups begin to see each other as important resources whose expertise cannot be reduced to simple categories of content and skill but as threads in the same cloth.

WORKS CITED

Blair, Catherine. "Only One of the Voices: Dialogic Writing Across the Curriculum." *College English* 50 (1988): 383–389.

Dillon, George. *Contending Rhetorics: Writing in the Academic Disciplines.* Bloomington: Indiana University Press, 1991.

Farris, Christine. "Giving Religion: Taking Gold: Disciplinary Cultures and the Claims of Writing Across the Curriculum." *Cultural Studies in the English Classroom*, eds. James Berlin and Michael Vivion. Portsmouth, NH: Boynton/Cook, 1992.

Kaufer, David, and Richard Young. "Writing in the Content Areas: Some Theoretical Complexities." *Theory Into Practice in the Teaching of Writing: Rethinking the Discipline*, ed. Lee Odell. Carbondale: Southern Illinois University Press, 1993: 71–105.

LeCourt, Donna. "WAC as Critical Pedagogy: The Third Stage?" *JAC: A Journal of Composition Theory* 16 (1996): 389–435.

McLeod, Susan. "The Foreigner: WAC Directors as Agents of Change." *Resituating Writing*, eds. Joseph Jangelo and Kristen Hansen. Portsmouth, NH: Boynton, 1995: 108–116.

Smith, Louise. "Opinion: Why English Departments Should 'House' Writing Across the Curriculum." *College English* 50 (1988): 390–394.

5

Finding Common Ground When WAC Writing Center Directors Meet Neurotic Pride

Mark L. Waldo and Maria Madruga

In an article published in 1988, Catherine Blair observed of English departments that they "should have no special role in writing across the curriculum—no unique leadership role and no exclusive classes to teach—not even freshman English" (383). Entrusting English with writing across the curriculum (WAC), she asserts, stems from the belief that the "English department has a special relationship to language and is, therefore, the department that knows the most about writing—in fact, the department that *owns* writing" (384, her emphasis). For Blair, however, this belief has no merit. While English does own its particular brand of writing within its "particular cultural context," so does every other discipline; and no one discipline's context for language is an innately privileged one. Her conclusion is that WAC should be taken from English, which then becomes "only one of the voices," and put into the hands of many disciplines, creating what she terms a dialogic cross-curricular program. Blair, we believe, is the first writer in composition studies to point out the potential difficulties which may emerge when campus-wide responsibility for writing is removed from English departments. This situation, she observes euphemistically, "could irritate [them]" (388). Why is the term "irritate" euphemistic? And why would English be irritated by sharing responsibility for teaching writing? What forms might this irritation take? And how may they be defused? In this essay, we want to address these questions, focusing on the often uneasy relationship between WAC writing center directors and English departments.

Almost any writing center director responsible for WAC can describe some conflict with English departments, even when the directors are themselves faculty members in English. These conflicts range from the mundane to the sublime: from minor jealousies generated when faculty in the disciplines consult the center director about using writing assignments instead of consulting, say, the director of writing in the English department; to debates with English over whether it should teach required writing courses at all (freshman composition), or attempt to teach courses for other disciplines (i.e., writing for the sciences, writing for business, writing for engineering); to fundamental differences in theory and practice which may surface over whose values, purposes, and forms for writing should prevail—those of one discipline or many. Each one of these conflicts stems, in large or small part, from pride of ownership; and each may result in irritation, or much more. We look to the source of these conflicts in an unusual arena—that of Third Force psychology, elderly in 1990s terms but still extraordinarily influential. But before we do, we want to offer a narrative which we hope will bring the problem substantially to life.

In 1996, a student graduated with an MA in rhetoric and composition at a university in Nevada. There, she had taken courses in rhetorical history, composition theory, applied linguistics, and writing in the academy. Her course work was supplemented by a varied menu of teaching in the freshman English program; tutoring for three years in a writing center, the home for WAC on her campus; and designing and coordinating a cross-curricular tutoring program for Native American students—an activity which helped her in her work with the diverse communities and cultures on her campus. She had a special interest in community college positions in the West and saw an advertisement for a tenure track position as an English/Writing Instructor and "writing lab director" at a community college in northern California—a seemingly ideal situation for her, and one for which she was qualified.

Asked to come to campus, she entered the interview process with confidence in her education, abilities, and experience. Each of the interviews went well, particularly that with the College's President. During each, she described her long and short term goals as a potential new faculty member. Her long term goal was to house WAC in the "Writing Center" while keeping it strongly connected to the writing program. As a part of the Center housing WAC, she would conduct assignment-design and paper grading workshops to help faculty integrate writing into the classrooms of all disciplines. The short term goal was to train tutors, work with developmental writing students, bring students into the computer writing world, and teach her composition classes. For his part, the President was excited about this prospectus. His only request was that she switch her long and short term goals, making WAC the priority, because the College had a strategic plan which depended on interdisciplinary teaching. Fifteen minutes after this interview, the President requested that she be hired on the spot.

This young professional's awareness of trouble began before her first semester started, at a very early meeting with the English Department. Asked to describe her priorities for the Center, she understandably presented the same vision she presented during her interviews. Far from the endorsement she received earlier, however, she was met with English faculty demands. Basically, they wanted her to focus on the sentence-level writing skills of the students in their courses through skills workshops, editing sessions, and computer-aided instruction.

Once the semester started, nonetheless, she began to do with the Writing Center what she had said she would do: to offer WAC workshops, train tutors in question-asking and collaborative techniques proceeding from global to local issues, develop the computer lab, work with basic writers, and open tutoring to students from all disciplines. English was far from supportive. English faculty particularly resented her WAC workshops, complaining to their (and her) Director about her audacity at presenting herself as a writing consultant to all the disciplines on campus. They also resented her resistance to focusing the Center's efforts on sentence-level correctness through tutoring and computing. Feeling more isolated, and hoping to confirm administrative support, she set up a meeting with the President. His response to her concerns was plain enough: he said she needed to work it out with the English Department. Following this meeting, the Vice President advised her to keep her head down and work hard. As long as she was successful, nobody would complain.

Though the political atmosphere outside the Writing Center seemed nothing short of dismal, the environment inside was dynamic. She hoped to lessen some of the English Department's discontent by documenting increasing use of the Center, and therefore kept detailed statistics of student and faculty traffic. From the spring of 1996, the semester prior to the inception of the WAC model, to the spring of 1997, student use increased 140 percent. In addition, the Center was now serving twenty-five disciplines. The English Department's lack of receptivity belied the growing support from other disciplines across campus, and from the students themselves.

At the first English Department meeting for the spring semester, her report of the Writing Center's accomplishments was met with critical attacks: "My students need a workshop on the use of commas." "Do you know anything about writing skills software?" "I had a student tell me that it was so noisy in the writing lab that she couldn't get any work done." In past meetings this Center Director had drawn from research and theory to support her practice. In addition, she had tried to point out what the Center could do for them: to tutor their students through techniques which would help them to become better revisors of their writing in both the short and long term, and to offer tutoring which opened itself to the student writers in other disciplines so that the responsibility for teaching writing might be increasingly shared. But this time she was tired and became immediately defensive. Instead of explaining what the Center could do for them, she simply responded that, as she had already explained, "the Writing Center utilizes the process of inquiry and collaboration, and no, we will not be loading any grammar software programs on the computers."

After that meeting the difficulties escalated: the Writing Center Director had finally tripped and English faculty seemed ready to use her mistake to its fullest potential. For a second time, she was called into the division Director's office where she was told to apologize to the English Department for her actions during the meeting. He told her that things didn't look good, and that her tenure committee, which consisted of four English faculty, were considering not renewing her contract with the College. Her story, decidedly bleak now, does not continue so, as we shall see.

In situations such as the one described above, a prospective writing center director explains what she will do if hired and when hired undertakes that activity with success. Then the shocking and unexpected happens: her early activities and accomplishments are not what the English department wants. They are, in fact, nearly opposed to English department desires. English sees its "writing lab" slipping away, perhaps still working with its students but with many others as well, and in ways different from before: not on sentence-level correctness alone but on the paper overall. It sees a faculty member hired by the department spending much of her time consulting with others, helping faculty in other disciplines to assign writing and lessening the responsibility for teaching writing that English has long borne. Faculty and students turn to the Writing Center, and not to those tradition-ally expert within the department, for consul in furthering the writing enterprise on campus. Resentments and conflict grow. As a member of the English department, whose performance reviews come from its members, this movement translates into something fierce for her. She is isolated, even spurned; her performance reviews are negative, and her job is threatened.

How could this phenomenon occur?

Before answering, we want to acknowledge the human complexities of such a question and offer a brief qualifier. People have individual personalities. People have personalities within communities, and communities themselves have personalities, in the Geertzian sense that they provide for their inhabitants "ways of being in the world," "forms of life," "varieties of noetic experience" (Geertz 1983, 155). These multiple personalities and visions will likely generate conflict in the best of circumstances because they rub against each other in ways which produce friction. In a healthy environment, this friction evolves new and better paradigms, models for solving problems. In an unhealthy environment, however, conflict may produce casualties, as individuals or communities cling to models with which they have grown comfortable and others try to change those models. This essay makes no effort to account for these variables because it cannot, the variables being as complex and numerous as the numbers of people involved in WAC Writing Centers, English departments, and faculty in the disciplines. Instead, it focuses on situations in which people explain in advance what they will do, are then hired, and in doing it are condemned or abandoned. Now to the qualifier. This explanation does not mean to take itself too seriously (it is hyperbole) or to render point by point applicability.

For this explanation we turn to Karen Horney, therapist and researcher into the neurotic condition, whose chapter "Neurotic Pride," in her work *Neuroses and Human Growth* (1950), is particularly applicable. We have changed Horney's referents from "the neurotic," the "person," "he," "his," and "himself" to the "the English department," "English," "it," "its," and "itself." Given that (and our apologies to Horney), here is the Third Force explanation of the phenomenon:

Even though god-like in [its] imagination, [the English department] still lacks the earthy self-confidence of the simple shepherd. . . . [English] still feels at bottom unwanted, is easily hurt, and needs incessant confirmation of its value. (86)

Neurotic pride . . . rests on the attributes which [English] arrogates to itself in [its] imagination, on all those belonging to [its] particular idealized image. Here the peculiar nature of neurotic pride comes into clear relief. [English] is not proud of the [the department it] actually is. Knowing [its] wrong perspective on [itself], we are not surprised that [its] pride blots out difficulties and limitations. (90)

The idealized image is a product of [English's] imagination. But this is not something which is created overnight. Incessant work of intellect and imagination, most of it unconscious, goes into maintaining the private fictitious world . . . through finding ways to make things appear different from what they are. (91)

In terms of subjective experience [neurotic pride] makes [English] vulnerable, and does so exactly to the extent that [it] is obsessed by pride. It can be hurt as easily from within as from without. The two typical reactions to hurt pride are shame and humiliation. [English] will feel ashamed if [it does, thinks, or feels] something that violates [its] pride. And [English] will feel humiliated if others do something that hurts [its] pride, or fail[s] to do what [its] pride requires of them. (95)

That any hurt to [English's] pride may provoke vindictive hostility is well known. It goes all the way from dislike to hate, from irritability to anger to a blind murderous rage. . . . What operates here is the straight law of retaliation. (99)

The quotes we have just remade are hyperbole meant, when applied to English departments, to amuse and to stimulate thinking about a problem and strategies for solving it. Even though it is hyperbole, there are many scholars within English whose publications tend to substantiate the points about English's uncertain history, its insecurity, its idealized image making, and its sense of vulnerability (Eagleton 1996; Ohmann 1979; and Parker 1967).

In an effort to define the problem, we want to isolate three phrases, "needs incessant confirmation of its value," "blots out difficulties and limitations," "to make things appear different from what they are," and then to place them in context. English departments have long been unsure of their value to the academy. Beyond many other disciplines, their work appears disconnected from that of others on campus and that needed by society. An exception to this claim is the teaching of writing, which the campus and society value highly. While teaching composition has, ironically, been thought odious by literature faculty (Hirsch 1982), it provides a sustaining confirmation of value. And, as Blair explains, English certainly imagines itself to have a special relationship with writing, to know the most about writing, and to produce the best writing and writers.

This impression of itself often leads English to blot out difficulties and limitations—two of which become most striking. First, English cannot teach writing by itself. A few (at most) composition courses over four or five years will not produce the better writers for which the institution and the public long. The effort must be much more broad-based and inclusive to achieve that result. Perhaps the degree to which English knows this is the degree to which writing across the curriculum succeeds. Even as English does not want to bear sole responsibility for writing, it does not want to lose its most public confirmation of value, and its belief in its heart that it can teach the best writing courses. Thus it may ignore or even resist the obvious need to change and to share, unnecessarily damaging itself and others in the process.

Second, what may have been vague a decade ago has now become almost a truism, that academic communities are in David Russell's terms a loose affiliation of separate disciplines, each with its own language and consequent frames for thinking, its own values, purposes, and expectations for writing (Russell 1991). Each department sees the world and makes meaning of it in a different way. Each faculty member and student have assimilated or are assimilating these differing ways of perceiving and making meaning. English is itself a discipline made up, as is every other discipline, of a variety of specializations, each again with its language. Given this fact; given that faculty are passing onto their students the language and culture of their disciplines, as a matter of duty and necessity; given that the work of a discipline could not be done without its language, it is hard to understand why English would want to make things appear different from what they are—to appear, that is, as if one language fits all, that fit coming from the values for writing held by English. This situation becomes clearer, however, when we realize that English (as with most disciplines) rarely recognizes its own values for writing as values at all, perceiving its judgements to be universals—its goods and bads for writing to be everyone's. To continue with the Horney schema, English thus fosters an idealized image, not proud of the department that it actually is, but of a department it has created in its imagination (i.e., English imagines itself to teach writing across the curriculum, but in reality the writing it teaches does not cross the curriculum). The difference between English and other disciplines lies in English's pride of ownership of writing and its position to act on that pride (to extend expertise in composition to "novice" faculty and students, to teach writing in other disciplines, to urge values for writing on cultures to which those values are alien); and in the endorsement of that pride and those practices by other disciplines ("Teaching writing is English's job," "they're the experts," and when their own students are not writing so well, "why isn't English doing its job?"). Given this context, the problem becomes formidable.

But does it mean that all WAC writing center directors have to become Third Force therapists, placing English on the couch? In a curious way, it does. When we delivered an abbreviated form of this paper to an audience at the National Writing Centers Association Conference at Park City, Utah (1997), its message clearly touched tightly strung cords. The response was largely enthusiastic and positive, perhaps predictably, because center directors involved in WAC have had negative experiences with English departments, some of them extremely negative. One very earnest person who had "problems" with the presentation, however, objected to its rhetorical effectiveness, its ability to "make the audience sympathetic" to its position. He further remarked that we cannot responsibly "trash" English departments based on the experiences of one community college teacher. (The experiences of one were all we offered at that point, though our conversation and consul with fellow professionals suggest that the conflict is wide-reaching.) About the presentation's rhetorical effectiveness, of course, we have no complaint. The presentation had hoped to persuade, as the essay does now.

In response to the complaint that English departments should not be trashed based on one community college teacher's experience, we offer the following: that first, he is right, one (or two, or three) person's particular experience does not prove the existence of a general condition; second, our purpose in presenting the narrative is not to prove a general condition (given the qualifiers already offered, such proof could not be arrayed); that third, the purpose was to suggest that such particular conditions do exist—that the experience of one community college teacher reflects in specific and non-specific ways the experiences of more than one, though one is more than enough; and finally, that this person's objection, to continue the hyperbole, implies the need to preserve an idealized image for English, to which we responded as therapists might, listening seriously, acknowledging concerns, seeking areas of agreement and, finding few, then looking for conciliation and compromise.

Horney remarks of dealing with those afflicted with neurotic pride: "Thus, when a friend or relative [an English department] behaves in an obnoxious fashion after we have liberally helped [it], we should not be upset over [its] ingratitude but consider how badly [its] pride may have been hurt by accepting help. And, according to circumstances, we might either talk to [English] about it or try ourselves to help [English] in a way that saves [its] face" (100). Horney's advice, translated, encourages conciliation and compromise between the WAC Center director and English, and, to a point, so do we. The road to establishing a viable WAC Writing Center while maintaining useful relations with English can indeed be potholed. What we suggest Writing Center directors do is to choose the principles about which they will not compromise and then those about which they will, all the while realizing that strong ties with English's writing program benefit both the center and English.

The principles about which no compromise is possible should be few, and those carefully thought through. That is, center directors must choose their arguments well. They may find themselves in conflict with English (or others) over numerous issues; but, to establish credibility, they must be selective, supporting the points which, from their knowledge and experience, if defeated would negatively impact the institution as a whole—students and faculty alike. And directors must have more than opinions to support these positions, and be more than defensive in presenting them. They need to have a thorough research base for their positions and present them with collegial assertiveness (for an effective model of change agentry within English departments see Gere and Smith 1979).

WAC Center directors also need to exercise the same kind of empathy, sensitivity, and communication skills with administrators and faculty, perhaps especially English faculty, that they encourage in the tutoring process with students. They need to ask questions, listen to concerns, collaborate to solve problems, act on good ideas, and demonstrate and then follow through on commitment. They need to wear many hats at once: that of therapist, arbitrator, teacher, student, visionary, researcher, and in-the-trenches toiler, to name only a few.

Writing Centers are the best place for WAC, as has been argued elsewhere (Waldo 1993). They offer definable space for expertise, with identifiable goals and services, which the campus needs to sustain WAC. Through their varying services for faculty and students, they encourage dialogue between diverse language communities. And they provide, in potential, a rhetorically neutral ground on which to carry out the program, perhaps the only such ground on the academic side of campus. What is meant by "rhetorically neutral ground," a confusing while important concept for establishing a WAC Writing Center? The term does not, and cannot, mean that Writing Centers have no agenda to persuade: they do, encouraging the use of writing as a way of learning and thinking critically all across campus. The term does not mean to suggest no strategy for tutoring with students or consulting with faculty. There is such a strategy. Instead, the term means that centers are in a unique position. They do not have their own language in the disciplinary sense and its consequent frames for thinking (yet). At the same time, they can be conscious of the varied discourses around them, resist preferring one set of values, purposes, and forms for writing over another, and, through inquiry and collaboration, help students discover what they want to do with their writing and faculty discover what they want students to do with their assignments. Thus, the term "rhetorical neutrality" wants not to imply something that centers cannot be, devoid of values for language, but something that they can be: places where all languages in the academy are equal and the people using them are treated equally.

And centers have made some strides forward during the last fifteen years. Many more directors are now tenured or tenure track, easing the difficulties they have with other faculty, and many more centers are now the homes for WAC. (A recent survey of Writing Center directors may provide some useful information about their status [Ballester and MacDonald, from a presentation at the NWCA Conference, 1997]. Evidently, fifty-one percent of center directors responding to this survey are tenure track; an important research project would be to find out how many directors were tenure track, say, ten to fifteen years ago, and how many centers bear responsibility for WAC; our impression of increases, beyond a glimpse at the survey results, is anecdotal.) Despite these successes, the problems generated by conflict remain. And conflict has been, in an unfortunate reversal of fortune, occasionally exacerbated by the increased importance of WAC Centers and their directors. People operating inside the institution's political structure, tenure track people, have more protection to act than those outside that structure. They have the mandate which the tenure track provides and may become even more threatening to English departments in their effort to initiate and sustain changes in attitude toward writing. Thus commitment to the enterprise and knowledge of how it might be made to work become essential. But conciliation and compromise are also important.

After the individual described in our narrative had clearly defined what she needed to maintain a WAC Writing Center, she decided to meet with English instructors in their offices one-on-one. She kept a file of their suggestions and implemented as many of them as she could. As had been expressed during the English Department meetings, many of the instructors wanted to send their students to work on grammar skills programs. She installed a skills program in a room adjacent to the Writing Center and compromised in other areas as well: providing an on-the-spot tutor, facilitating a research paper workshop, and even allowing one English instructor to bring her entire class in to have tutors assist her in checking their bibliographies. As a consequence, she began to notice a drastic change. Instead of walking through the English Department and hearing doors close before her, people began to say hello. One teacher even cornered her in the break room and in front of everyone told her how well her students were writing with the help of Center tutors. This teacher followed up her comments with a memorandum announcing this to the Writing Center Director's supervisor and the Vice President.

Obviously, one-on-one meetings and compromises did make a difference in the English Department's acceptance of the Writing Center. Critical for her as its Director, nonetheless, was to remain tenacious about principles which established it as the campus home for WAC. By maintaining its integrity, in just one year the amount of time students spend in the Center has doubled and it now serves over 60 percent of the academic disciplines on campus.

Her response to the situation, we think, was effective. She identified principles about which she would not compromise. The first insists on maintaining the integrity of disciplines as language communities with their own values, purposes and forms for writing (Bazerman 1988; Blair 1988; Russell 1991; Myers 1990; Becher 1993; Berkenkotter et al. 1994). Recognizing the varying languages of the academy has serious implications for WAC and tutoring practice. It means that WAC consultants (who may come from disciplines different from those of the faculty with whom they consult) should use techniques based not on prescription, an expert telling a novice how to teach writing, but on inquiry and collaboration, one person asking questions in an effort to help another make discoveries on his or her own. Question asking helps faculty to link writing assignments to goals they have for learning in their courses, to design assignments pertinent to their students, classes, and disciplines. To show how this process works and provide one measure of its effectiveness directors might turn to Bean (1996) or Waldo (1996).

The second principle is that the tutoring process should be hierarchical, not in the sense that experts prescribe solutions to novice writers but that tutoring sessions move from global to local issues. Tutoring may certainly include help with editing and proofreading, but in a WAC (or any) Writing Center it makes sense to focus on issues relevant to the paper overall. Does the paper meet the goals of the instructor's assignment? Is it consistent with the writer's purpose? Are the organization, content, form, and tone appropriate? Is there coherence within and between paragraphs? Addressing global or local issues, tutors do not want to tell students what to do. (The tutors may be, after all, from disciplines with values for writing differing from their own.) Instead, they want to use question asking and conversation to help writers themselves resolve any problems. Their goal, as a friend of ours once said, is "perpetually to put themselves out of business." Research done at University of Nevada, Reno's Writing Center suggests that students internalize the questions tutors ask during sessions (Johnston 1996). The questions go underground, as Lev Vygotsky observes of the disappearance of the running commentary in young children—becoming a part of a writer's thinking and evolving his or her efforts to become an independent rewriter. In addition to Scott Johnston's dissertation, there is ample evidence for the writing center director to turn to support collaborative methods should such a case need to be made (Bruffee 1984; Harris 1992; Lunsford 1995).

After identifying principles about which she would not compromise and arraying research sources to support her position, the director from our narrative determined areas of compromise and conciliation. She consulted with English faculty individually, asked questions, discovered common ground, and acted on concerns. Loading an editing skills program in a separate room, she conceded a point upon which English appeared intractable but also one upon which she would not base her college's Center. Thus English faculty felt included in the establishment of a Center which, in their view, would benefit them and their students, while freeing it to do its cross-curricular work. Whether what happened meant that English no longer felt ownership of writing is unclear. The story, of course, continues. Her Center now serves students and faculty from the large majority of disciplines on campus, and she is an increasingly valued member of the faculty. We believe letting go of ownership is, nonetheless, critical to the success of WAC and WAC Writing Centers. Ownership of writing belongs to those communities in which writing occurs, for teachers making assignments and students writing them. If writing centers are to be WAC Centers, then that truth, and not neurotic pride, must be recognized and sustained.

WORKS CITED

Bazerman, Charles. "How Language Realizes the Work of Science: Science as a Naturally Situated, Social Semiotic System." *Shaping Written Knowledge: The Genre and Activity of the Experimental Article in Science*. Madison: The University of Wisconsin Press, 1988.

Bean, John. *Engaging Ideas: The Professor's Guide to Integrating Writing, Critical Thinking, and Active Learning in the Classroom*. San Francisco: Jossey-Bass, 1996.

Becher, Tony. *Academic Tribes and Territories: Intellectual Enquiry and the Cultures of Disciplines*. Buckingham, England: The Society for Research into Education & Open University Press, 1993.

Berkenkotter, Carol, Thomas N. Huckin, and John Ackerman. "Social Context and Socially Constructed Texts." *Landmark Essays on Writing Across the Curriculum*, ed. Charles Bazerman and David Russell. Davis, CA: Hermagoras Press, 1994.

Blair, Catherine Pastore. "Only One of the Voices: Dialogic Writing Across the Curriculum." *College English* 50 (1988): 383–389.

Bruffee, Kenneth. "Collaborative Learning and the 'Conversation of Mankind.'" *College English* 46 (1984): 635–652.

Eagleton, Terry. "The Rise of English." *Literary Theory: An Introduction*. Minneapolis: University of Minnesota Press, 1996.

Geertz, Clifford. *Local Knowledge: Further Essays in Interpretive Anthropology*. New York: Basic Books, 1983.

Gere, Anne Ruggles, and Eugene Smith. *Attitudes, Language, and Change*. Urbana, IL: NCTE, 1979.

Harris, Muriel. "Collaboration Is Not Collaboration Is Not Collaboration: Writing Tutorials vs. Peer-response Groups." *College Composition and Communication* 43 (1992):

369–383.

———. *Teaching One-to-One: The Writing Conference*. Urbana, IL: NCTE, 1986.

Hirsch, E. D. "Remarks on Composition to the Yale English Department." *The Rhetorical Tradition and Modern Writing*, ed. James J. Murphy. New York: MLA, 1982.

Horney, Karen. *Neuroses and Human Growth: The Struggle Toward Self-realization*. New York: W. W. Norton, 1950.

Johnston, Scott. "Basic Writers and Peer Tutoring." Dissertation, University of Nevada, Reno, 1996.

Lunsford, Andrea. "Collaboration, Control, and the Idea of a Writing Center." *The St. Martin's Sourcebook for Writing Tutors*, ed. Christina Murphy and Steve Sherwood. New York: St. Martin's Press, 1995.

Myers, Greg. *Writing Biology: Texts in the Social Construction of Scientific Knowledge*. Madison: University of Wisconsin Press, 1990.

Ohmann, Richard. *English in America: A Radical View of the Profession*. New York: Oxford University Press, 1979.

Parker, William Riley. "Where Do English Departments Come From?" *College English* (Feb. 1967): 339–351.

Russell, David R. "The Triumph of Specialization." *Writing in the Academic Disciplines, 1870–1990*. Carbondale: Southern Illinois University Press, 1991.

Waldo, Mark L. "The Last Best Place for Writing Across the Curriculum: The Writing Center." *WPA: Writing Program Administration* 16 (1993): 15–27.

———. "Inquiry as a Non-invasive Approach to Cross-curricular Writing Consultancy." *Language and Learning Across the Disciplines* 1.3 (1996): 6–23.

6

When a Writing Center Undertakes a Writing Fellows Program

Richard Leahy

The Writing Center at Boise State University has launched a WAC effort similar to a writing fellows program, which we call The Write Project. This is a Writing Center-WAC partnership with a difference: the two programs are branches of the same agency, run by the same people. To combine a writing fellows program and a Writing Center is probably not unique, but it is not the norm; most writing fellows programs operate independently of Writing Centers, even though they share many concerns in common. I do not presume that my discussion of our venture will persuade many Writing Centers to follow our example. I do propose that the combination, though it complicates the work of our Writing Center considerably, is beneficial to our Writing Center's relations with faculty and students, and to our competence as tutors of writing. It has taught us things that our previous models of tutoring and tutor training did not, particularly about issues of rhetoric and directiveness, and about the nature of our relationship with faculty and students. It has brought us into partnerships with faculty and students that we have not been able to achieve in any other way.

ABOUT THE WRITE PROJECT

We launched the project because, a year ago, the Writing Center was given full responsibility for Writing in the Disciplines (WID) but no additional budget. We needed a way to make our WID presence felt on campus at minimal cost. We had already been publishing a WID newsletter for ten years, and it had established a solid following. We had recently set up a Web site and an online writing lab (OWL). We had, over the years, been involved in several different partnerships with faculty and classes all over campus. But except for ongoing work with the nursing department, they tended not to last: instructors' efforts to get their students to use the Writing Center usually came to nothing. Though we do not know all the reasons why these efforts failed, one is certainly that Boise State is a 90 percent commuter campus. A great proportion of the students are on campus only to attend their classes. We wanted a way to involve entire classes in a WID partnership, and the writing fellows model presented itself as a way to do it.

As in typical writing fellows programs, we assign writing assistants (WAs) to classes in various disciplines. In a participating class, students submit drafts of their papers, the WAs read them and write suggestions for revision, and then the students revise the drafts and submit them to the instructor for grading. Classes taking part have included American literature, communications, construction management, engineering, history, economics, physical education, and general business.

The Write Project operates like most writing fellows (or rhetoric associates) programs. In a participating class, students write two or three papers per semester. Two weeks before a finished paper is due, the students must submit complete drafts. The drafts are read by writing assistants, who write extensive comments and suggestions for revision. The students then revise their papers and submit the revisions to the instructor to be graded. They are strongly encouraged to consult with the WA or someone else in the Writing Center during the revising process.

Any faculty member may submit a request to have one class included each semester. As a general rule we take requests first come, first served. Faculty who have used the project before get no special priority. We hope to always have a mix of old and new faculty, and so far that has happened without our having to work out any priority procedures. Some faculty do not want to use the project every semester, because they sometimes have no classes for which the project will work.

Writing assistants work with two or three paper assignments per semester because, in order to help students improve, the WAs need to see a significant amount of writing. The first assignment allows the WA to determine the strengths and weaknesses of each student's writing. A subsequent assignment allows WAs to see whether, and how much, students have improved. Very often the second set of drafts is noticeably stronger than the first. Some of the improvement undoubtedly comes from the students' getting used to what the instructor expects. Some, though, comes from the revision practice students got on the first assignment; they learn how to revise more effectively and how to apply that knowledge to the next set of drafts.

Established writing fellows programs usually compensate the fellows with flat stipends, currently about $300–$400 per semester. Their budgets run in the range or $30,000 a year or more. We have had to operate, so far, out of our regular Writing Center budget of $23,000, which has meant that we have had to find a way to give just compensation and still run the project on a shoestring. Our solution has been to pay by the paper, taking into account the number of drafts read and average length of the drafts.

When we began the project, we borrowed heavily from the wisdom and experience of those who had gone before us. The writing fellows director at Brigham Young University, Deirdre Paulsen, gave generously of her advice and support, and our continuing conversations about running a program have been of immeasurable value. Rhoda Flaxman of Brown University, Barbara Sylvester of Western Washington University, and Joyce Kinkead of Utah State have also generously shared their experience and expertise.

CEMENTING A PARTNERSHIP: PURPOSES OF THE PROJECT

The purposes of a writing fellows program had already been well established for a dozen years or more before we began. Tori Haring-Smith identifies two principal aims of a writing fellows program. The first aim is that faculty should assume a shared responsibility for supporting the writing of their students. What our faculty learn as soon as they sign up for The Write Project is that they are entering a three-way partnership with the WAs and their students. Just as the students are responsible for submitting drafts of high quality or at least high potential, and just as the writing assistants are responsible for providing feedback that is full, thoughtful, diplomatic, and helpful, so the faculty are responsible for designing good assignments and following the ground rules of the project to make sure it works as it should.

The second aim is "the association of writing with learning" (Haring-Smith 1992, 176). Writing as a mode of learning involves much more than two sets of drafts and revisions as required in a writing fellows class. It requires copiousness, an element of learning to write that rhetoricians have always recognized. Students should write every week, every day, about their understanding of the course material. The project does not require this kind of writing-for-learning, though faculty are encouraged to include it. What the project does address is revision, one of the most important aspects of writing and learning. Students' failure to revise, or to understand revision, has always been one of the weakest links, if not the weakest, when teachers have tried to make writing assignments an important part of their course. The project is designed so that revision is at the core. It could even be said that revision is what the program is all about.

Haring-Smith has identified three features of a writing fellows program that distinguishes it from a Writing Center.

1. The project takes place all over campus, rather than requiring students to come to the Writing Center.
2. All students in a class are involved, strong writers as well as weak. And students do not have to self-identify as needing help with their writing.
3. The project "assists individual faculty members with assignment design and models for them in a direct and immediate way methods of responding to student writing" (179).

From our point of view, of course, these features serve not to distinguish The Write Project from the Writing Center, but rather to extend and enrich the center's traditional role. Nor is such a project the only way to achieve the results listed by Haring-Smith; Writing Centers on other campuses are achieving similar results by other means. The project provides the structure that works for us.

The "direct and immediate" modeling of response is of value to instructors. It is, in a way, more efficient than teaching faculty in workshops about responding to student writing. Workshop instruction has to be fairly abstract, and we never know whether faculty are going to go back and apply (or apply correctly) what they have learned. The project allows us to work with faculty individually. Some of them undertake major revisions of their assignments after debriefing with the WAs on what worked and what did not. The hidden power of the project lies in the fact that faculty teach themselves how to design effective writing assignments. They sign up for the project thinking it is a service, but once they are involved they quickly find out that it is less a service than a partnership. In order to work with the project, they have to be willing to change as much as they want their students' writing to change.

TRAINING WRITING ASSISTANTS FOR THE PROJECT: RHETORICAL ISSUES

Because our project is a function of the Writing Center, the WAs must play dual roles: they tutor in one-to-one sessions and respond in writing to student drafts. To prepare WAs for both roles, we have revised our training course and weekly staff sessions to include intensified instruction in rhetorical theory, study of research on written response, practice in writing responses to student drafts, and instruction on how to work with faculty in the project and how to manage draft-reading time.

Before we started the project, I had already been interested in rhetorical theory as a component of writing assistant training (Leahy 1995). Boise State University's writing curriculum, even for writing-emphasis majors, was not strong on theory (a deficiency the program is now starting to address). The WAs, though good writers themselves and veterans of several writing classes, did not know how to talk about writing issues and strategies or how to analyze the rhetorical effectiveness of their clients' writing. I had become a proponent of the idea that all writing is persuasive in some way. I had also come to see tutoring itself as a rhetorical-persuasive act, with WA and client shifting back and forth, in many complex ways, between being the persuader and the one to be persuaded. With the project and the new demands it imposed on the training program, our rhetorical training became more focused and formalized.

Our training program uses Classical rhetoric as a basic theoretical framework. We find that training in rhetorical theory is important for learning both how to give written response and also how to tutor. Tutors do not necessarily know how to analyze and talk about writing just because they themselves are good writers; for years as a Writing Center director I made that mistaken assumption. When I started introducing rhetorical theory into some of the staff training sessions, I discovered that it was a new world to them. They found it a fascinating way to look at writing, and they actually began applying it to their work and their own writing.

I do not intend to sell Classical rhetoric as *the* theoretical framework for tutoring and writing fellows programs. Classical rhetoric is the subject of considerable controversy: not only about whether it is a viable system for today's rhetors, but also—if it is considered viable—how it should be adapted to contemporary writing pedagogy. I am convinced, however, that every Writing Center and writing fellows training program needs some kind of theoretical rhetorical framework, one that is explicit and constantly reexamined, if it is going to provide comprehensive training. Without a comprehensive system, WAs' knowledge of rhetoric tends to be fragmented, made up of isolated bits of lore about writing strategies. Consequently, the help they provide to clients can be unsystematic and even haphazard. Directors and trainers should choose the system they believe in most strongly. We use Classical rhetoric because it offers us a systematic, flexible way of generating, thinking about, and responding to writing in all disciplines (and because it is the system I have taught and know best). As Kathleen Welch (1990) has argued, Classical rhetoric is an adaptable, rich, and comprehensive system for generating written discourse. For us, it provides a handle on many of the problems WAs encounter, both in the project drafts and in tutoring.

Classical rhetoric is sometimes misunderstood as being a rigid system of rules: it is seen as prescribing everything in a doctrinaire way, especially in the canon of arrangement. Critics of contemporary use of Classical rhetoric, such as C. M. Knoblauch and Lil Brannon (1984), blame Classical rhetoric as contributing directly to the rise of Current-Traditional rhetoric. This is an attitude many of the WAs I work with have to unlearn. I am not sure where they have picked it up. Perhaps they confuse Classical rhetoric with the Neoclassical period they study in literature survey classes, where Classicism can appear rule-bound, offering little artistic freedom. This common attitude toward Classical rhetoric is what Kathleen Welch calls the Heritage school, as contrasted with the Dialectical school, which views Classical rhetoric as a flexible system, a powerful generator of text in many genres, and highly adaptable to contemporary writing (1990, 9–11).

In our training program, we align ourselves with the Dialectical school. We study the relationships among the five canons of rhetoric (invention, arrangement, style, memory, delivery); the three means of persuasion (ethos, pathos, logos) and kairos, literally "the opportune moment" or awareness of the rhetorical situation, the dynamic relationships among audience, occasion (or exigence, the conditions requiring discourse on a subject), and purpose.

The five canons, arranged in the traditional order, can give the impression that they are a description of the process of writing or composing a speech: first, the writer invents, then arranges what has been invented, then adds style, and so forth. Such an impression leads to an impoverished view of the canons, a view that they are just like the early linear, non-recursive models of the writing process put forth in the 1960s and early 1970s. The canons become productive if they are seen as constantly involved in each other. Richard Coe has pointed out that "[t]he division of classical rhetoric into [the five canons] did not imply that these are "stages" in some ideal writing process. . . . The linear division is made so that students can concentrate on learning one thing at a time" (1990, 16).

When Aristotle proposed a definition of rhetoric, he did so in a provisional mode, consistent with the pioneering nature of his work: "Let rhetoric be [defined as] an ability, in each [particular] case, to see the available means of persuasion" (trans. Kennedy 1991, 36). Aristotle was looking for a definition that would cover the broadest possible application of the term. In our training, it makes sense to extend persuasion to all writing. Even the personal-experience writing so common in our first-semester writing curriculum can be dealt with as persuasion. At the very least, student writers must persuade readers that they have something to relate that is worth reading. They must find some meaning in their experiences and persuade readers to give assent to those meanings. Even when students in technical communication compose "parts" lists, they must persuade readers that the lists are complete, accurate, and placed in the arrangement that the reader needs. Seeing the available means of persuasion in each case calls for a broad repertoire of invention strategies and the use of all the other canons, interwoven with each other.

Although our basic theoretical orientation is toward classical rhetoric, we borrow freely, not to say eclectically, from other systems. We especially borrow from Romantic-Expressivist rhetoric. The most compelling reason for this is that it is endemic in the culture in which our Writing Center exists. The freshman writing program is strongly oriented toward Romantic-Expressivist rhetoric, which means that not only our clients and many of the teachers we interact with, as well as the writing assistants themselves, take it as a given.

In the canon of invention, Romantic-Expressivist rhetoric's major contribution was to popularize freewriting, brainstorming, and clustering. These are powerful strategies. They are the ones I always begin with in my own writing. They are the ones the WAs most often teach their clients and suggest on Write Project drafts. Often, though, these are the only invention strategies student writers use, and they are limited. They are essentially non-systematic systems; they can pull out ideas the writer might otherwise not have discovered, but they are still hit or miss. Most textbooks have by now gone beyond them and are including more systematic strategies like cubing; Jacqueline Berke's twenty questions; Aristotle's twenty-eight *topoi*; Kenneth Burke's pentad for examining motivation; and Young, Becker, and Pike's tagmemic invention. These strategies, it seems to me, are all Classical at heart because in their different ways they all aim at completeness. They prompt the writer to explore all possible aspects of a subject. They are in spirit very much like the Classical idea of *topoi*— literal "places" outside the confines of one's own head where one can look for ideas. *Topoi* act as a corrective and complement to the Romantic idea that one should look deep inside for inspiration. The *topoi* are based on the assumption that inspiration often does not come when it is needed.

The difference might appear to come down just to competing metaphors, but there is more to it than that. The classical rhetors saw themselves as operating as part of a community that shared the same body of knowledge, values, and opinions (Crowley 1994, 7–9). It is enabling for inexperienced (and experienced) writers when they learn to think of their writing as part of a community's quest for knowledge and understanding, rather than a lonely, individual struggle to make private sense out of experience.

In helping Writing Center clients develop their repertoires of invention strategies, we find Berke's twenty questions especially useful. We print them on wallet-size slips and keep supplies of them on the tables for use during tutoring sessions. When the WAs respond to Write Project drafts, they use the twenty questions as a guide to suggesting ways for the writers to develop their drafts more fully. Also useful to us in invention are the Ladder of Abstraction as adapted by Jay King in *Demystifying Writing* and the TRIAC as presented by Chris Anderson in *Free/Style*:

(T): starting a thesis, topic, or theme
(R): restating the theme, refining, restricting it
(I): illustrating the theme or thesis, giving examples of it
(A): analyzing the thesis or the examples
(C): concluding, closing (90).

The canon of arrangement may be the locus of most misunderstanding about Classical rhetoric. The parts or the oration with their Latinate names smack of rigidity and control: exordium, narration, partition, confirmation, refutation, peroration. Reading the Classical rhetoricians, though, one finds that they were not rigid. They disagreed with one another on several points of arrangement. They suggested alternatives, as Quintilian, the author of the *Rhetorica ad Herennium,* does in the following passage:

The kinds of Arrangement are two: one arising from the principles of rhetoric, the other accommodated to particular circumstances. . . . [F]or example, if we should begin our speech with the Statement of Facts, or with some very strong argument, or the reading of some documents; or if straightaway after the Introduction we should use the Proof and then the Statement of Facts; or if we should make some other change of this kind in the order. (Benson and Prosser 1988, 194–5)

Such changes in order are not made arbitrarily, however; they are made for a reason:

[N]one of these changes ought to be made except when our cause demands them. . . . If our cause seems to present so great a difficulty that no one can listen to the Introduction with patience, we shall begin with the Statement of Facts and then recur to the idea intended for the Introduction. If the Statement of Facts is not quite plausible, we shall be-

gin with some strong argument. It is often necessary to employ such changes and trans-
positions when the cause itself obliges us to modify with art the Arrangement prescribed
by the rules of the art. (Benson and Prosser 1988, 195)

In other words, it is important to know the parts and what each is for, to be
aware that arrangements can vary—and also to realize that the choice of variation must be guided by an awareness of the rhetorical situation and the strengths
of our material.

Romantic-Expressive rhetoric handles arrangement mostly on the level
of what works for this piece of writing. That is a welcome corrective to the impoverished Current-Traditional rules, which offer little beyond the five-
paragraph theme. It is useful if "what works" is considered in light of the audience and the rhetorical situation. Classical rhetoric, in fact, essentially teaches
the same principle. It puts a theoretical foundation under "do what works,"
however, by providing a matrix in the six parts of an oration. Once student writers learn the system, they learn how to vary it depending on the occasion, audience, and purpose.

Our most helpful resource on arrangement has been Richard Coe's
Process, Form, and Substance. For argument, Coe has a good explanation of
Classical arrangement and the clearest exposition of the form of purpose of
Rogerian argument I have yet found (1990, 388–408). For more general purposes, Coe provides excellent advice on how organizing can work as part of the
composing process (199–229). He also has one of the best, most rhetorically
oriented discussions of titles, beginnings, middle paragraphs, and endings (170–
191). One of Coe's strengths is that he always explains not just how something
is done, but why: the reasons each strategy is suited to certain rhetorical situations.

Style is the canon in which Classical rhetoric most clearly shows the
way to greater control for the writer. Neither Current-Traditional nor Romantic-
Expressivist rhetoric does much about style that student writers can find very
useful, outside the general categories of clarity and honesty—principles that
technical communicators need to deal with more than other writers do. Most
teachers today do not really have the tools to talk about style. They grade on
style—who among us has not given one paper an A and another a B because the
A paper has a more sophisticated style?—but they do not know how to teach it
(Ronald 1993, 55).

The teachers cannot really be blamed. For the most part, nothing in
their (our) training prepares us to talk about style. Consequently we tend not to
talk about it. Instead we tend to use a term that is a questionable substitute:
voice. I have heard colleagues in my department tell freshman students that they
are "really beginning to write in their own authentic voice." The students may
nod and smile and be pleased with the compliment, but they have no idea what
they have done differently that has started to put their own authentic voice in the
writing. When clients come to the Writing Center puzzled about voice, we try to

avoid talking about voice and nudge them in the direction of style, about which they can do something.

The Classical approach to style offers control over one's writing because students learn a set of specific strategies. The more they practice the strategies, the more they will find opportunities to use them. We do not make much use of the actual elements of Classical style. It is concerned with topics such as the distinctions among high, middle, and low styles and with figures of speech (tropes and schemes). Knowledge of a few classical strategies comes in handy, such as the various forms of parallelism, antithesis, polysyndeton and asyndeton, and metaphor and simile. But we have found the most useful resource to be Ann Raimes' section on style in her handbook, *Keys for Writers*, entitled "The Five C's of Style": Cut, Check for Action, Connect, Commit, and Choose your Words. Raimes has collected a group of stylistic strategies that student writers can quickly apply to their own writing. Most useful of all is her "Connect" section, in which she demonstrates the known-new contract and topic chains. Our other important sources for style are Chris Anderson's enlightening discussion of cumulative and periodic sentences (1992, 118–123) and Richard Coe's section on cumulatives, alternative sentence structures, and balance and parallelism (1990, 239–254). These three provide WAs with a means of talking about style and explaining to writers, both in the Writing Center and on project drafts, how to attack stylistic problems in their writing.

My remarks on memory have to be more tentative. Memory and delivery have often been dismissed today as irrelevant to writing. But work has been done to show that they are indeed relevant, in new ways (Reynolds 1993, 1–13). Our Writing Center staff has only begun to explore its relevance to the writers they tutor and the Write Project drafts they read.

Memory in Classical times consisted mostly of mnemonic devices by which an orator could remember the parts of a speech. It stressed visual imagination. The *Rhetorica ad Herennium* contains a fascinating and, to modern readers, a rather bizarre account. The rhetor started with a place, such as a house or public building, and "placed" objects in various rooms, so that when he imagined walking through the rooms in a certain order, the objects he placed there would remind him of the reasons and evidence he was going to use at that point in the speech (Benson and Prosser 1988, 294–299). Quintilian, though skeptical of the use of physical locations as overly burdensome, also advised using objects as symbols to help jog the memory (Matsen, Rollinson, and Sousa 1998, 228–229).

Writers have little use for such mnemonic tricks, which were designed for oratory, but they still need to cultivate memory. The *ad Herennium*'s claim that memory is "the guardian of all the parts of rhetoric" still holds true. Memory works at many levels and at many stages of the writing process and overlaps all the other rhetorical canons. Memory aids invention by bringing to bear everything the writer knows that is connected with the subject. This includes all forms of knowledge: knowledge from reading, from conversations, from personal experience. It includes seeing connections between ideas and between facts and general truths. Memory aids arrangement by enabling the writer to hold all the different parts of a piece of writing in mind at once and relate them to each other. Memory aids style by enabling the writer to remember the structure of a sentence from beginning to end, remember different kinds of structures, remember words, remember patterns (rules) for punctuation. Failure in any one of these efforts can result from a failure of memory as much as anything else. Memory aids delivery, too, by helping the writer maintain visual consistency.

We have only begun to examine the potential of memory in tutoring and in giving written response to drafts, but we have turned up a few clues. Certain kinds of sentence-level errors, such as subject-verb agreement and dangling modifiers, and especially mixed sentence constructions, might be treated as problems of memory. A writer struggling with what to say or how to say it can forget where a sentence is going. Memory problems may occur more easily at the paragraph level and may be partly responsible for paragraphs that switch topics in the middle.

At the whole-essay level, the role of memory is even more certain and obvious. When I asked the WAs to reflect on the problems of memory they saw in students' drafts, a majority of them cited two. They wrote that student writers forget what the assignment instructed them to do, and they forget what their thesis is. Consequently their writing goes off in the wrong direction, either from the start or halfway through the essay. Several WAs suggested that students' memory problems might stem from failure to understand what they are asked to do, or what focus they had set for themselves.

When I asked the WAs to write about how we can help students with memory, they were not able to come up with anything very specific. The problem is that our clients come and go; many only make one visit to the Writing Center. A writing class is able to build a collective memory of writing lore because it stays together over a period of months. A Writing Center like ours does not have that luxury. In the general discussion following our writing exercise, we seemed to agree at least that to approach our clients' problems as problems of memory would at least be of some help. We could at least urge student writers to apply their memories more: not only to recalling what to say but also to how they were saying it.

But these aspects of memory are only part of the story and perhaps not the most important. Janine Rider argues persuasively that memory is the faculty that not only allows us to know; it enables us to create (1995, Chapters 2 and 6). These are exciting ideas whose implications few writing theorists and, as far as I know, no theorists of tutoring writing have begun to explore.

Delivery in Classical times included everything we would call performance, mainly voice control and gesture. Today, delivery has gained enormous importance in technical communication, where placement of text and graphics, white space, use of color, and other considerations are understood to have rhetorical significance. In the technical communication program in my department, the document production courses—one upper division and two graduate—are mainly courses in delivery. But in composition courses and other courses, too, we see more and more students playing with visual delivery as they learn to do more with their word processors.

Undoubtedly we will be dealing with visual rhetoric in some Write Project courses eventually. Already we have seen drafts in which students experiment with the look of their documents on the page. WAs reading Write Project drafts from engineering and construction management classes are already having to respond to the clarity and effectiveness of tables, graphs, and illustrations. The chief rhetorical aspect of delivery is that it reflects the writer's ethos. A visually sloppy, inaccurate, or confusing draft sends the message that the writer does not care much about the paper or what the reader thinks of it.

Our training program for the project consists of a number of readings on written response. Currently we are using Sommers, Podis and Podis, Lindemann, and Straub, in that order. Other good material keeps appearing—for instance, a recent article by Peshe Kuriloff exploring commonalities among writing conventions of many disciplines.

The most difficult, prolonged effort needed in training WAs for the project is teaching them to write well-developed, text-specific comments. This characteristic is number one in the list of traits identified by Richard Straub and Ronald Lunsford in their study of responses written by composition experts (1995, 347-374). Well-developed, text-specific comments are the most important aspect of a reader's response. It is difficult to train the WAs to do this, not because they are being dense or stubborn about it, but because such comments are hard for anybody to write without practice and a definite strategy.

The best strategy we have found so far was suggested by Gay Lynn Crossley in a Four C's workshop. Crossley asked participants to write their interpretation of what a sample draft was saying. That one simple direction helped me as much as any other piece of advice I have found in the literature of responding. By telling the writer first what I thought the draft was saying, I found it easy to move on to a specific response to how the draft said it. The strategy was close to the "sayback" strategy of Peter Elbow and Pat Belanoff (1995, SR–9) that I had used in my classes for years but had not connected with the kind of response I wanted the WAs to write. Now I ask them to make it the primary strategy for all responses in the project.

In a staff meeting at the beginning of the semester I handed out a draft and asked everyone to write a response to it. Of the fourteen new trainees, eleven wrote lists of disjointed notes about problems with the draft and no suggestions for revision. Three managed to write full sentences and paragraphs. The ten returning WAs, who had worked with the project for a year, without hesitation wrote well-developed responses diagnosing the drafts's strengths and weaknesses and suggesting concrete strategies for revision. This was encouraging evidence that our training program appears to be effective.

EVALUATING THE PROJECT: ISSUES OF EXPECTATION
AND ASSUMPTION

We evaluate the project in every class at the end of each semester. Questionnaires are filled out by faculty, students, and WAs. At the end of the first year, one WA, Dallas Hightower, did a comprehensive study of the results as an internship project. The results were strongly positive. So far, all of the faculty have been pleased by the results and would use the project again. Of the students, 70 percent were pleased with the help they received on their drafts and would be willing to take part in another Write Project class.

We discovered that all parties involved in the project—faculty, students, and WAs—generally hold a realistic view of what the project can be expected to accomplish. Some misconceptions surfaced, though, and they are worth examining.

The faculty generally seemed to understand the limits of the project. A couple of faculty, however, seemed to assume that the WAs would function rather like teaching assistants and do much more with the class than their role prescribed—such as reading multiple drafts and visiting classes as substitute teachers when the instructor was absent. On the other hand, at least one instructor expected too little: "I want the writing assistant to just look at the writing, and I'll respond to the content." Writing, for this instructor, appeared to consist of grammar and punctuation, not the entire piece of writing as an act of discovery and communication.

One instructor apparently assumed that revision is a simple, mechanical suggestion-to-change procedure, a form of fixing what is wrong with the paper. She required her students to use *all* the WA's suggestions on their drafts. The students themselves, many of them, could see the problem with that. They were aware that one person's response to a draft, however expert that person may be, cannot be accepted uncritically. They also understood that dealing with a reader's response to a draft involves a complex rethinking of major aspects of the paper as a whole. We have worked with these instructors as diplomatically as we can to correct their misperceptions. Classes for which the instructors are unable, or refuse, to adjust their use of writing assignments to the project are not included in subsequent semesters. In hope of defusing misconceptions, we added to the project's faculty handbook a section on the nature of the revising process and how writers should think about feedback.

Some students appeared to harbor the same simplistic idea about the revision process as some of the faculty. They tried to use everything the WAs said about their drafts and were disappointed—either that the comments did not solve enough of the problems, or that the papers did not get higher grades (we make it a point never to promise that). Or they tended to regard the WA's comments as the "whole truth" about their drafts and did not take the initiative to regard their own drafts with a critical eye. We are trying to correct this by explaining to students that they alone must assume ultimate responsibility for the quality of their revisions.

Students frequently expressed the concern that the WAs were not fully qualified to respond to their drafts because they were not familiar with the subject matter of the class. This is not a new issue; it has been debated before with respect to tutoring Writing Across the Curriculum (Hubbuch 1988; Kiedaisch and Dinitz 1993). We are not yet convinced that this is as serious an issue as the students believe. The instructors would not have asked to take part in the project if they thought the WAs could not adequately respond to the drafts. They apparently think, as Hubbuch argues, that a naive tutor can provide valuable feedback to writers when they have not made themselves clear. The students' concern might come from something so simple as the WAs' practice of asking for clarification of confusing passages by writing comments like "I don't understand what this is saying." Perhaps the writers assumed the WAs could not understand the subject, whereas they were actually trying to prod the writers to try for clearer wording. We may just need to change our phrasing in such comments. However, I do not believe we can shrug off the issue that easily. In fact, WAs who have other majors can lend important credibility to their work with classes in their majors. We have evidence of this in a very successful collaboration that one WA, a history major, has established with a history professor in his course on historical writing.

The writing assistants, too, held some unrealistic assumptions about what the project could accomplish. Some of them tended to assume that faculty should be made to abide strictly by our guidelines and rules. It is true that we have our ground rules and expect faculty to abide by them—for instance, by not suddenly saying they need drafts back as soon as possible instead of giving us a week. It is also true that some faculty forget the ground rules and have to be reminded. What the WAs did not understand, though, was that dealing with faculty often demands negotiation and compromise—and that I was not in a position to make any of the faculty do anything.

Several of the WAs wished we had a rule that students must bring their drafts to the Writing Center for further consultation before handing in their revisions. Ideally, that would be an excellent rule; it is standard in some writing fellows programs. We have a logistic constraint, however: if all the Write Project students tried to visit the Writing Center, they would jam the appointment calendar and prevent other students from using the center. The WAs do urge students in the project to visit the center. Sometimes, when a draft has especially knotty problems, the WA will write a note to the effect, "There are some things I need to ask you about your draft before I can respond to it. Please make an appointment to meet with me in the Writing Center."

The WAs, of course, encounter the same difficulty that instructors do when dealing with student papers. They find it easy to identify specific weaknesses but hard to identify specific strengths. But, as tutors sensitized to the danger of discouraging the writer, they tend to play down the weaknesses or describe them in general terms. The students' evaluations across the board, in a wide variety of classes, indicated that students wanted more specific suggestions on their drafts. Going through the evaluations the first time, we did not know what to make of that comment. Did the students want more suggestions that were specific, or did they want the suggestions that were already there to be more specific? We wondered if students were just displaying a "tell me what to do and I'll do it" attitude, surrendering ownership of their writing. But then I read through the comments on a collection of sample papers, and I understood what the students were saying. Reading the comments on a sampling of drafts, there were several times that, if I had been the writer, I would not have understood how to think about revising. In fact, the papers needed both more specific suggestions and more specificity in the suggestions that were there. Here again, I found that we have a recurring need to stress text-specific written response.

ISSUES OF DIRECTIVENESS

When I described our project to another Writing Center director, she told me that it was inconsistent with Writing Center practice because it was "too directive." I have to admit that I myself hung back from starting the project for some time for the same reason. It seemed out of step with what I was training my WAs to do.

Important work has been done, however, that questions whether the nondirective techniques of tutoring are the only (or always the best) way of giving feedback. The work of Lisa Ede and of Irene Clark, and especially of Linda Shamoon and Deborah Burns, have gradually won me over. Let me offer two reasons why I am comfortable with directive techniques.

First, directive techniques are not necessarily incompatible with tutoring. Quite the contrary, as Shamoon and Burns argue, sometimes they are the best techniques. The experience of faculty across the disciplines calls into questions the assumption that directiveness is counterproductive, that it does the work for the student, that students are going to passively accept direction and not actively learn from it. Shamoon and Burns offer multiple examples of testimony from both students and teachers that they learned the most from, exactly the kind of directiveness that Writing Centers shun. Burns recounts an experience with her dissertation director:

[He]added transitions when needed, showed me how to eliminate wordiness, and formalized my vocabulary. In addition, he offered specific suggestions for rewriting entire paragraphs, and he always pointed out areas where I had lost focus. The most important thing he did for me was to write sentences that helped locate my work in the field of Dickens studies. . . . I learned that I was so immersed in the research and articulation of the new ideas I wanted to explore in my thesis, I had neither the time nor the experience to fully understand how to write an extended piece of scholarly work in the discourse community. . . . After I watched my director work with my text, and after I made the necessary changes, my thesis and other academic writing was much less of a mystery to me. (1995, 138)

Burns observed further that this professor did the same with other graduate students' writing, with similar results. "[H]e took their papers and rewrote them while they watched. They left feeling better able to complete their papers, and they tackled other papers with greater ease and success" (138). Shamoon and Burns discovered in a series of WAC workshops that many faculty had the same experience.

Over and over in the informal reports of our colleagues we find that crucial information about a discipline and about writing is transmitted in ways that are intrusive, directive, and product-oriented, yet these behaviors are not perceived as an appropriation of power or voice but instead as an opening up of those aspects of practice which had remained unspoken and opaque. (139)

Shamoon and Burns argue that, in the pages of *The Writing Lab News-letter* and the *Writing Center Journal* and in electronic discussion, the ideology of tutoring writing is "process-based, Socratic, private, a-disciplinary, and non-hierarchical or democratic" (137). I suspect that one reason Writing Center or-thodoxy so strongly favors non-directive techniques is that it is, at heart, strongly Romantic-Expressivist in its persuasion. It privileges the writer's own-ership of a piece of writing and assumes that the same writing processes are "global and transferable" (136) to writing in all disciplines.

Second, the assumption that written comments are "too directive" ig-nores the fact that modes of comment run a whole gamut. Knoblauch and Bran-non did pioneering work by distinguishing between "directive" and "facilita-tive" comments. Straub and Lunsford, in their study of the response styles of twelve composition experts, refined the distinction into twelve different modes. Among the more directive modes, they identify the "corrective," "evaluative," "imperative," and "advisory." Among the more facilitative are "problem-solving," "heuristic," and "reflective" (1995, 166–174). Writing assistants' comments, like those of the teachers in the study, display the entire range of response modes. They must learn to make judgments, or educated guesses, as to which modes are most likely to contribute to effective revision and student learning.

And finally, written response is becoming increasingly common as more Writing Centers begin to offer online tutoring and response to drafts—which is almost exactly the same as the written responses we make to drafts in the project.

FUTURE DIRECTIONS FOR THE PROJECT

The Write Project is only the beginning of what we hope will be a growing Writing in the Disciplines program. Now that the project is fairly well established, we can see more clearly where to go next. The project should turn out to be a starting place for other activities.

The clearest effort that emerges is faculty development. The project creates a demand; faculty working with the project find out what they do not know about designing assignments, about advising students about their writing processes, and about responding to student writing. Instructors who were at first drawn to the project by the prospect of getting papers that were easier to read find themselves wanting to know more about how to use writing in their teaching. We have started working on plans to reestablish a series of faculty seminars that have been successful in the past. Veterans of the three-week summer sessions and the full-semester seminars of past years still report that the seminar was the best thing that ever happened to them as teachers, that what they learned permanently changed the way they teach.

A new issue will arise eventually: if the project continues to be successful, how much bigger can it get? At present, the size of the project is limited to the size of the Writing Center staff. We can handle ten to a dozen classes each semester. It is unrealistic to think that the project can continue indefinitely if it stays that small. If we can not come close to meeting growing faculty demand, faculty will feel discouraged from asking to be included. Successful programs at other schools work with numbers many times the size of ours. The program at Brown University, for instance, involves about half of its 5,000 undergraduates and 80 writing fellows (Haring-Smith 1992, 178).

One promising avenue is to train students as WID liaisons between content-area classes and the Writing Center. At the time of this writing, we are piloting a satellite program in three section of a Spanish literature course. The instructors found five Spanish majors willing to serve as WAs for one credit of internship. For part of that credit, they underwent a short series of training sessions in the Writing Center. For the rest, they are responding to student drafts (written in Spanish). So far the experiment is working. We may try to add other departments to the WID liaison project. A possible source of liaisons may be the "fourth credit" service learning program the University plans to implement. Honors students and strong student writers might fulfill their fourth-credit obligations by serving as WID liaisons in courses they have taken in their majors.

Though The Write Project exerts a certain amount of strain on the Writing Center's resources and the writing assistants' time, we are convinced that it was a good move for us. It has given the Writing Center a higher profile on campus and has helped us get established in our new role as the center for writing in the disciplines. The writing assistants believe in the project. They have come to view written response as valuable and effective, even though it is not as satisfying and generally not as effective as face-to-face tutoring. They enjoy the professional relationships they establish with the faculty—relationships which encourage their own sense of professionalism—and they work hard to encourage thoughtful revision from the students.

The project has helped us to focus on rhetorical theory and to take a more truly rhetorical approach to all of our work. It has prompted us to examine in new ways issues concerning the training of writing assistants, issues of directiveness in tutoring and written response, and issues of the expectations of faculty, students, and the writing assistants themselves. We have learned that the relationship between the Writing Center and the project, on one hand, and the faculty and students, on the other, is one of partnership. In order for the partnership to work, both sides have to contribute a substantial amount of effort in order to reap the greatest benefits.

WORKS CITED

Anderson, Chris. *Free/Style: A Direct Approach to Writing*. Boston: Houghton Mifflin, 1992.

Aristotle. *On Rhetoric* , trans. George A. Kennedy. New York: Oxford, 1991.

Benson, Thomas W., and Michael H. Prosser. *Readings in Classical Rhetoric*. Davis, CA: Hermagoras Press, 1988.

Clark, Irene L. "Collaboration and Ethics in Writing Center Pedagogy." *Writing Center Journal* 9 (1988): 3–12.

Coe, Richard M. *Process, Form, and Substance*. 2nd ed. Englewood Cliffs, NJ: Prentice Hall, 1990.

Crossley, Gay Lynn. Workshop presentation for "Responding to Student Writing: Gearing Comments to Our Teaching Styles, Students, and Course Goals." Richard Straub, Chair. Conference on College Composition and Communication Convention. Phoenix Convention Center. 12 Mar. 1997.

Crowley, Sharon. *Ancient Rhetorics for Contemporary Students*. Boston: Allyn and Bacon, 1994.

Ede, Lisa. "Writing as a Social Process: A Theoretical Foundation for Writing Centers?" *Writing Center Journal* 9 (1989): 3–13.

Elbow, Peter, and Pat Belanoff. *A Community of Writers*. 2nd ed. New York: McGraw-Hill, 1995.

Haring-Smith, Tori. "Changing Students' Attitudes: Writing Fellows Programs." *Writing Across the Curriculum: A Guide to Developing Programs*, eds. Susan H. McLeod and Margot Soven. Newbury Park, CA: Sage, 1992. 175–187.

Hubbuch, Susan M. "A Tutor Needs to Know the Subject Matter to Help a Student with a Paper: ___Agree ___Disagree ___Not Sure." *The Writing Center Journal* 8.2 (1988): 23–30.

Kiedaisch, Jean, and Sue Dinitz. "Look Back and Say 'So What': The Limitations of the Generalist Tutor." *The Writing Center Journal* 14.1 (1993): 63–74.

Knoblauch, C. H., and Lil Brannon. *Rhetorical Traditions and the Teaching of Writing*. Portsmouth, NH: Boynton/Cook, 1984.

Kuriloff, Peshe C. "What Discourses Have in Common: Teaching the Transaction Between Writer and Reader." *College Composition and Communication* 47 (1996): 485–501.

Leahy, Richard. "Rhetorical Analysis in Writing Assistant Training." *The Writing Lab Newsletter* 20 (1995): 1–4.

Lindemann, Erica. *A Rhetoric for Writing Teachers*. 3rd ed. New York: Oxford, 1995.

Matsen, Patricia P., Philip Rollinson, and Marion Sousa. *Readings from Classical Rhetoric*. Carbondale: Southern Illinois UP, 1990.

Podis, Leonard A., and Joanne M. Podis. "Improving Our Responses to Student Writing: A Process-oriented Approach." *Rhetoric Review* 5 (1986): 90–98.

Raimes, Ann. *Keys for Writers*. Boston: Houghton Mifflin, 1996.

Reynolds, John F., ed. *Rhetorical Memory and Delivery: Classical Concepts for Contemporary Composition and Communication*. Hillsdale, NJ: Lawrence Erlbaum, 1993.

Rider, Janine. *The Writer's Book of Memory*. Hillsdale, NJ: Lawrence Erlbaum, 1995.

Ronald, Kate. "Style: The Hidden Agenda in Composition Classes or One Reader's Confession." *The Subject Is Writing*, ed. Wendy Bishop. Portsmouth, NH: Boynton/Cook, 1993. 53–68.

Shamoon, Linda K., and Deborah H. Burns. "A Critique of Peer Tutoring," *Writing Center Journal* 15 (1995): 134–151.

Sommers, Nancy. "Responding to Student Writing." *College Composition and Communication* 33 (1982): 148–156.

Straub, Richard. "The Concept of Control in Teacher Response: Defining the Varieties of 'Directive' and 'Facilitative' Commentary." *College Composition and Communication* 47 (1996): 223–251.

———, and Ronald Lunsford. *Twelve Readers Reading*. Cresskill, NJ: Hampton,1995.

Welch, Kathleen. *The Contemporary Reception of Classical Rhetoric: Appropriations of Ancient Discourse*. Hillsdale, NJ: Lawrence Erlbaum, 1990.

7

A Writing Center without a WAC Program: The De Facto WAC Center/Writing Center

Muriel Harris

Reflecting on the twenty-fifth anniversary of Writing Across the Curriculum (celebrated in 1995), Barbara Walvoord takes a long look at WAC's past in order to assess where it should be heading (1996, 58–79). She looks back at WAC as an academic movement and concludes that, among other steps to be taken for the health of WAC's future, WAC Programs need to connect to Writing Centers. She writes as if WAC and Writing Centers, at least in some institutions, have gone their separate ways despite overlapping and reinforcing interests. Among the many configurations and varieties of WAC/Writing Center connections, she notes the absence of a consistent linkage. While many WAC Programs have connected in productive ways with the campus Writing Center, it is true that some WAC specialists have not perceived there to be lines of connection—a phenomenon I observed first hand a few years ago. When a nationally recognized WAC specialist came to my campus, it was clear from this person's remarks and responses to questions in public forums that the person seemed well meaning but clueless as to what Writing Centers do beyond some vague sense that they repair remedial writers in some way.

But the perspective of some WAC specialists that Writing Centers have little or no apparent connection to WAC is neither a universally nor even a widely held one. In the descriptions of various programs in Toby Fulwiler and Art Young's collection, *Programs That Work: Models and Methods for Writing Across the Curriculum*, there are a variety of models for ways Writing Centers and WAC Programs can and do work together. At some institutions WAC Programs and Writing Centers coordinate their efforts; in other cases the administration of both is delegated to the same person. Mark Waldo, in "The Last Best Place for Writing Across the Curriculum: The Writing Center," argues for a somewhat different configuration—situating WAC within the Writing Center. In yet other cases, there are WAC Program directors who recognize the need for a

Writing Center when there is none and work actively to bring one into existence. For example, Pat McQueeney, in "Proposing a Writing Center: Experts' Advice," details the rationale in her proposal for a Writing Center on her campus and notes that their WAC Program needs the support service that the faculty want for the writing in their courses.

Yet another variation on this theme of connections between Writing Centers and WAC Programs is the Writing Center on a campus where there is no officially sanctioned or institutionalized WAC Program. Such is the case on my campus, Purdue University—a large land grant, research-oriented university where to varying degrees, faculty with varying goals and varying awareness of what writing can do to enhance learning assign writing in their courses. For reasons discussed below, our Writing Lab has become a de facto WAC Writing Center, that is, a Writing Center where there is no WAC Program but where we meet with all students working on writing who seek our tutorial help, where we recognize a need to respond to faculty interest in using writing in their courses, and where—we hope—we try to nurture an interest in developing more formalized WAC Programs on our campus. From my perspective, as we attempt to work with faculty who interact with our Writing Lab and to meet with their students in tutorials, I can see how mutually advantageous a WAC/Writing Center relationship might be, and I offer the example of our Writing Lab, a de facto WAC center, as a case study in what a Writing Center situated in a context like ours can and cannot do.

Such Writing Centers can, if resources permit, take on some faculty development as well as the tutorial support for students writing in various courses. But, in addition, a closer look at what a Writing Center with no institutionally supported WAC Program cannot achieve is also a rationale for why WAC Programs are needed on a campus committed to strong integration of writing into all disciplines. For those who forecast the end of institutionalized WAC, a clearer sense of what a Writing Center cannot achieve alone is a strong argument for maintaining a WAC Program where there is the commitment to its goals. Even if the WAC Program is situated in the Writing Center, as Waldo argues for, it has to be an institutionally supported WAC Program, not a bottom-up attempt by the Writing Center to launch a WAC-like program of its own.

While Walvoord and McQueeney argue for the WAC/Writing Center connection from the perspective of WAC directors, I thus add—from a vantage point inside a Writing Center—my argument for such a linkage. Without a WAC Program, our Writing Lab can achieve certain goals but is limited in its ability to bring about the self-sustaining changes a WAC Program seeks. Looking at what we can and cannot do in our Writing Lab is also another argument for Walvoord's insight into how reinforcing a WAC/Writing Center relationship can be. When there is careful, thoughtful integration and mutual working out of goals and responsibilities, each can complement and strengthen the other's work. But without institutionally provided resources and institutional sanction for WAC, a Writing Center has limits beyond which it cannot go in working with students Writing Across the Curriculum and the teachers assigning that writing. This case study will attempt to flesh out the particulars of that statement and to provide a clearer sense of what a Writing Center can contribute to WAC Programs as well as what it cannot reasonably be expected to accomplish and what might be unrealistic to incorporate into the Writing Center's mission statement or future goals. As Stephen North cautioned, in his reconsideration of the idea of a Writing Center, a Writing Center's mission should match its resources and should not "be seen as taking upon its shoulders the whole institution's (real or imagined) sins of illiteracy" (1994, 17). But, matching its efforts to its resources, a Writing Center can work to develop campus-wide awareness of how writing can enhance learning and how it can be used to help students become proficient in the disciplinary thinking and writing they will need when they enter those fields.

GUIDELINES AND GOALS FOR WAC PROGRAMS

When using the term WAC both in this essay or in my own thinking and planning for our Writing Lab, I have found it useful to keep in mind the defining features of WAC as a movement. Otherwise, a Writing Center without a WAC Program can fall into limited—and limiting—perceptions of Writing Across the Curriculum, thinking of it merely as any writing done in any course with the WAC Writing Center being any center which offers a few faculty workshops and tutorial assistance with writing in any course. Writing Across the Curriculum as the particular movement Walvoord was examining in her article—the movement that has spawned national conferences, books, articles, an electronic listserv, and the book in which this essay appears—has broader, more substantive defining features. WAC, as Susan McLeod has written so eloquently, is a transformative program in that it seeks to change the way teachers and students use writing in the curriculum (1992, 3). Beyond using writing as a way to measure or evaluate mastery of a subject and beyond grading writing as a means of improving grammatical proficiency, WAC promotes writing as a tool for learning and as a way to write and think in discipline-specific ways. McLeod adds that WAC also encourages writing to learn and learning to write in all disciplines (1992, 5). Her description of what a WAC Program needs in terms of combining top-down and bottom-up support also impinges on what a Writing Center can and cannot do without a program that can be called a Writing Across the Curriculum program:

A WAC Program needs strong administrative support, but it also has to be a bottom-up phenomenon, usually starting with a few committed faculty members and growing as others see how successful these faculty have been. Profound curricular and pedagogical change can come about as a result of a WAC Program, but such change will not take place unless it comes from the faculty themselves. And change takes time. Successful WAC Programs start slowly, phasing in various components over a period of years as a consensus develops that the program is useful. (1992, 6)

The emphasis on faculty here reinforces both Toby Fulwiler's description of WAC as "teacher centered" (3) and Walvoord's cautionary comment that because WAC is intended to change teaching, WAC Programs need to work with teachers directly, usually through workshops or linked courses or team teaching. The choice to focus on teachers was a deliberate one made by early WAC proponents, Walvoord notes, and faculty development is therefore a key ingredient in a WAC Program. But extended faculty development can exist only where there is institutional support, and that support can take a number of forms such as encouraging attendance at retreats, workshops, or seminars with inducements such as release time or extra funding, providing writing fellows or teaching assistants, limiting class size, offering course reduction, or finding some means of lessening the load in other ways to compensate for the increased work that WAC requires. There also has to be some institutional recognition that such work is valuable, and if this is in the form of being incorporated into the review process, the reward is particularly strong.

Without some form of compensation and without some means of bringing teachers together for faculty development so that they become aware of what they want to do and how they might achieve the new goals they set for themselves, a WAC Program can falter. There are other factors that must be present as well. As Jody Swilky notes, in her discussion of faculty resistance, there is a falling off of faculty interest when there is no follow through after a workshop. A workshop or intensive training can bring great expectations and can fire teachers up to plunge in, in new and challenging ways. But then, with no follow up and the onset of reality (which is never quite what the workshop might lead the newly inspired to expect), interest wanes. Teachers retreat, fall back to old patterns, and drop out. Swilky thus concludes that the short seminar approach for faculty training has serious limitations in producing strong follow through. And, as already mentioned, Pat McQueeney argues for an additional component in WAC, a strong support system such as a Writing Center, for without that faculty resist taking on WAC work by themselves.

RATIONALE FOR A DE FACTO WAC WRITING CENTER

If a Writing Center exists in an institution where there is no WAC Program to focus its full attention on instituting WAC goals, why then might a Writing Center attempt to be a de facto WAC Writing Center? As a Writing Center director in this context, I have to thread my way through a number of complex considerations in deciding how we will expend our limited resources. How do I respond when a faculty member across campus assigns all seventy-five students in her class to see a Writing Lab tutor before handing in their papers, and about two-thirds of them come in the morning the paper is due? If the other third of the students from that class schedule appointments beforehand and cause us to turn away other students as they fill up the appointment book—particularly the students in our writing courses in the English Department who constitute the largest group of users—what is my response, given the fact that the

English Department funds us and that the University has no history of funding for services crossing school lines? How should I respond to phone calls or visits from faculty who want to know about adding more writing to their classes? And how much time should I invest in responding to such a request, given the fact that I can not provide the kinds of extended workshops and seminars we know are needed?

If we offer brief workshops on various writing topics and class visits to publicize our Writing Lab, what do we do if there are so many responses that we seriously have to decrease our available time for tutoring? Do we agree to do workshops anywhere on campus or only in composition courses? If an instructor in another field is truly interested in using the Writing Lab in the most appropriate manner he can, including an offer to come to our staff meeting to coordinate with us, do I encourage his interest? What if eight or fourteen more faculty do the same? (That might seem like a large number to some, but on a campus with over a thousand faculty and perhaps another thousand graduate teaching assistants, fourteen requests would be a tiny fraction of the University's instructional staff.) If one of the purposes of our OWL (Online Writing Lab) is to provide a campus resource on using the Internet for writing research papers, should we be offering classroom workshops for instructors in other disciplines interested in seeing how this all works and how OWL can be coordinated into their classes? These and other questions come up regularly in our Writing Lab, and because we have always made our services available to any writer in the University, drawing boundaries is neither easy nor obvious. How do I determine what are appropriate Writing Center responsibilities (in a large institution with administrative oversight dispersed in various ways, our responsibilities are not clearly defined), which requests fall within our perceived mission and goals, and when do we have to admit that without more extensive resources and programs, we are only offering Band-Aid WAC help? Writing Center theory and practice is drenched in discussions of how to avoid Band-Aid writing help to students, but de facto WAC Writing Centers also need to think about how to avoid Band-Aid WAC help.

However, there are a number of reasons that argue for taking on some of the work of assisting writers from all disciplines even if the center can not do it all or do it in a way that will be substantive or lead to self-sustaining change— and even if we agree (as I do) that Michael Pemberton raises valid considerations for rethinking the Writing Center/WAC connection. One of the theoretical justifications for tutorial work is the Writing Center claim that all writers benefit from tutorial collaboration, especially as they move on to more complex writing challenges (Harris, "Collaboration" 1992 and "Talking in the Middle" 1995), and we have a commitment in our Writing Lab to enact that principle, to keep our doors open to all writers. Since Writing Centers are student-centered, it would also be difficult for us (unless mandated to do otherwise) not to respond to students who come in asking for help.

Moreover, we have a commitment to providing tutorials that are as effective as we can make them. If there are obstacles that are likely to diminish the possibility that we are assisting writers, we have to improve those conditions if possible. One of the major impediments to helping a writer is a writing assignment so poorly designed that it can only provoke bad writing. A tutorial that focuses on helping the student become a better writer as she writes a paper in response to such an ill-conceived assignment is a study in frustration and, too often, defeat. Some years ago, several Writing Center colleagues and I offered a session at the Conference on College Composition and Communication dealing with how to cope in the Writing Center with what we called "Assignments from Hell" (AFH's, as they are familiarly known in our Writing Lab). The flood of attendees at that session, with people cramming and shoving to get in, attested to the high frequency as well as high level of frustration Writing Center specialists experience with this problem. Writing Center tutors need to deal, somehow, with students trying to write papers in response to AFH's, and there is little we can do when the assignment is from the darkest depths of Hell, even more horrible than we might have otherwise imagined. In my early years as a Writing Lab Director, I was complaining to a colleague about the problem of students trying to cope with poorly written assignments, and in his astute Southern manner, he answered with a proverb, "You don't want to waste your energy swatting mosquitoes when you really need to drain the pond."

The source of the AFH problem, of course, is the teacher, not the student, and to start draining the pond, we need to find ways to help teachers master the complex art of designing effective writing assignments. That can range from calling the instructor and gently attempting one-to-one consultation to holding faculty workshops, and some of the responses we have come up with in our Writing Lab are discussed below. But the point here is that if Writing Centers want to help students in truly effective ways, we have to dip a toe (or, more likely, both feet) into faculty development. And that assistance is needed across the curriculum of an institution, especially in large institutions when there are students coming to the center from all corners of the campus where faculty may even be award-winning teachers and cutting-edge researchers but have never stopped to think about the elements of an effective writing assignment in their field.

Another compelling reason for a Writing Center to engage in some WAC work when there is no WAC Program has to do with the public image of the center. A Writing Center on a campus with no WAC Program becomes the lightening rod for faculty questions about using writing in their classes or faculty complaints or faculty interest in helping particular students. And a Writing Center, if it is working well, draws students who have heard from other students how valuable their tutoring experience was. Part of the success of a Writing Center is the campus-wide perception of it as being responsive to user needs, and by users, I mean faculty and students. Writing Centers that draw tight boundaries around what they can and cannot do, that carefully limit their services and conserve resources, that train tutors to confine their assistance only to what is possible or required of them are soon known to be just that—not responsive. Campus perceptions are important to the health of a Writing Center, particularly one that relies on voluntary attendance, and it does not bode well for a center to be perceived as being less than helpful. Moreover, a non-responsive center is not true to basic Writing Center principles of being nurturing and supportive. A number of different strands of Writing Center theory and pedagogy (e.g., feminist theorizing on nurturing practices that promote learning; borderlands or contact zone theorizing that promotes the center as the place for different cultures to meet, literacy theorizing that looks at the role of a center to provide a space for different literacies, etc.) reinforce the view of the Writing Center as being positioned to help students, regardless of the source of the writing assignment or problem.

Moreover, if a Writing Center advertises on its publicity materials, as many do, that it welcomes all students, it should do just that—welcome all students. An added bonus in a Writing Center open to all students is the sense of accomplishment tutors feel when helping students with complex writing tasks in various disciplines. The collaborative effort is truly collaborative when it is particularly apparent in the tutorial that while the tutor brings rhetorical knowledge to the conversation, the student brings disciplinary knowledge. This is a powerful enactment of tutorial theories of collaboration. From another theoretical perspective, Writing Centers have always welcomed challenges for new ways to work with writing. Some see this as a reason for the health of the Writing Center concept, that Writing Centers are flexible enough to move forward easily. While curricular changes happen slowly, Writing Centers can respond quickly and energetically to changing climates for writing instruction. Writing Center practice can thus move forward by experimenting and trying out and seeking new ways to help writers and to assist with new forms and genres of writing that students in various disciplines are engaging in. This has led some Writing Center enthusiasts to view Writing Centers as being on the cutting edge of current practice, and certainly there is a freedom to explore opportunities and challenges. One example of this is the rapid growth of online writing labs—known by the acronym OWL—that have become resources for faculty and students, and our OWL, as discussed below, has certainly developed into a campus-wide resource on writing.

Finally, from the perspective of administrative concerns, there is yet another rationale for being a de facto Writing Center. A Writing Center that to some degree relies on demonstrating its effectiveness through statistics showing high (or steadily increasing) usage will find that opening its doors to all students is one more bit of insurance that the center will be used. Initiating contact with faculty, holding faculty workshops, or responding to faculty contacts for help make faculty more aware of the center and more likely to refer their students to the center. And when a Writing Center builds a strong constituency among the faculty across campus, the center builds a strong base of support that helps it grow and prosper. Given these broader reasons for a Writing Center to engage in WAC efforts, I turn now to our Writing Lab—who we are in terms of our institutional setting, what we do to fill the gap in WAC efforts, and finally what we cannot do to fully implement the goals of a successful WAC Program.

THE INSTITUTIONAL SETTING FOR OUR DE FACTO WRITING CENTER

Purdue University is a huge institution—with 35,000 students on my campus—that has a strong centralized administration overseeing ten academic schools, all of which are decentralized to the extent that they control their own curricula and core requirements. Some of these schools, such as Pharmacy and the ten schools of engineering within Engineering, have nationally mandated emphases on communication skills as part of accreditation requirements (see Eric Hobson and Neal Lerner's "Writing Centers/WAC in Pharmacy Education: A Changing Prescription" in this book for a closer look at one School of Pharmacy's institutionalized WAC Program). Of the engineering schools, some more than others are also responding to pressures from the world that hires their graduates to improve their students' communication skills. Their responses vary, but the most common model has been to hire a writing specialist who works closely with the report writing in a course, usually an upper-level one. This is the case in several of the engineering schools (the School of Chemical and Metallurgical Engineering, the School of Mechanical Engineering, and the School of Civil Engineering).

In a somewhat different arrangement, the School of Management has a small staff of writing professionals to teach writing courses and offer writing support for Management students. Some of the students from these and the other schools on campus come to the Writing Lab, either because of faculty or staff referral (or a friend's recommendation), and some come in with papers after having acquired the habit of working with a tutor in their composition courses. In addition, graduate students also appear in our Writing Lab with drafts of course papers, dissertation proposals, and other writing projects. Although the other land-grant institution in our state—Indiana University—has a university-wide WAC Program, Purdue's structure is such that curricular requirements are handled within each school, and it is not likely that this will change in the foreseeable future. If WAC enters the curriculum here, it is more likely that it will be at the school level and not campus-wide.

Within the School of Liberal Arts, a recent and very extensive core curriculum revision effort resulted in a recommendation for instituting a WAC Program, but the lack of funding has kept that from becoming a reality. The English Department, with a large writing program (first-year composition, advanced composition, business writing, technical writing, creative writing, etc.), still provides most of the writing instruction on campus and enrolls in its upper-level writing courses students from various majors, some of whom are required to take the courses as part of their majors in their schools. Thus, the Writing Lab, housed in and funded by the English Department, has attempted to meet the need for writing support for both the faculty and students in writing courses as well as provide campus-wide writing assistance. But we exist on the usual tight English Department budget and perennially cope with the usual maximum strain on our resources.

Our Lab's largest constituency are the students in both first-year and upper-level writing courses, though, as noted, many of these students are fulfilling writing requirements in their own schools. We also work with undergraduates and graduate students writing papers in a variety of courses across campus, though our statistics show that 40 percent of these students are enrolled in the School of Liberal Arts. That is, when we exclude the students in our first year writing courses, 40 percent of the remaining students are Liberal Arts majors, though all other schools in the University are represented in this group. By this I mean that when we exclude all students in first-year writing classes from the statistical survey of usage, the remaining group includes students writing in courses in all schools in the University, a further demonstration that we do serve the entire University. In the majority of cases across campus, where faculty are incorporating writing into content courses, they are left to their own devices to structure assignments and to figure out how to respond appropriately to that writing. The faculty have diverse perceptions of how writing can be used and how it can be evaluated, and they vary greatly in the degree to which they are willing to make contact with writing resource people and places to assist them.

In this setting, the English Department houses the Writing Lab which I, as a tenured faculty member, direct. We have two staffs of tutors funded by the department: one staff is composed of graduate students who work with all students who seek tutorial help (except for students in our developmental writing program) and another staff of undergraduate peer tutors who are integrated into the developmental writing program, attending one class a week and tutoring every student in that program every week in the Writing Lab. An additional staff of peer tutors is funded by other sources in the University to assist with resumes and job applications. We also have a support staff consisting of a professional person who acts as secretary and general assistant, a receptionist, and work-study students who provide clerical and reception assistance. Although I report usage statistics, our services have grown so complex that no single number adequately represents our work. We work with about 6,000 students a year in tutorials or workshops or brief phone consultations, we give out hundreds and hundreds of handouts on writing skills to students and instructors who come in to ask for materials, and our OWL recorded about 1,500,000 hits (excluding graphics) last year, over 40,000 of which were initiated on campus. This vast usage, coupled with numerous awards from Internet companies (the usual handouts from four-star ratings companies so that the site will then post their award and thereby promote traffic for that company), is the kind of "good news" news that universities like to promote about themselves. In the flurry of articles in university publications that mention the success of our OWL, the description of its services is a highly effective means of getting the word out to faculty around campus that OWL is a resource for them too.

OUR WRITING LAB'S WAC EFFORTS

The major expenditure of our resources is for tutoring and working with all students who come to the Writing Lab. However, because WAC is a teacher-centered movement, this discussion of our de facto WAC efforts focuses primarily on the assistance we offer instructors in terms of faculty development and faculty support (though, of course, faculty support does encompass offering one-to-one assistance to their students when they assign writing). Faculty consultations occur most often in response to instructors who contact me with a question or complaint or whom I contact after they have begun to refer students to the Writing Lab. If the assignment that brought some students in is an AFH, I try to initiate a conversation with the instructor that can offer some help with revising the assignment. And there are other opportunities for contacting faculty across campus. If I notice a sudden surge of papers from a particular course in economics or political science, I can contact the teacher to establish lines of communication. Sometimes, that line is merely a thin thread, but other times, it can turn into a productive relationship. Some consultations are initiated by faculty who have called to ask for help in writing essay exam questions or who want some feedback on an assignment they are about to hand out or who want some information about how they can use the Lab for their students. If possible, I try to invite more interaction than a single phone call or meeting provokes, and in some cases, that has worked. In other cases, teachers look upon that one interaction either as sufficient or as the extent of the time they can devote to the topic.

Phone conversations and personal consultations are, seemingly, reactive responses, but they can also be the result of proactive efforts: sending out publicity notices, offering my services to departments when I meet administrators from that department, and reminding teachers whom I meet that the Writing Lab is a resource for them as well as their students. A more structured proactive approach is to offer my services for campus workshops on popular topics such as using writing in the classroom or evaluating papers. Faculty workshops are effective in that participants are there because of some interest in the topic, and useful contacts are made in those workshops. In addition to the few who are attracted to the workshop for the sole purpose of complaining about how badly students write these days, I meet teachers who begin to think about using the Writing Lab and about how they should assign and respond to writing. Even a brief introduction in a workshop or a short phone conversation can also be the opening to explain why our Writing Lab is not a grammar fix-it shop and why we do not proofread papers. If possible, by moving the conversation in appropriate directions, I can promote the notion of writing as a tool for learning. By being known on campus as a person willing to help with writing, I have been invited to departments to talk with instructional staff who are grading writing assignments, and I have been asked to talk to majors in various fields about the importance of writing in their future careers. Another result of all these efforts, I hope, is simply to keep the topic of using writing on the academic table.

Our most focused large-scale WAC effort is our OWL (Online Writing Lab; http://owl.english.purdue.edu). A number of forces have spurred the growth of our Writing Lab's OWL, and one of them has been a challenge to serve the campus—both faculty and students—in ways we are not normally able to do. Online, we are providing a WAC-like service, one that expands on a familiar service in most Writing Centers—offering print materials on writing skills from our cabinets of instructional handouts developed originally to accompany tutorial talk. It also, as Irene Clark discusses in her chapter in this book on the role the Web plays in the Writing Center, expands the space for working with writing to include a virtual space as well as a physical one. Our OWL, originally an e-mail service that is now primarily (in terms of usage) a Web site, includes among its resources a large number of handouts on writing. We have offered these materials to all faculty on campus who are invited to download and use them in their classes or refer their students to the materials which are available in any campus computer lab or anywhere they can access the Web or e-mail. Making materials on writing available to students and faculty is easily done online, and the Internet is a perfect means for our Writing Lab and any other Writing Center to make those materials available to any teacher for any course anywhere in the world. Thus, we have heard (informally) that our OWL is listed as the "writing assistance" on Web course pages beyond Purdue in fields as diverse as anthropology, medicine, engineering, and geology, as well as in institutions all over the world.

Across campus, we have had numerous requests for workshops on using OWL as a resource. In addition to providing online materials on writing (including assistance with citing electronic sources), OWL was set up to help writers search the Internet for information. At present that includes a collection of Internet search engines, and under development will be online materials on using search engines effectively and evaluating sources. Thus, we offer various services because of OWL, and our workshops around campus are usually tailored to the specific teacher's need to help that class use the Internet when writing papers and to the teacher's additional need to think about how to incorporate use of the Internet in his or her curriculum.

In this way, our OWL is a resource both for students and faculty, but working from the perspective that WAC is a faculty movement, our OWL also assists faculty development. One section of our OWL is labeled as "Teacher Resources," and here we have useful links on teaching writing as well as links to WAC pages at other institutions. This provides our faculty with the means to read about WAC Programs as well as to read WAC papers and online versions of WAC newsletters (such as the excellent one at Boise State University). Some institutions with WAC Programs have flourishing and rich Web sites where their faculty can find resources on using writing in their disciplines, and our OWL becomes the conduit for our faculty to have access to those same materials. We hope that by developing that part of our OWL site further, we can be more proactive in offering easily accessed information about using writing effectively.

In addition, to assist faculty who want to know more about how to grade English as a Second Language (ESL) papers, we are developing the ESL resources for teachers, including materials on responding to ESL writing. We hope that teachers in all fields will visit that section of our OWL to gather ideas for how to evaluate papers written by ESL students, and we also hope that it will deter some teachers from reacting too harshly to minor surface errors in ESL writing. If we meet up with such problems when the ESL student comes to the Writing Lab desperate for proofreading help (because of unrealistic teacher comments about the need to fix the errors in the paper), we can suggest to the teacher that he or she consider the suggestions offered on OWL for how to respond to ESL papers. Again, the purpose is both to help instructors and also to improve tutorials by having students come in for appropriate kinds of tutorial help.

LIMITATIONS TO OUR WRITING LAB'S WAC EFFORTS

While we provide faculty support and some faculty development, there are limitations to what our Writing Lab can hope to accomplish on a campus with no WAC Program. In Toby Fulwiler and Art Young's *Programs That Work* and other discussions of WAC, there are a number of recurrent themes in descriptions of successful WAC Programs, factors that are of crucial importance in creating the sustained transformative change that McLeod defines as necessary for WAC integration in the curriculum. The retreats and workshops that start off an instructor's introduction to WAC are intended to immerse teachers, to bring them together in collaborative ways, to create what Mary Jane Dickerson, Toby Fulwiler, and Henry Steffens describe as "engaged faculty" (1990, 46). In their WAC Program at the University of Vermont: "Instructors go away from our two-day workshops full of good feelings, enthusiasm about teaching, a renewed interest in their own writing, and, of course, with some ideas about the ways to implement more writing into the courses they teach. Perhaps even more important, however, is the sense of community they discover at the workshops" (46).

Joyce Neff Magnotto and Barbara R. Stout describe the "spirit of collegiality [that] develops" (33) in extended workshops, and they detail some of the ground that must be covered, introducing faculty to the complexities of writing processes, to "re-examin[ing] pedagogies in light of WAC values" (32), to various kinds of writing beyond the traditional forms they knew as students, and so on. Without the opportunity to engage in such extended dialogues with faculty or to provide contexts for the kinds of enriching collegial interaction and collaboration described by Magnotto and Stout, we cannot expect that our short workshops will provide the stimuli needed for substantive change. Moreover, without the means to encourage or provide extended individual consultations and follow up, we have to realize that our efforts will fall prey to various problems. As Judy Gill notes, such assistance is needed because when reality sets in, "instructors don't see the improvement they had hoped for, they are frustrated and their earlier anxieties and skepticism may return"(1996, 168). An inference that Swilky draws from her analysis of teacher resistance to using writing is that "to assist teachers who are serious about changing their pedagogy, we need to collaborate with instructors as they revise their courses" (1992, 58). Clearly, sustained interaction cannot be provided by a Writing Center without resources provided for such work.

But even if our Writing Lab were to apportion our resources so that we could somehow set up more workshops or use some of our time to offer more faculty consultation, there has to be some incentive for faculty to plunge in to course revision and to take on the labor-intensive work of interacting with more student writing. Some faculty are, of course, motivated by a genuine desire to be good teachers, but even they are not likely to be able to sustain that interest in an institution that does not reward them for the effort in some way, either through course support (e.g., offering release time or providing graduate student or writing fellow assistance) or recognition at review time. Worse yet, when the institution has made no overt commitment to WAC and when it encourages by rewarding research efforts, some faculty members may find themselves quietly warned by mentors not to devote so much effort to teaching because they will, finally, be reviewed for promotion and tenure (and salary raises) on the basis of research. Without institutional support in terms of rewards for the teacher, the most well-meaning teacher will eventually figure out that all this work may be personally and intellectually rewarding but is not a strong career move. In these days of tight job markets for academics, faculty catch on fairly quickly. At my university where research is encouraged and valued, how could I reasonably expect faculty to come to extended workshops or to devote the necessary time to those consultations that we would offer if we could when we can not provide the kinds of stamps of approval they need to survive in their jobs? As Malcolm Kiniry, Ellen Strenski, and Mike Rose note, in their description of the University of California, Los Angeles' cross-curricular writing program ("UCLA"), "[r]esearch universities. . . are just not structured to reward scholars for spending time assigning and responding to student writing" (1990, 30). Even in successful WAC Programs, there are what Dickerson, Fulwiler, and Steffens describe as mixed messages:

All the forces in the university, from department to college and university level, conspire to make research and publication more important than teaching. No matter what we say or do, our program [University of Vermont's Faculty Writing Project] asks instructors to think and do more about their teaching than the university rewards them for. And though we promote the workshops in part by suggesting that faculty will learn how to assign and assess student writing more effectively and efficiently, etc., thoughtful teaching does take more time—time away from something else. (1990, 59)

But given all this, for a Writing Center that is a de facto WAC Writing Center, there should be some recognition that there is merit in assisting with small changes even when there may be no likelihood of large-scale ones. Without a WAC Program for extended and extensive faculty development, a scaling down of expectations is necessary in order to acknowledge that merit. Part of that scaling down is to recognize what happens in our Writing Centers in other contexts. That is, when Judy Gill reminds us that in Writing Centers, we are not likely to see many of the students again and have learned to live with "not seeing the fruits of our labors" (1996, 175), it is no great stretch to expand this to de facto WAC Writing Center efforts as well. We should remember that we can contribute in ways that we may not see and that there is a lot more fruit out there than we are likely to be aware of. But to complete the picture, I need to switch to a water metaphor. Some days in the Writing Lab as I watch students come and go, I worry that we are trying to empty the ocean with a teaspoon. I had a similar sense when reading the comments on an end-of-the-semester evaluation from a faculty member across campus, several of whose students had come to the Writing Lab: "Thanks for your assistance, but Tim's paper still had a few grammatical errors that slipped through your net." But in that same pile of teacher evaluations was one from another faculty member with whom I had talked after he initially sent two of his "miscreants" (his term) to the Lab (both had some grammatical errors in their papers): "Matthew is beginning to write critically and thoughtfully now. I am not sure about Loni but she did have a tighter grip on her conclusions in that last paper. Thanks for your efforts—and for that reprint on using micro-themes." In that pile there were no evaluations from any of the biology instructors with whom I had met, the instructors in quiz sections who graded papers for a large lecture course. The faculty member who directed that course had contacted me about her interest in adding writing to the course. She and I talked and later agreed to a follow-up meeting with a graduate student Writing Lab staff member interested in working with faculty across the curriculum. After he met with her, she called to ask if I would talk with her staff since they would be the ones interacting with the student writing. I had difficulty determining what the agenda for my visit to the staff meeting would be, but when I arrived, the faculty member enthusiastically informed me that she had allotted ten minutes for my part of her staff meeting and asked if I could introduce the Writing Lab and its services, talk about writing and its importance in a biology course, and suggest to these quiz section instructors how to work with writing in their quiz sections. She assumed that I could adequately cover all that in ten minutes. In a de facto WAC Writing Center, you win some and you lose some, and it is never quite clear which is which.

WORKS CITED

Dickerson, Mary Jane, Toby Fulwiler, and Henry Steffens. "The University of Vermont." In *Programs That Work: Models and Methods for Writing Across the Curriculum,* Toby Fulwiler and Art Young eds. Portsmouth, NH: Boynton/Cook, 1990. 45–63.

Fulwiler, Toby, and Art Young, eds. *Programs That Work: Models and Methods for Writing Across the Curriculum.* Portsmouth, NH: Boynton/Cook, 1990.

Gill, Judy. "Another Look at WAC and the Writing Center." *Writing Center Journal* 16.2 (1996): 164–178.

Harris, Muriel. "Collaboration Is Not Collaboration Is Not Collaboration: Writing Center Tutorials vs. Peer-response Groups." *College Composition and Communication* 43 (1992): 369–383.

———. "Talking in the Middle: Why Writers Need Writing Tutors." *College English* 57 (1995): 27–42.

Kiniry, Malcolm, Ellen Strenski, and Mike Rose. "UCLA." In *Programs That Work: Models and Methods for Writing Across the Curriculum*, Toby Fulwiler and Art Young eds. Portsmouth, NH: Boynton/Cook Heinemann, 1990. 29–43.

McLeod, Susan H. and Margot Soven, eds. *Writing Across the Curriculum: A Guide to Developing Programs.* Newbury Park, CA: Sage, 1992.

McQueeney, Pat. "Proposing a Writing Center: Experts' Advice." *Writing Lab Newsletter*, forthcoming.

North, Stephen. "Revisiting 'The Idea of a Writing Center.'" *Writing Center Journal* 15.1 (1994): 7–19.

Pemberton, Michael A. "Rethinking the WAC/Writing Center Connection." *Writing Center Journal* 15.2 (1995): 116–133.

Swilky, Jody. "Reconsidering Faculty Resistance to Writing Reform." *WPA: Writing Program Administration* 16.1–2 (1992): 50–60.

Waldo, Mark L. "The Last Best Place for Writing Across the Curriculum: The Writing Center." *WPA/Writing Program Administration* 16.3 (1993): 15–26.

Walvoord, Barbara E. "The Future of WAC." *College English* 58 (1996): 58–79.

8

Writing Centers as WAC Centers: An Evolving Model

Peshe C. Kuriloff

Some years ago, when an uninformed administrator suggested doing away with our Writing Center on the grounds that Writing Across the Curriculum courses would provide all the instruction students needed, I fought that position vehemently. The Writing Center, I argued, is the instructional safety net for the writing program. We can not just abandon students who do not have the luck or inclination to end up in one of our courses during any particular semester. We have a duty to provide support for anyone who seeks it. If we set high standards, as I have always insisted we should, then we must assist those who have difficulty meeting them. In addition, Writing Centers serve an essential function in the implementation of goals for any writing program.

The goals for writing programs vary, but the standards I am advocating now have little to do with skill acquisition or the surface features of writing. As the concept of Writing Center has matured, expectations about what goes on there have changed. As early as 1984, Stephen North spoke up for the critical importance of serving the writer and refusing to separate Writing Center work from the mainstream of academic inquiry. More recently, Irene Clark and Dave Healy (1996) have taken that notion a step further in urging that Writing Centers challenge rather than acquiesce to institutional ideology and practice. This progressive effort to position the Writing Center more centrally and to assign it a more activist role in the institution merits notice. To the extent that Writing Centers locate themselves at the hub of the academic wheel rather than on the periphery, they stake out space previously occupied only by classroom instruction. Can tutoring or one-on-one conversations about writing actually claim equal status with classroom learning? Those of us who have worked in Writing Centers know that they can and they should.

In order to claim academic integrity, the work of the Writing Center must become integrated, structurally and theoretically, into the intellectual work of the university (Grimm 1996, 524). Writing Centers need to affiliate themselves with ideas and practices that have a direct relationship to what goes on in the classroom. This "new breed of Writing Center," as described by Mark Waldo, is closely allied with critical thinking and learning theory (1993, 16). Affiliation with Writing Across the Curriculum (or alternatively, promotion of Writing Across the Curriculum as a concept where programs do not already exist) offers a natural path to integration. Outreach to instructors and movement into classrooms across the curriculum provide a structure; participation in various conversations about disciplinary discourses and the methodologies of teaching and learning offers a theoretical frame. To the extent that a Writing Center operates independently, on the model of a skills center or remedial tutoring center, it not only isolates itself but it undermines the goals most WAC Programs struggle valiantly to promote. When the writing program speaks with a single voice, students and faculty hear a consistent message, learn better, and respond more enthusiastically to the demands placed on them. Writing Centers that function autonomously and deliver a message at odds with classroom instruction risk marginalizing their practice.

With that said, I do not want to undermine the idea of the Writing Center as a center for activism. I do want, however, to emphasize the potential gains to Writing Centers that provide a home for the interdisciplinary partnerships that often define Writing Across the Curriculum. By nature, WAC Programs exist in fragments, courses in many different departments related by a writing emphasis that hardly competes with the courses' departmental affiliations. Instructors, even when trained together in faculty workshops, may barely acknowledge the dotted line that connects them to the writing program. Writing Centers offer an opportunity to overcome some of the weaknesses inherent in the nature of WAC, particularly the potential for fragmentation and, as a result, the dilution of goals. By seizing the initiative, they can promote a common mission, centralize resources, advocate for an approach to writing instruction that is reinforced consistently across the curriculum, and position themselves at the heart of the academic program.

PRINCIPLES OF WAC

In spite of differences, most WAC Programs share a healthy respect for the discourse conventions of different disciplines. They have accepted a model of writing instruction rooted in socialization rather than skills acquisition (Bizzell 1982). Even programs that focus primarily on using writing as a tool for learning, rather than on mastering a writing process that leads to finished, discipline-appropriate text, emphasize discipline-specific modes of inquiry. They attempt to teach students that writing occurs in a context and that familiarity with the context is a necessary although not sufficient condition for successful communication. A skills-based approach to writing instruction, conveyed either through a more traditional English writing program or through the Writing Center or both gives students a contradictory message. In the context of writing isolated from other subjects and other natural contexts, a correct paper is a good paper; but in courses in other disciplines and in professional contexts, correctness only carries the writer so far. Writers who do not understand the conventions of writing in a field will not be well received by the more specialized readers to whom they must address themselves. They need to know about language and language structures, but they also need experience with the modes of inquiry and presentation, the rules of argument and evidence, the vocabulary, and the style expected of writers in their situation.

Attempting to separate language issues from issues related to context can easily create a false sense of security in a writer and a writing tutor or teacher. Students need appropriate instruction in evaluating writing situations, locating the information they need about customs and conventions, and cultivating an appropriate style and voice in order to manage their communications in the academy and in the world. Like any good safety net, the Writing Center needs to resist fostering dependency and empower students by giving them the tools they need to succeed on their own. Such tools include increased self-consciousness about their writing strategies, increased understanding about audience and reader/writer relationships, and mastery over relevant discipline-based conventions. Writing Centers willing to take on this mission play a critical role in both supporting and defining the goals of Writing Across the Curriculum.

At the University of Pennsylvania, I am fortunate enough to direct both the WAC Program and the Writing Center as a single unit. As a result, the two features of the program have grown up together and support each other both philosophically and practically. As Muriel Harris points out in another article in this volume, Writing Centers without WAC Programs can reach out to faculty but cannot provide the sustained attention and expertise required to implement WAC alone. Situating WAC in the Writing Center, as Mark Waldo recommends, has definite advantages, but none that is greater than integrating them under the same rubric. When Writing Centers and WAC team up, the potential for influencing faculty, students and the curriculum increases exponentially. Such has been the case at my institution, and the lessons we have learned may help others to position their Writing Centers, as we have attempted to do, at the heart of our program.

OPERATING PRINCIPLES FOR THE WRITING CENTER

Traditionally, Writing Centers focus on improving students' texts, often with little or no reference to the content of the text. In many institutions, conversation about the meaning of the text is taboo, on the grounds that such conversation may improperly influence the writer's thinking (as opposed to influencing the writing which is a desirable end). Advice about the mechanics of writing, even about organization and style, meets established criteria for appropriateness only to the extent that it separates itself from any discussion about ideas. In many instances, consultants have no problem conforming to these criteria because they are unfamiliar with the content of many of the student papers they advise. They can not evaluate the ideas because they know nothing about them.

Short of becoming experts in all disciplines, what kind of expertise can writing consultants offer? Like other instructors, they can teach students about writing as content as well as coach them through the process of creating and refining text. Writing Centers affiliated with Writing Across the Curriculum need not reject instruction in paragraph or sentence-level features of writing or in mechanics, but they do need to rethink their approach to such instruction. Working on the construction of sentences, isolated from their meaning, threatens the principle that even basic decisions about writing occur in a larger context. Even when consultants do not share the student's context, they can recognize its validity. For example, a consultant could choose to focus on the internal problems in the following opening sentence from a sociology paper, helping the student to improve syntax and style: "Women and men have differing attitudes on sex because of differences in pressures exerted on them by their peers: men tend to stress the conquest of a sexual encounter while women value the emotional aspects more." Such a focus, however, would miss the important fact that the writer seems ignorant of some of the basic conventions of how to present social science research. The revised sentence might be better written but no better at framing a proper social science analysis.

Helping student writers identify and analyze the contexts for writing offers them access to tacit knowledge frequently unavailable in any other location. Thinking about writing, along with doing it, raises the content of the interaction between student and consultant to a higher intellectual plain. It also redefines the nature of the interaction in a way that makes it more similar to, and often more enlightening than, interactions between other teachers and learners. For example, a student struggling with a text analysis may be having difficulty with the text, the assignment, or the crafting of prose that adequately expresses the student's thinking. In a conventional conference, only the student's text would get attention. In a WAC-based conference, however, conversation would be likely to extend to the assignment, the work being studied, the method of analysis, and the discourse conventions required for the particular field. This type of interchange might seem more appropriate between the classroom instructor and the student. A writing consultant engaging a student writer in a dialogue about a method of analysis or the student's understanding of the text might seem to be crossing the imaginary boundary between "writing" and "content." Judith Langer has shown, however, that many classroom teachers have no explicit knowledge of their own discipline-specific ways of thinking (1992, 84). As a result, they tend to emphasize content issues rather than the rules of argument and evidence which would clarify their expectations and better serve as a guide for student writing (83). For a writing consultant, the student's ability to explicate his/her thinking goes to the root of writing. Discussing writing apart from thinking would seem like cheating the student of valuable feedback and the opportunity to learn more about the subject and about writing.

Reinventing the Writing Center as a WAC center opens the door to all sorts of conversations about ideas, about methodologies, about teachers' intentions and learning outcomes that used to be restricted, even prohibited in the context of discussion about writing. It also broadens the definition of writing to resemble more closely the type of intellectual activity that occurs in the classroom, in the laboratory, or even over the dinner table in a dormitory dining room. The interchange between a WAC consultant and a student writer consists less of prescriptive feedback on the writer's text (This is a comma fault. Don't use the passive voice.) and more of questions about the writer's intentions (Why did you choose this particular example? How does this point connect to the one above?), audience (Can you assume that your readers are familiar with this author's work?), and disciplinary or course conventions (Is it customary to begin a sociology paper with an anecdote? In Art History, must you describe the painting first before you talk about the artist's work in general?). WAC consultants do not know the answers to these questions; they know instead that asking such questions assists writers in thinking through their goals, helping them to see what they have achieved and what they have not, and directing their attention to issues that merit rethinking. In this context, consultants may sometimes venture into fields unfamiliar to them and beyond their expertise. In these situations, however, they depend on writers to accept responsibility for their work and to make their own decisions about evaluating and changing what they have written. When consultants take this step, they should also remind students that their course instructors or teaching assistants can best explicate the material or clarify the conventions. When students know what questions to ask their instructors, they are often more successful at obtaining the information they need to write well. Closing the loop, by talking with a writing consultant and then going back to the instructor, helps students perceive writing more accurately as the complex intellectual activity it is and as more fully integrated with the thinking on which good writing depends.

IMPLEMENTING WAC CENTER PRINCIPLES

Positioning a Writing Center as a WAC center changes the structure and composition of the center in significant ways. Traditionally located in English departments and staffed by English instructors or outsiders with expertise in writing and editing, Writing Centers must generally work to acquire the interdisciplinary focus necessary to take a leadership role in promoting Writing Across the Curriculum. David Russell has illustrated how, "By recognizing the disciplinary organization of knowledge . . . WAC has been able to appeal to faculty members from many departments, whose primary loyalty and interest lay in a discipline, not in a particular educational philosophy or institution" (1992, 41). Much of the success of a WAC center, consequently, hinges on its credibility as a place that values all disciplines and their discourse conventions. In order to achieve this status, WAC centers must take discourse conventions seriously and make an example out of their willingness to learn about fields different from their own. From the beginning, they must welcome teachers from all fields to collaborate in ongoing efforts to learn about disciplinary discourses and teach them to students.

Many instructors, especially in non-writing-intensive fields, in the social sciences and sciences, may not recognize the contribution they can make to this type of collaboration. The notion of discipline-based discourse may seem strange to faculty educated in a tradition that equated writing with correctness and, perhaps, a sense of style but acknowledged no connection between how well students learn and how well they write. There is, however, in my experience, a convincing logic to presenting writing and thinking as a joint venture, and many instructors are persuaded by it. They also respond well to inquiries about discourse practices in their disciplines. Specialist teachers, in particular, who require science writing or business writing as opposed to a more literary style, welcome efforts to make their students more versatile writers and more able to conform to expectations different from those established in their English classes. At Penn, the Writing Center, along with the WAC Program, fall under the aegis of the school's Writing Committee. This group of dedicated faculty understand and support the goals of WAC and serve as ambassadors to other departments and schools. An advisory board or faculty committee composed of instructors from many different departments can greatly bolster the credibility of a WAC center. In addition, these well-informed faculty can provide resources including disciplinary expertise, sample student papers and assignments, and can help to educate their less knowledgeable colleagues in different fields.

Contributions to the acquisition of knowledge about disciplinary and professional discourses appear regularly in the composition journals and in new books dedicated to such exploration (see, for example, Charles Bazerman's *Shaping Written Knowledge: The Genre and Activity of the Experimental Article in Science*). Writing Center consultants need not reinvent the wheel, but in any specific college or university settings conversations among faculty in different fields about their expectations for student writing serve an important purpose. They spread the sense of ownership for teaching writing across disciplines and departments, and they create a richer environment for students learning to write. By sponsoring these conversations through faculty workshops, bringing in distinguished speakers, or simply hosting brown bag discussions on writing in a specific field, as we often do, the WAC center becomes a center of inquiry about nothing less than the structure of knowledge and how it gets communicated. For example, a graduate student writing consultant from Philosophy offered the following point of view on the subject of informal fallacies at a gathering on writing in philosophy: "These often have picturesque names, such as 'begging the question,' 'the strawman,' etc. These are associated with certain conventional philosophical practices, such as a great drive for clarity and precision, the 'principle of charity,' the providing of counterexamples, etc. But all of these return in one way or another to the basic structure of argumentation....It is for this reason that certain words, such as logical connectives (e.g., 'and,' 'or,' or 'therefore') tend to cause the blood of philosophers to get hot" (Michael

McShane, 11 April 1996). What type of discussion could possibly be more integral to the mission of higher education or more likely to position the Writing Center at the hub of intellectual activity in the institution?

STAFFING AND TRAINING

The staff of a WAC center by definition brings experience in many different discourse communities and familiarity with a variety of discourse practices to the effort of helping students improve their writing. Whether they come with skills in teaching writing or not, ongoing training and collaboration can facilitate their ability to read and respond helpfully to all kinds of writing. As a first step, they need to accept, as Lee Odell points out, that "judgments about the quality of writing cannot be separated from judgments about the quality of meaning making reflected in that writing" (1992, 98). As Odell argues, they must also give up often ingrained but unhelpful generalizations about what constitutes "good" writing (89) and seek to acquire at least a basic knowledge of common discourse conventions in disciplines other than their own. They must also become familiar with the expectations of faculty in different departments and with the features of successful papers in various fields.

At the University of Pennsylvania, we employ graduate students from different departments and schools in the role of writing consultant. As newcomers to their own discourse communities, they quickly catch on to the value of identifying disciplinary discourse conventions and making them public. In monthly meetings, many of which focus on the presentation of different disciplinary conventions and practices, they readily share both their own work and student papers from their individual disciplines and courses in which they have assisted, and they help each other identify the conventions and features of discourse that help students communicate successfully or inhibit their success. For example, an English department writing fellow might offer illustrations from student papers of claims that are well supported by quotations and, in contrast, of quotations that are used without explanation or elaboration. Because they benefit directly from these discoveries about disciplinary discourse, which often help them think and write about their research more successfully, the consultants bring energy and commitment to the task. Their growing understanding of the role conventions and expectations play in academic communities makes them both better teachers and learners.

The staff of a WAC center accepts collaboration as the norm, because in a multidisciplinary environment, no individual possesses all the pieces of the puzzle. General acknowledgement that the center is greater than the sum of its parts, that consultants have much to learn from each other, encourages both humility and a joint sense of purpose. In our center, consultants from different departments and backgrounds take responsibility for conducting our monthly staff meetings that introduce their peers to conventions of disciplinary discourse, particular genres of writing in their fields, or issues related to field-specific writing, such as the positioning of the observer in ethnographies or the use of the historical present. Often consultants in different fields get together to talk about genres that cross disciplines, like interviews, and to investigate how readers can identify the field of a paper from the writing conventions it observes. Questions raised might include: "How can we recognize a paper as history, rather than sociology?" or "What conventions are required in interdisciplinary fields, like women's studies, area studies, or folklore?" Answers to these questions assist consultants in offering the best possible feedback to their students. The following selection from a Writing Center presentation reveals a consultant who has used her insights into her field to inform both her scholarship and her teaching and is seeking to share her insights with her peers:

Because folklore is multidisciplinary, it necessarily draws on and is informed by many fields, methods, and critical approaches (anthropology, literary studies, sociology, psychology, history, to name a few). Conventions for presenting ideas, organizing arguments and offering evidence, therefore, are varied. The best suggestion for those beginning to write in the field is to examine as models the scholarly work in the field . . . Other scholars' interpretive categories and questions can provide useful models for your own writing/thinking; looking at the kinds of questions that get asked in a discipline will help you understand the basic motives/approaches informing what is (or has been) considered worth exploring. (Nancy Watterson, 30 April 1993)

Writing consultants with this level of disciplinary self-consciousness and this type of training appropriately belong at the center of a WAC Program. Their interactions with each other, combined with their experience of the variety of student writing to which they must respond, gives them a unique meta-view of the curriculum and of academic discourse. Since they come from various fields and departments to work together in the Writing Center, when they go back to their departments, they take the knowledge and information they have gained with them. There is no need for the center itself to proselytize. The utility of the information the consultants bring back, communicated by knowledgeable insiders, rather than outside experts, speaks for itself and raises the credibility of the writing program as a joint venture among all faculty and departments.

Hiring staff from inside the institution that reflects its diversity accomplishes several purposes at once. It eliminates the pressure on the director to attempt to educate staff members about the many types of papers they will be reviewing, because staff members can educate each other. It creates closer working relationships with different departments which, when members of their own departments work there, may take some pride of ownership in the center. It enables staff members to refer to each other for specialized knowledge and expertise, offering students the most complete and sophisticated assistance with their writing. In addition, it helps students begin to understand the role of context in writing, particularly the importance of understanding the expectations of your audience, which greatly helps to further the mission of Writing Across the Curriculum.

WAC CENTER AS RESOURCE CENTER

In a recent report of their study of enduring WAC Programs (1997), Susan McLeod and Erica Miraglia point out that enduring programs tend to have more components and to affiliate themselves with other educational movements, such as critical thinking or learning communities. One interpretation of this tendency suggests that any program emphasizing improved undergraduate education is likely to team up with others. Another, however, highlights the role WAC can play as a resource to faculty and curriculum developers across campus. The wealth of information and insight gleaned by WAC instructors needs to be disseminated. WAC Programs can and often do make their resources available to the institutional public on demand. Any faculty member can look for and expect to find approaches to teaching thesis-generation or argumentation in the WAC resource center. Faculty can gather under the auspices of WAC to exchange ideas about improving teaching effectiveness through requiring writing or through other means that participants might suggest. As a result of the WAC Program's willingness to act as an institutional resource center and open its files, little curricular reform takes place on many campuses without at least referring to, if not including, Writing Across the Curriculum.

Two features of WAC make its resources particularly valuable to faculty across the curriculum. The multidisciplinary character of WAC lends credibility to its offerings, especially if the program takes pains to gather resources from many different contexts, to keep an up-to-date library, and to stay current with teachers' concerns. In addition, a Writing Center well integrated into the mainstream academic program and affiliated with, if not part of, the WAC Program has status that a remedial center (or a center perceived as remedial) lacks. Faculty will more readily trust resources derived from classroom situations they recognize and fellow instructors who have confronted the same challenges.

WAC Programs have access to resources likely to excite interest in many faculty members struggling to do a good job. In WAC Programs that offer faculty seminars, the WAC resource center can provide ongoing support and stimulation for those who have already shown an interest in Writing Across the Curriculum. For faculty who do not participate in training seminars or for whom they are not an option, the WAC center can offer dialogue and new ideas as well as access to tried and true methods of nurturing student learning and improving their writing. Topics often of interest to faculty include determining the number and length of writing assignments to require in a course; teaching research and library skills; crafting writing assignments that promote good writing; and responding efficiently and effectively to student papers. Faculty often welcome advice, as well as materials, from writing consultants who can contextualize these questions and help instructors think them through.

A well-equipped WAC center should focus on the needs of instructors as well as students. Along with grammar texts and style books, files of sample assignments in different courses, writing-related handouts, and model student papers can provide invaluable information to instructors often isolated in their own classrooms and departments. Just as students gain perspective from reading each other's papers in peer review sessions, instructors gain from perusing each other's assignments and comparing standards of evaluation in other courses to their own. Many faculty members spend considerable amounts of often unproductive time editing students' texts and writing unhelpful comments, such as "vague" and "awkward" in the margins. They react enthusiastically and appreciatively to strategies for responding efficiently to writing that shorten the time the instructor spends on students' texts. By anticipating the needs and interests of faculty, and keeping adaptable materials at hand, the Writing Center director and staff provide a specific service even many teaching and learning centers do not offer.

Feedback probably constitutes the most critical resource a WAC center can offer faculty. Because Writing Centers, especially Writing Across the Curriculum Centers, interact with so many students from so many courses and departments, they have critical knowledge about what writing-related curriculum and teaching strategies work and which ones fail or elude numbers of students. To the extent that we identify ourselves as serving the needs of students and student learning, we have an obligation to use feedback to improve learning. We further this goal by strengthening those aspects of teaching, such as the crafting of writing assignments, over which we have some authority and, in some cases, in conjunction with a WAC Program, even some control. For example, our handbook for new writing fellows, which we also give to new WAC faculty, features a chapter on creating writing assignments. Offering those guidelines, especially to new faculty but also to those whose students struggle to understand and respond to their assignments, can help to prevent a lot of bad papers.

Even though not all faculty value feedback, enough do to make the enterprise of gathering data and feeding it back constructive. Without personalizing the feedback, the Writing Center director and consultants can speak from experience in endorsing some practices, such as detailed feedback and revision, and discouraging others, such as assigning only one long paper at the end of the term. They can explain to faculty where students have difficulty or misunderstand instructions and suggest ways of clarifying the instructor's expectations, so that students can more readily attempt to fulfill them. They can offer concrete examples of exercises and assignments used in similar contexts that have worked well. They can describe individual cases of students who have struggled or succeeded in a given set of circumstances and report patterns of student response to certain types of writing activities, courses, or disciplines. Instructors are often surprised to hear, for example, that many students find both vague assignments (write a paper about *King Lear*) and overly prescriptive ones (a laundry list of questions to cover) difficult, and that they write better when their teacher's expectations for the paper are clearly communicated. Creating this feedback loop and conveying vital information gleaned from students to their instructors (as well as translating instructors' expectations for students) helps make the WAC center a valuable resource to all participants in the teaching and learning process.

THE WAC CENTER AS AN OUTREACH CENTER

As a resource center, the WAC center may advertise its resources but generally makes few demands on faculty, only welcoming those who choose to take advantage of the available materials and expertise. The role of outreach center requires more person-to-person initiative, although before we reach out to faculty, they often first reach in. Where WAC Programs exist, writing-intensive courses have their own identify and qualifications; faculty affiliated with the WAC Program make a commitment and take advantage of resources presented as a product of their affiliation with the program. What happens to other faculty, however?

A WAC center can accommodate any faculty member who uses or assigns writing whether or not writing becomes a central feature of the course, greatly expanding opportunities to interact with instructors and students in different fields and contexts. The center can offer partnerships with individual faculty or with departments in efforts to raise standards, improve learning, or emphasize the importance of writing well. At our institution, we routinely partner with departments by providing support for senior thesis writers, students required to present senior projects, and students conducting independent research. We also work with individual instructors who want to encourage drafting and revising procedures on a particular assignment by sending a consultant to speak with their students and then encouraging the students to bring their work to the consultant in the WAC center. In quite a few cases, WAC center consultants have helped to redesign courses by instituting deadlines for parts of a writing project and procedures for obtaining feedback through the center and revising. The center has also worked closely with university reference librarians to ensure that faculty educate students about research methods, data bases, and the Internet, and that students perceive writing research papers as a combined activity requiring both research and writing skills to complete effectively.

In a university setting like ours, opportunities for partnerships proliferate. Most recently, efforts to promote and evaluate uses of instructional technology have led us to discussions about and innovations in uses of e-mail and listservs (after all, they do write those messages). A new online writing advice service has led to considerable debate among writing instructors and consultants about the character and value of this type of interaction, particularly when focused on a student's text. The central role of the WAC center has made it a natural source of criteria for framing this kind of debate and presenting the results to interested parties across campus. The WAC center also has insight to offer educators eager to promote writing courses as a regular feature of distance learning.

In many colleges and universities departmental affiliations are so strong that faculty fail to acknowledge the extent to which courses in different departments share intellectual activities and learning outcomes. Even if we expect students to think and present their thinking differently in different fields, there are writing strategies and goals that cross disciplinary boundaries. In this age of specialization, WAC centers can play a unique role in bringing faculty from different departments together to discuss common concerns and formulate potential partnerships and joint ventures. The WAC center might help to broker interdisciplinary majors or minors by suggesting places where disciplines overlap or intersect; it might call attention to omissions in general requirements by focusing attention on the critical need for all students to get sufficient practice in writing as they satisfy requirements; and it might highlight ways in which courses can teach related skills, such as critical thinking, or even quantitative reasoning, through the use of writing.

THE WAC CENTER AS A MODEL FOR TEACHING AND LEARNING

By focusing on writing conferences, on one-on-one consultation as essential to the process of teaching and learning about writing, WAC centers present a model of instruction from which any teacher can learn. Through WAC conferences, the nature of the transaction between writer and reader comes alive in a way it cannot when the writing consultant lacks the experience or expertise to role play a real reader. For so many student writers, their readers are vague presences they perceive standing in the front of a room at a podium, strangers whose ways of thinking are completely foreign to them. Writing consultants who can legitimately represent themselves as sample readers of a text offer the student an opportunity to concretize the vague image they have of the reader, to get to know the reader as a person, to ask questions and gain insight into the text as it appears to a person for whom it was intended.

In many classroom settings, the transaction between writer and reader that motivates so many writers to write gets lost or ignored. The written response professors routinely offer students, often to justify a grade, gives writers no glimpse of the gratification they can experience by successfully communicating carefully crafted ideas to a chosen reader. In writing conferences between attentive readers and struggling writers, however, writers gain insight not only into their texts but into the relationships they have an opportunity to create through their writing. As one student commented on an evaluation form, "No one ever showed as much interest in my writing before." In my experience, that chance to interact with a real reader accounts for the overwhelmingly positive feelings visitors to our Writing Center express about their writing conferences.

In the process of teaching students about the transaction between writers and readers, WAC consultants also reinforce the pedagogy of writing instruction employed in many WAC courses by endorsing the value of thoughtful revision based on feedback. They can encourage students to return for further consultation as they like, teaching them to develop and refine their writing one step at a time, at a pace few classroom situations allow. The instruction in writing process that students receive in the WAC center complements and often deepens the instruction they receive in their classes. Writing conferences often send students back to the classroom with new insight and new understanding of the content as well as the process of writing. Minimally, they go back to class with a set of intelligent questions about, for example, what constitutes appropriate evidence, the answers to which will help them refine their thinking and better equip them to meet their professors' expectations for writing and learning.

The work of the WAC center need not, however, simply support mainstream classroom instruction by making it more effective or support student achievement by helping student writers get better grades. As Charles Bazerman argues, "Explicit teaching of discourse holds what is taught up for inspection. It provides the students with the means to rethink the ends of the discourse and offers a wide array of means to carry the discourse in new directions" (1992, 64–5). The interactions that take place between classroom instructors and writing consultants have the potential to change classroom pedagogy, and the interactions that take place between students and consultants can help students master strategies that lead to permanent improvement in their learning and writing, not just an improved text. WAC has traditionally identified itself as a reform movement, seeking to change the status quo; WAC centers can certainly further those efforts to promote change by taking an activist stance toward the curriculum in which their work is embedded (Walvoord 1996, 69).

I have come a long way since my initial defense of the Writing Center as a necessary safety net. The Writing Center is a central component of the WAC Program I direct, guided by the same philosophy, staffed by the same instructors, sharing the same resources. WAC meetings take place in the Writing Center which houses all of our materials: books, journals, articles, sample assignments, sample handouts, information about disciplinary discourses, general statements about issues like plagiarism and gendered language, and model papers from many different courses with which we have interacted. Although no situation is ideal, the identification of our entire writing program as a WAC Program, certainly makes positioning the Writing Center as a WAC center a lot easier. The center has accrued credibility as a result of its integration into WAC and can represent the program with integrity in a public context.

This integrated approach to writing and the unified message an integrated program can deliver give it clout that no single component could amass alone. Finally, nothing gets attention faster than success, and a writing program that fosters a consistent approach to writing across departments and reinforces that approach at all levels is likely to succeed. From a strategic point of view, the clout success brings opens the door to activism. If and when the writing program achieves status equal to that of other academic units, its opportunities to influence the academic program increase dramatically. At this stage, certainly a mature stage in the evolution of Writing Centers and writing programs, the writing program can help to shape rather than participate in, or simply respond to, the established curriculum. As many of us have already discovered, there are some virtues to maturity. The specter of power and influence that looms before Writing Centers can inspire us all.

ACKNOWLEDGMENTS

I would like to thank the dozens of graduate student consultants who have worked in the Penn Writing Center over the last fourteen years, particularly Michael McShane from Philosophy and Dr. Nancy Watterson from Folklore and Folklife who are quoted in this article.

WORKS CITED

Bazerman, Charles. "From Cultural Criticism to Disciplinary Participation: Living with Powerful Words." *Writing, Teaching, and Learning in the Disciplines,* eds. Anne Herrington and Charles Moran. New York: MLA, 1992. 61–68.

———. *Shaping Written Knowledge: The Genre and Activity of the Experimental Article in Science.* Madison: University of Wisconsin Press, 1988.

Bizzell, Patricia. "Cognition, Convention and Certainty: What We Need to Know About Writing." *Pre/Text* 3 (1982): 213–243.

Clark, Irene L., and David Healy. "Are Writing Centers Ethical?" *WPA: Writing Program Administration* 20 (1996): 32–48.

Grimm, Nancy. "Rearticulating the Work of the Writing Center." *College Composition and Communication* 47 (1996): 523–548.

Langer, Judith A. "Speaking of Knowing: Conceptions of Understanding in Academic Disciplines." *Writing, Teaching and Learning in the Disciplines,* eds. Anne Herrington and Charles Moran. New York: MLA, 1992. 69–85.

Miraglia, Erica, and Susan McLeod. "Whither WAC? Interpreting the Stories/Histories of Enduring WAC Programs." *WPA: Writing Program Administration* 20 (1997): 46–65.

North, Stephen. "The Idea of a Writing Center." *College English* 46 (1984): 433–446.

Odell, Lee. "Context-specific Ways of Knowing and the Evaluation of Writing." *Writing, Teaching, and Learning in the Disciplines,* eds. Anne Herrington and Charles Moran. New York: MLA, 1992. 86–98.

Russell, David R. "American Origins of the Writing Across the Curriculum Movement." *Writing, Teaching, and Learning in the Disciplines,* eds. Anne Herrington and Charles Moran. New York: MLA, 1992. 22–42.

Waldo, Mark L. "The Last Best Place for Writing Across the Curriculum: The Writing Center." *WPA: Writing Program Administration* 16.3 (Spring 1993): 15–26.

Walvoord, Barbara. "The Future of WAC." *College English* 58 (1996): 58–79.

9

Situating Writing Centers and Writing Across the Curriculum Programs in the Academy: Creating Partnerships for Change with Organizational Development Theory

Karen Vaught-Alexander

Many Writing Centers (WCs) struggle to overcome misconceptions about what WCs do and who should come to them, while Writing Across the Curriculum (WAC) Programs often grapple with faculty resistance to re-situating Writing in the Disciplines (WID), instead of writing being the sole responsibility of the freshman year composition (FYC) program or the English Department. WCs and WAC Programs are best situated to mediate misconceptions and resistance concerning both programs—through collaborative partnerships.

This partnership is not new but belongs to the rich history of writing and writing programs in the academy. This history, in which disciplinary writing and writing tutorials evolve, is a story of misconceptions about academic writing and resistance to changing those—a highly relevant story to those of us who direct those programs today.

As David Russell chronicles in *Writing in the Academic Disciplines, 1870-1990, A Curricular History,* in the 1870s, writing gained a new role—as a means to disseminate new knowledge not just to a general reader but to specialized audiences, who shared unique disciplinary discourse conventions. At the same time began the almost 130-year-old lament about the inability of college students to write. The nineteenth century solution to this problem, a general composition course for the freshman year, emphasized correctness in grammar, spelling, and usage. By the turn of the century, as one or two general composition courses did not succeed in teaching students to write, even with remediation or tutorials, universities began to try cross-curricular writing approaches. In the ensuing cycles of attempts to improve academic writing skills, whether through cross-curricular or general composition courses, writing was still separated from disciplinary learning, thinking, and content (1991, 1–32). Writing was misconceived as a generalizable and mechanical skill—a misconception that we still face.

Although the disciplines historically have resisted seeing writing as part of their fields, they did use writing for evaluation of student performance or admission into professional contexts: essay exams beginning in the 1840s (Russell 158), course term papers in the late 1860s or research seminar papers or theses in the late 1880s (78–92), laboratory notebooks and the laboratory report in the 1890s (92–94), the written analysis of cases in business schools beginning at Harvard in 1908 (129–132), and the turn-of-the-century recognition of technical writing's "myriad letters, reports, contracts, specifications, and proposals addressed to audiences with varying interests and technical backgrounds" (120), especially for engineering professionals. Those of us writing program administrators (WPAs), who direct WAC and Writing Centers today, may recognize these academic and professional writing genres, as well as the resistance of disciplinary faculty to see writing as a legitimate part of their field's thinking and learning.

Woven into Russell's history of academic writing can be found the beginnings of today's Writing Center and even its early connection with writing in the core courses (261). In the 1930s at Colgate University, a writing tutorial or "preceptor program" had been transformed by 1949 into The Functional Writing Program's writing lab, with Jonathan Kistler, as its director. Students whose "papers received a grade of C or below rewrote them with help from the FWP's writing lab" (262). Perhaps the misconception that Writing Centers work with remedial or poor writers can be traced to such early practices. Presaging the potential for partnerships between WID and Writing Centers, Kistler worked with disciplinary faculty to fine-tune their writing assignments; the faculty taught and graded the writing (263). Student writing improved; faculty were enthusiastic.

At about the same time, because of a survey indicating that student writing did not improve during the undergraduate years, the University of California at Berkeley organized the Prose Improvement Committee (PIC). Rejecting remedial composition courses as ineffective elsewhere, this committee developed a program in which each discipline's paper graders and teaching assistants, who helped students rewrite papers and discuss their paper assignments, were trained in a special writing techniques course. Although the PIC approach did not involve a Writing Center, this training of disciplinary graders and teaching assistants may be seen as a harbinger for Tori Haring-Smith's 1980's pairing of courses and trained writing fellows at Brown University or the 1990's WAC-based Writing Center staffed by trained cross-disciplinary peer tutors described by Margot Soven. The PIC promoted faculty discussions about writing as learning, as developmental, and as connected distinctly to the disciplines—all tenets of the later WAC movement. WPAs today, like Jody Swilkey, have noted similar broader campus acceptance of WAC Program change, when a cross-disciplinary committee initiates the reforms.

Neither the FWP or the PIC lasted more than ten years, before enthusiasm and participation waned. Russell indicates from his research that typically such programs are even more short-lived due to institutional inertia or the loss of dynamic leadership (268). Why do such innovative partnerships between

Writing Center and WAC Programs fade, even when they appear to overcome misconceptions and resistance about writing?

Cross-disciplinary programs, whether WCs or WAC, do not fit into the typical discipline-organized structures or priorities of the university (268). According to Susan McLeod in *Strengthening Programs for Writing Across the Curriculum,* WAC Programs tend to survive after the "first stage" by securing internal funding or internal support systems or by collapsing WAC into Writing Center, general education, freshman year, or faculty development programs. Current WPA positions like mine often combine previously separate positions of WC, WAC, FYE, or even FYC, especially in "second stage" WAC institutions. Carol Hartzog in her 1986 survey of writing program administration commented that no one formula produces a successful writing program (12); writing programs must fit the intellectual and academic structures of their respective institutions (xii), addressing the local needs of the institution, the departments, and the student body (xii). Such observations are insightful and practical. Tori Haring-Smith et al. in *A Guide to Writing Programs: Writing Centers, Peer Tutoring Programs, and Writing Across the Curriculum* and Gary Olson in *Writing Centers: Theory and Administration* give us stories, powerful with details and theory, about strategies used by successful WC and WAC Program administrators to meet the needs and challenges of their particular institutions.

As Art Young and Toby Fulwiler in *Programs That Work: Models and Methods for Writing Across the Curriculum* further caution, successful WAC Programs, like successful WC programs, cross disciplinary boundaries and organizational structures to create a community of faculty and students engaged in teaching and learning. This point of strength, however, positions such programs and their WPAs ambivalently in terms of budgeting priorities, organizational chains of command, and faculty status. Hartzog did find typical administrative lines of reporting for writing programs: program directors report to one academic unit, usually the chair of the English department or a separate departmental writing committee, or they report directly to a dean or provost, to a cross-disciplinary advisory board. Thus, writing programs may have different lines of reporting for various aspects of the program, that is, for the WC or WAC director to report to the dean but for FYC director to report to the English department chair (1986, 14–18). Each institution creates its own unique combination of writing programs and positions.

But how does any WPA use these to develop a WC or WAC Program with that "right institutional fit"? Certainly Russell's historical overview, Haring-Smith et. al.'s, Olson's, McLeod's, and Young and Fulwiler's stories, and Hartzog's survey research indicate that the right fit often includes or assumes some kind of partnership or collaboration between WCs and WAC Programs.

What partnerships are needed for developing successful programs? In *Intersections: Theory-Practice in the Writing Center,* Joan Mullin and Ray Wallace challenge WPAs in charge of WCs to look for new theory to inform our practice.

Most of us administer such programs for our departments or institutions without any background in organizational systems or change, yet our programs and our careers hinge on our success in implementing or resisting such changes. For navigating the bureaucratic structures of our institutions—between the Scylla and Charybdis of organizational resistance and change—organizational development (OD) theory, modified for the academy, offers hope. In the process of informing practice with OD theory, other key partnerships for institutionalizing successful WC and WAC Programs will emerge.

Based on the social and behavioral sciences, OD theory works to create change, planned change, within the social and cultural structures of an organization. Collaborative problem-solving and consensus for solutions forge ownership for change across the organizational hierarchy. Redefining organizational roles and incentives, along with interventions in knowledge or skills and the subsequent changing of attitudes, are the primary goals for positive change and implementation of innovation (Beer, Eisenstat, and Spector in Kolb, Osland, and Rubin 1995, 665). According to Burke and Hornstein, "organizational development is a process of planned change—change of an organization's culture from one which avoids an examination of social processes (especially decision making, planning, and communication) to one which institutionalizes and legitimizes this examination"(qtd. by French, Bell, and Zawacki 1994, 6–7). The culture of the organization, its group and individual social processes, past experiences with change, even individual personalities—all combine to determine how and if change, implementation, and evaluation are even possibilities in a particular academic organization.

Certainly in the academy, WC and WAC administrators are familiar with program reviews, annual budget requests, and planning documents, but OD theory makes transparent how and why our academic organizations implement or cannot implement this planning and change. With our English studies or composition and rhetoric degrees in hand, WPAs often expect logic and evidence from research to create improvement or change in their programs. Change, however, is not that easy for any organization, and for the academy, it becomes even more complex or even impossible.

According to Wendell French, Cecil Bell, Jr., and Robert Zawacki in *Organizational Development and Transformation: Managing Effective Change,* organizational change in the corporate world follows a generalizable pattern. Some catalyst for change occurs: as a result, the CEO, other administrators or managers, as the change agents, recognize the problem and begin the problem-solving stage. An OD consultant analyzes the problem, in the context of surveying and interviewing the organizational culture, its groups and individuals. Any change requires support from top leadership, especially for a organizational transformation, a second-order change. Formal work teams air differences and brainstorm possible solutions to the problem. From these groups, potential solutions can be selected, planned, and narrowed to one that supports a common vision for the organization. Discussions with respect for resistance must occur, or that resistance will later sabotage the change. Supervisors must also fund necessary resources, interventions, and incentives to prepare groups and individuals for change.

The key for long-term change is a change in roles and knowledge, leading to changes in attitudes. First-order change can be implemented relatively easily because it involves improvement in existing structures and roles. More difficult to implement, second-order change may produce little or no initial improvement. But astute change agents know to wait for the change's "learning curve" before evaluating the change. In a business culture, on-going change and evaluation have been institutionalized as the norm: the change catalyst is the bottom line, that competitive edge in profits, productivity, and accountability. The business culture expects to spend time and resources periodically in the change process, whereas the academy places more value on disciplinary, rather than organizational or program, research. After all, once an academic program works well, is it not best to leave it alone?

But organizations and change do not work that way. As Rick Maurer in *Beyond the Wall of Resistance: Unconventional Strategies That Build Support for Change* points out, change is a cycle. First, a seemingly successful program will experience random incidents, presaging potential problems. Then, someone, usually the change agent, recognizes that a problem exists and brings it to the attention of the group. Next, potential solutions are generated, leading to group consensus and collaboration about implementing the change. Timing is critical: neither too fast for consensus nor too slow for enthusiasm. Loss of team members during a change cycle may push the change cycle back to earlier stages. Key to positive change is the embracing of resistance, the respecting of those who see problems in present solutions. If there is no resistance, something is wrong. Resistance is normal. Only when resistance is open, will successful change be integrated into the very fabric of the organization. Resistance may also lead to discussions and disclosures that make the change impossible. Timing is critical. Even the loss of one key individual or one change in circumstances can hinder or stop the change. When such events occur, Maurer advises to let that change die and wait for the next cycle to bring the problem back to the organization's attention. Even a successful integration of change will gradually unravel with time and changing situations. The cycle never stops, although it may speed up or slow down (1997, 65–73).

This cycle of change explains what can happen to our WC and WAC Programs. A new dean or chair may not see the Writing Center as a priority for improving writing in the disciplines, but rather may view large numbers of upper-division center clients as a problem, an indication of the failure of the FYC program. Suddenly funding for the Writing Center program may be threatened, despite a history of budgetary increases based on client usage. A new provost may prefer centralized program administration under the deans rather than campus-wide administration models, putting even a successful cross-disciplinary WC or WAC Program at risk. A new rank and tenure policy may decrease incentives for teaching excellence, causing faculty to opt for workshops on grant proposal writing, rather than designing effective WAC writing assignments or giving a priority to using the WC. Our programs face the continual challenge of this cycle of change. We need to recognize that it exists—and not ignore those little, and not so little, changes that can ultimately affect our program's development or existence.

Academic institutions pose special resistance to change. Gervase R. Bushe and Rami Shani in *Parallel Learning Structures: Increasing Innovation in Bureaucracies* classify universities, as professional bureaucracies similar to governmental agencies or hospitals (1995, 150). Universities tend to have "a fairly low degree of consensus on organizational means and end and a number of competing factions with roughly equal power," often leading to an "inability to create a coalition strong enough to direct the organization" (150). Obviously the academy's complex organizational structures create leadership, planning, and communication challenges for cross-organizational WC and WAC Programs.

Our awareness of the academy's competing sub-cultures—identified by William H. Bergquist in *The Four Cultures of the Academy* as the collegial, the managerial, the developmental, and the negotiating—can help us work more productively with what most of us now label "campus politics" or "good old boy networks." Because each of these academic subcultures has values and assumptions that conflict with those of the other subcultures, the WPA of a cross-disciplinary program must somehow appeal to, or at least not threaten, the unique combination of sub-cultures comprising its academic institution.

Based on the British and German university traditions, the collegial subculture values faculty autonomy in teaching and scholarship, with loyalty to the discipline over that to the university. Faculty governance and primacy in decision-making are believed to supercede the mission of the university, planning of administrators, or needs of students. Effective teaching and informed curricula are believed to evolve naturally from disciplinary knowledge and research. Faculty and programs in the Colleges of Arts or Sciences (CAS) are strongly tied to this subculture (Bergquist 1992, 17–56). WC and WAC directors, even those with academic teaching appointments and tenure, may be marginalized. We run programs that challenge collegial assumptions about effective teaching, disciplinary loyalty and boundaries, and curricular autonomy. If our WPA positions are allied with English departments, we often are separated by our program and teaching responsibilities from the rest of the department (Hartzog 1986, 63–71).

According to Bergquist, the managerial subculture inherits its emphasis on hierarchical authority and top-down leadership from the American junior college and the Catholic university traditions. It values educational outcomes, competence in teaching and leadership, accountability of programs, cost containment, instructional delivery efficiency, and clearly defined lines of authority. Administrators see themselves in control of mission, curriculum, financial funding priorities, and academic personnel. Institutional research, especially empirical designs and quantitative summative evaluations, presumably guide the managerial culture to rational and equitable program decisions. In reality, the managerial culture, while valuing such research, may exercise its authority to set its own agenda, leaving faculty and programs feeling powerless and isolated from key decision making (1992, 57–87). In the organizational chart of the academy, a program director does not fit the usual lines of authority, often being held accountable for programs in which no clear authority, only responsibility, has been given. Even when we compile annual reports replete with quantitative evaluations that validate program funding, managerial agendas may or may not be swayed. Professional schools, because of their close alliance with the business world or the public schools, often align themselves more with the values of the managerial culture, leading to potential campus schisms between the professional school faculty and the Arts and Sciences faculty. WC and WAC directors must craft programs that accommodate diverse goals and values.

Advocating faculty development, curriculum development, institutional mission and long-term planning, is Bergquist's developmental culture (93). A marriage between collegial and managerial cultures, the development culture in which WPAs work often pleases neither (102). Because the developmental culture values innovative teaching strategies, interdisciplinary approaches to curriculum, and collaborative problem-solving, it violates the collegial culture's beliefs about effective teaching based on research, disciplinary specialization, and academic autonomy. The managerial culture views the developmental culture's hypothetical spirit of inquiry and collaborative problem-solving as slow and indecisive. Developmental faculty run the career risk of being perceived by their collegial peers as less scholarly or rigorous and of being labeled by the managerial culture as less professionally accountable or focused (93–124). As WC and WAC administrators, we clearly reside within this subculture. Ironically these developmental values endanger the collegial and managerial support and resources that we need for successful program development and implementation.

The negotiating culture with its collective bargaining and faculty unionization is more prevalent in public institutions, rather than private colleges and universities in which the collegial and managerial cultures dominate (129–131). Faculty who gravitate to the negotiating culture usually teach at an institution with little faculty governance, low faculty trust, high teaching loads, low salaries, and a prevalence of nontenured or part-time faculty (131–139). Faculty senates or faculty welfare committees often serve the function of unions in institutions dominated by the collegial culture. The managerial culture sees itself in charge of these cost containment and academic personnel issues (154–163). As participants in the negotiating culture, we advocate for professional standards in program appointments and pay, which can polarize our relationship with the managerial culture and can further separate us from the collegial culture's disciplinary-focused roles and values.

Using Bergquist's cultural analysis of the academy, the WPA, whether of a WC or a WAC Program, clearly does not fit in any one subculture. Our programs bridge, often precariously, the conflicting values of these subcultures. Our WPA academic appointments, usually housed in the collegial culture, leave us without direct lines of authority for our interactions in the other cultures. We teach in the collegial culture; we administer our programs in the collegial and managerial; we lead faculty training, curricular innovation, and pedagogical reform in the developmental; we advocate for work load and pay for instructors, staff, and assistants in the negotiating. In an academy that values specialization and loyalty to one culture, we interact with all. Even as our Writing Centers and WAC Programs are praised for their support of students and faculty across programs, disciplinary faculty and programs are not likely to advocate funding for these special programs at the expense of resources for their own disciplines. Bergquist's cultural analysis of the academy begins to explain what WPAs have documented about their programs and professional lives: the pitfalls of WPA programs and appointments, the competing factions inherent in our academic institutions, and the recognition of our work as change agents in a complex bureaucratic setting.

Much of our WPA literature relies on surveys, case studies, and histories of successful, and not so successful, Writing Centers or other writing programs. What will Writing Centers and WAC Programs gain if they use OD theory? In the following case study of a fully institutionalized Writing Center Program and a not-so-successful writing-in-context proposal, the significance of using OD theory for long-term program planning development becomes clear. We can attribute program successes to something other than lucky circumstances, and we can contextualize program setbacks as something other than professional and personal incompetence.

ACADEMIC BUREAUCRACIES AND PARALLEL LEARNING STRUCTURES: CREATING LEARNING PARTNERSHIPS AND A LEARNING SUBCULTURE AS A NEW WAC AND WC WPA

Most bureaucracies are slow to change. A bureaucracy's strength lies in its predictable performance, but such predictability also sets up inabilities to adapt and change. Its centralized control leads to more focus and decisiveness, but information about needs to change may not be told to key decision-makers, who tend to see any mention of organizational problems as disloyalty or whining. Specialization leads to task accountability, but specialization also produces individuals who are less flexible and who cannot see the big picture. Bureaucracies group individuals by function or specialty for efficiency in organizational production; however, functional grouping also divides organizations into subcultures with conflicting or competing goals, making organization-wide change very difficult (Bushe and Shani 1991, 1–9). The academy with its four subcultures faces the learning and change problems of any complex bureaucracy .

As a new Ph.D. and new WPA in the fall of 1989, I was given one year to learn campus politics well enough to initiate needed programs. The job description in the Modern Language Association job list asked that the candidate develop a WAC Program and a WC; teach freshman, advanced, and business writing, as well as occasional courses in linguistics and literature, with a course load of five courses rather than eight in two semesters. The Integrated Writing Program (IWP) was the name chosen to describe my overlapping administrative roles in the FYC, WC, and WAC Programs. Because of this overlap, pedagogical and curricular partnerships were easily constructed among these jointly directed programs.

This blending of programs, however, also yielded ongoing confusions about lines of reporting, program funding, and administrative authority. The freshman composition program was always housed under the authority of the chair of the English department, but the WC and the WAC Programs with no clearly defined line of reporting constructed its authority sometimes from the IWP Advisory Committee, other times from the CAS dean and the departmental chairs, in other instances the professional school deans and their respective curriculum or writing committees, and from time to time, the academic vice-president. The exciting prospect of developing these WC and WAC Programs overshadowed my nagging concern that no one shared any consensus on how these programs fit into the existing organizational structures. Meanwhile, developed at the same time as the IWP, the Freshman Seminar (FS) program had been carefully shaped by faculty consensus with clear lines of reporting to the deans and the academic vice-president and with established program funding sources. Necessary curricular changes for the FS program had already been approved by the curriculum committee and the academic senate; monies for faculty development and for the director to work on program evaluation and improvement were in place. None of that was true for the IWP position—then or even now.

For this IWP grass roots position, my on-campus interview included all academic units in the process, giving all ownership for my hiring. All the deans and the academic vice-president interviewed me. The academic vice-president had been president at a university with a flourishing WAC Program and later provided the upper administration leadership and support that any cross-disciplinary program requires.

I gave a campus-wide presentation on WAC and Writing Centers. Interested faculty, not just those in the two departments in which I was to teach, were given the opportunity to make appointments to chat with me. Once I was hired in late January 1989, I began to receive letters and long distance phone calls about writing assignments at the University, even though my appointment did not begin until August. By mail, I distributed a survey about the writing needs and interests of faculty and programs, so that I could develop appropriate workshops for the fall. This campus-wide involvement with faculty, programs, and deans had already begun to create parallel learning structures in the university's bureaucracy.

Parallel learning structures operate in tandem with a bureaucracy's normal structures. They are opportunities for groups to learn, discuss, and problem solve without affecting the organization's normal operations. Parallel learning creates an opportunity for openness and innovation in organizational groups used to competition and compliance. Questioning and doubting, taking risks and confronting ambiguity—are all part of parallel learning (Bushe and Shani 1991, 9–12), along with a steering committee, a vision statement, study groups, time for inquiry, complete support from the top of the hierarchy, feedback among study groups and steering committee, experimental implementation of change, and system-wide diffusion and evaluation. Parallel learning structures span various levels of power and status in the organization, creating optimal discussions for decreased resistance to later program development or change. These informal learning structures prepare the organizational culture for positive change, setting up more open discussion and flexible roles than a departmental meeting or formal forum. IWP workshops, consultations with individual faculty and programs, and semester-long seminars created key informal and formal learning structures for subsequent WC and WAC Program development.

In academic program development, parallel learning structures do not threaten the established organizational bureaucracies of separate schools and departments. The university, grounded in the Catholic liberal arts tradition, was strongly managerial in the professional schools and upper administration, while the College of Arts and Sciences's (CAS) departments fully identified with the collegial culture. As Bergquist predicted, this division created cultural differences between the professional school and CAS faculty and programs. I was often asked by my CAS colleagues how I could possibly work with "faculty from that school." Meanwhile, the CAS departments did not work together as a unit like the other schools; instead the departments and their chairs pursued independent and often competing agendas for scant resources and status. In CAS especially, I continued to be seen as the "long arm" of the English Department, an extension of the FYC program. This confusion between my role within the English Department and my role for the other aspects of the IWP confounded my networking with CAS departments, although not with individual faculty from those departments. The usual CAS chain of command is vested in chairs and deans. Program directors often lack that direct link to budgeting sessions and planning meetings, so crucial for explaining their priorities and requests. Within the English Department, I coordinated FYC adjuncts in terms of curricula, pedagogy, hiring, placement, plagiarism incidents, course observations, scheduling, and teaching evaluations. The lack of clarification of my various roles within the IWP's WAC and WC roles and the English Department's writing program set the stage for future misconceptions and confusion.

In 1989–1990, I established a dual learning strategy: 1) to network within each unit, building trust and support by providing consultations and workshops on field-specific needs, and 2) to provide campus-wide workshops. At this same time, another cross-disciplinary program, the FS program provided the new IWP and university faculty with additional opportunities for learning partnerships, outside the usual disciplinary boundaries. In the fall of 1989, I became a member of the FS Advisory Committee and in 1994 began teaching a FS course. Over the years, the FS director and I worked as partners in planning that would accommodate our shared faculty development and pedagogical goals.

Professional school accreditations were all occurring within the next few years. These accreditation review standards include emphasis on communication skills and critical thinking. The IWP and its director formed consultation partnerships with these schools to achieve their accreditation goals, while further achieving its own goal of networking and building learning structures.

In 1989–1990, the IWP and the engineering writing committee developed an engineering writing program with a school-wide writing for engineers pamphlet, praised by the engineering accreditation review, and leading to a collaborative professional publication (Kuhn and Vaught-Alexander 1994). This past year, the School of Nursing integrated critical thinking, the American Psychological Association (APA) research and writing goals, and required WC conferences with course curriculum guidelines.

Over the next few years, the following parallel learning structures formed IWP partnerships that crossed university subcultures and organizational hierarchies: 1) the IWP Advisory Committee with representatives from all the academic units; 2) the Common Curriculum Document, an extension of the mission statement, describing critical thinking, communication, and knowledge-based proficiencies for graduates of the university; 3) continued networking within organizational units through consultations and specialized workshops; 4) workshops and semester-long seminars often in tandem with the FS program; 5) adjunct writing faculty and the English Department's common course goals for the FYC course; 6) a newsletter *Writing UP*, highlighting one faculty member's writing, cooperative learning, or critical thinking assignment, reviewing new IWP library acquisitions, and announcing workshops and seminars.

PARTNERSHIPS FOR "SECOND ORDER" CHANGE: THE IWP'S DEVELOPMENT OF A WRITING CENTER STAFFED BY WRITING ASSISTANTS FROM THE DISCIPLINES

The IWP Advisory Committee, similar to Bushe and Shani's steering committee and study groups, functions as an ad hoc committee, rather than a standing committee. It convenes by e-mail or in face-to-face meetings when program advice or input is needed. Committee members are usually volunteer representatives, although a few departments have rotating appointments. This committee, as well as the academic vice-president, sanctioned the WC pilot and established the Integrated WC philosophy and WA training.

Inspired by a 1990 Conference on College Composition and Communication (CCCC) workshop highlighting the writing fellows programs of Tori Harring-Smith, Barbara Sylvester, and Margot Soven, the IWP Writing Center began as a 1990–1991 pilot, operating on a $500 budget with one workshop-trained, English-major writing assistant (WA) who held conferences at a desk in my crowded office. By 1991–1992, the WA program had three writing assistants: one English and Performing and Fine Arts major, one English education major, and one history. They were trained in a one-hour directed studies class; conferences were held in my office and in the adjoining hall area. The nursing

dean helped me secure funding to continue the WA program during their summer school program.

In 1992–1993, a year of especially scant resources, the WA program,
with supporting letters from all the professional schools and most CAS departments, expanded its budget to twelve writing assistants for the regular academic
year with two in the summer. The School of Nursing allowed its study lounge to
be converted into our present WC. I now teach a 400-level, three-hour-credit
course for training the WAs. As part of their training, they do case study research, usually focused on a disciplinary writing issue. Case studies on freshman
biology writers, freshman history writers, or upper-division engineering writers
are shared with faculty in these fields, further validating the value of discipline-
specific WAs. Case studies are kept on file so that each year our on-site database
of WC research grows. The IWP has its own budget line within CAS, with
monies for the WA salaries and supplies for WAC faculty development. Appeals for increases in budget are made to the CAS dean and the academic vice-
president, although this program serves all schools and faculty.

The WC and its WA program are successful due to partnerships—
within and across individual academic units. It is an accepted and expected part
of academic life. From the initial involvement of the IWP Advisory Committee
in determining center philosophy to the annual nomination of the WAs by
faculty in that field, the academic units are key partners in the WC program.
This nomination policy establishes faculty trust in the competence of the student
selected. Faculty members are more comfortable in a working relationship with
a student already known to them. The prospective WAs, in turn, see their
nomination as a disciplinary honor and have a vested interest in responsibly
working as a WA for their major-area departments after their training class.

The IWP Advisory Committee decided our WAC-based Writing Center
should serve all students, not just those requiring remediation. Some professors
require whole classes to bring their drafts to the WC to emphasize that writing
improves with revision and trained peer review. Less skillful writers can become
better ones; already good writers become even better. Faculty members can request writing tutorials for students who need intensive work on Lower Order
Concerns (LOCs) like grammar and mechanics. These sessions last longer than
other sessions focused on Higher Order Concerns (HOCs) in which students are
asked questions and given feedback on organization, selection of evidence, etc.
WAs host a table at freshman orientation as well as an open house for faculty
and clients in the fall. The use of informational bookmarks and five-minute WC
introductions by a WA to a whole class have been especially useful in getting
clients to come to the WC voluntarily. Specially trained WAs or the WC director also provide group conferences and in-class "portable" workshops for specific style sheets, MCAT essay practice, peer review, and particular requested
topics like conciseness.

Carefully the IWP Advisory Committee crafted the center philosophy
to increase student involvement and avoid ghost writing. Seated at round tables
to promote interaction, new clients fill out an information sheet which reports

writing background and writing attitudes. After the initial getting acquainted and a request for an explanation of the writing assignment, our conference protocol includes the setting of conference goals by the client. Clients read their papers aloud or ask the WA to read it for them. Clients are handed a pencil and paper for their notes on the session. The WA and client negotiate appropriate goals and strategies for improvement or revision, just as they work collaboratively to compose the conference report at closure.

This WAC-based WC is a support system for clients and faculty. We set up a cooperative, triadic partnership for writing improvement among the faculty member, client, and WA. Each year, policies and procedures are fine tuned by faculty, client, and WA feedback (i.e., triplicate conference reports composed and signed by client and WA). These reports with copies for faculty member, WC, and client provide a summary of conference emphases as well as other suggestions for the client to consider before turning the paper in. Each semester, faculty ask WAs for their opinions on the clarity of a writing assignment. One faculty member, whose assignment caused the frustration and confusion of many clients, asked the WAs who had worked most with the assignment to send suggestions for improving the assignment for next semester. This WC team is a partnership for improving writing strategies for clients and improving writing assignments for faculty, while giving the WC input for its own improvement.

The university WC is not an extension of the English Department's FYC program, although the center certainly works with that program too. Faculty, beyond those on the advisory committee, have begun to appreciate the difference between general writing assistance and assistance with disciplinary writing by a trained reader from that field. From 1990–1997, the center evolved from an English-major-based program in which writing was equated with style, grammar, and mechanics—to a Writing Across the Curriculum Program in which WAs translated across fields through assignments and center summary sheets—to a Writing in the Disciplines Program in which WAs in the field are seen as irreplaceable for helping with certain assignments.

The program has moved individuals and groups from first-order change (improving what existed, namely, in 1989 untrained Blue Key volunteer writing tutors who worked one night a week) to second-order change (transforming ideas about writing in the disciplines and creating on-going learning structures among faculty, WAs, and clients). For my academic organization, a direct second-order change would have been too difficult, too radical, too time-consuming. This second-order change began as a less threatening, first-order change, a "right fit" for my campus culture.

No WAC workshop or seminar can create the parallel learning structures of a WC, staffed by cross-disciplinary WAs. I had no idea how powerful these partnerships would become. I call the writing assistants, my gentle subversives. As they interview faculty about disciplinary expectations for our center's summary sheets, they ask questions to clarify their understanding of a writing assignment, they form the day-to-day partnerships that inform our WC and

WAC practice. Whereas some faculty may be reluctant to ask me about the wording of a writing assignment, they are more comfortable talking about their disciplinary writing expectations with a WA who is a member of their discourse community. The WAs function as translators for WAs from other fields and mentors for clients in the thinking, rhetorics, and expectations of their fields.

These WC partnerships enrich disciplinary writing experiences for faculty and students alike. The enter now has WAs from all the professional schools, Army and Air Force ROTC, and CAS departments including most recently ones in Spanish, German, and mathematics and computer science. I determine which fields need more than one WA for the next year, given the previous year's center usage. WC usage and WAC faculty-development workshop participation also became useful for professional school accreditation reports this year, further forging WC and WAC partnerships.

IN THE MIDDLE: "EXPERT" POWER PARTNERSHIPS AND RESISTANCE TO A WRITING-IN-CONTEXT AND FRESHMAN YEAR EXPERIENCE PROGRAM PROPOSAL

Those who create change must be seen as legitimate sources of power. In the developmental culture of the academy, WC and WAC administrators supposedly have their own "expert" power, from research and theory or outside experts. Yet those of us who work with writing-related programs know that some of our disciplinary colleagues may choose to privilege personal experiences or anecdotes about the teaching of college writing over what decades of composition research shows. Our expert power becomes questioned in ways few other disciplines are questioned by colleagues:

What ever happened to the teaching of grammar through work sheets and drills? That's the way that Miss Smith taught me and I learned how to write. Or I learned the most when Mr. Jones wrote more on my paper than I did in bright red ink and gave me a D for one punctuation error. We want results, not just all this emphasis on writing process. When I send students to the WC, I expect the papers to be perfectly edited if the WAs are doing their jobs.

IWP faculty development can begin to address such misconceptions with individual faculty. Semester-long seminars and the May Workshop of the IWP have been successfully institutionalized, as well as program and individual consultations. Faculty document attendance at these to show university service and dedication to teaching. These faculty development partnerships of the IWP do not disturb academic autonomy, disciplinary power or status, or work load. They are voluntary and optional. But as a result, the same faculty participate year after year, and others never do.

From 1995–1997, a learning subculture of twenty-six individual faculty, participants in the IWP and freshman seminar workshops and seminars, joined the IWP director in experimenting with course portfolios and reflective thinking, culminating in their contributions to *A Practical Guide to Course Portfolios*: *Writing, Thinking, Learning Across the Curriculum*. Faculty, as well as the IWP director, have presented and published papers as a result of their working with the IWP. This expert power creates significant change in individuals and their individual assignments. Programmatic change, however, violates the collegial culture's academic autonomy that such individual changes validate.

To create broad-base or program-level change, WPAs need to form partnerships with other sources of power. Organizational Development theory recognizes four other possible sources of power: the organization's legitimately constituted authority (in the academy a president, provost, dean, or chair), coercive power (this is the way it is), trust-based power, and common vision power (Jick 1993, 622–623). Trust-based power emanates from past successful experiences with collaborative problem-solving. In academic institutions with scant resources and stories of those who "were done wrong," trust-based power is especially difficult to cultivate. Common vision power ("the vision thing," as Jick calls it) unifies and inspires those, who normally could not agree on a shared view.

Grass root changes emerge from trust-based and common vision power. Top-down changes use authority and coercive power. When WPAs feel powerless, they may not have formed these power partnerships, they may not know how to use the power they have (as Edward White [1990] tells us about WPA power, "use it or lose it"), or they are not placed clearly in the power hierarchy of the institution.

So where are WPAs on the organizational chart of the academy? As program directors, we appear to be the academic equivalent of a middle manager. OD theory tells us that middle managers are in a pivotal position for initiating and creating change. That is good for program development. Unfortunately, that middle position also can trap WPAs in the potential powerlessness of the Middle.

According to Barry Oshry's "Converting Middle Powerlessness to Middle Power: A Systems Approach," "Middles" live a hectic and frustrating organizational and personal existence, working in "other people's spaces and other people's agendas" (1995, 403). Originally emotionally and physically healthy, competent professionals in middle positions can become burnt-out, powerless, confused, devalued wrecks—not meeting the expectations of the "Tops" or the "Bottoms." Middles soon get the "milquetoast" reputation of being nice, hard-working, well-intentioned, but wishy-washy weak and ineffective. They exhaust themselves trying to please both the Tops and the Bottoms with compromise after compromise, and, in the process, please neither. Oshry urges Middles to take a systemic look at what is really happening: "Above has its agenda for Below, and Below has its agenda for Above. . . . We slide into the Middle. . . . We feel that it is our responsibility alone to resolve their issues and conflicts" (404).

Somehow Middles must let the Tops and Bottoms work our their own issues. If Tops want to give garbage to the Bottoms, Middles should neither agree to deliver the garbage nor fight the battle for the Bottoms. If Bottoms have a problem with a policy of the Tops, Tops and Bottoms need to work these issues without using the Middles as the whipping post. Middles need to find their own agendas and work to resolve those. According to Oshry, Middles need to master the Middle Space by concentrating on forming partnerships with other Middles, with the Tops and with the Bottoms. "Middles who empower themselves and others. . .are Top when they can be. . .are Bottom when they should be, who coach and facilitate. . .a different order of Middles. . .they value themselves and bring value to their systems" (412). In our academic organizations, we Middles need to negotiate productive partnerships with the Bottoms, the collegial culture; the Tops, the managerial culture; and other Middles, the developmental culture.

Such partnerships are crucial for positive change. The IWP Advisory Committee spent 1994–1996 trying to formulate a more clearly articulated description of WAC, bringing input on the proposal from departmental and school-wide meetings. The idea was to move from our present voluntary diffusion model to a Writing-in-Context (WIC) model, with department-agreed-upon courses designated as having writing assignments that used the writing process and were given grades for writing quality. The proposal itself was based on collaborative action research, an in-depth survey of the university's writing assignments: what kind of writing was assigned, what steps in the writing process, if any, were assigned, and what about writing was graded. The WAs conducted the survey and compiled each department's results. The successful WAC-based WC program provided a support system for drafting and revising of WIC assignments that encouraged faculty to move to this next stage. The deans and the academic vice-president also supported the proposal, as they had the WC pilot.

The overall results of a 1995 survey showed that many courses were already meeting the proposed WIC requirements. The IWP Advisory Committee felt sure that the WIC pilot proposal would be readily accepted by the Curriculum Committee. WIC was a voluntary designation; the survey showed that writing assignments, typical of a WIC program, were already being used by many faculty. What could go wrong? What could create resistance to such collaborative, consensus-seeking proposal?

Resistance is to be expected with any change. We know that from Rick Maurer and other OD experts. So perhaps the question here should be—how can resistance to change be reduced? Don Bryant in "The Psychology of Resistance to Change" points out that individual and institutional attitudes, as well as present and past experiences with change processes, need to be considered. Have past changes for the individual or institution been beneficial or detrimental? Some resistance can be assuaged by tying change to improvement, improvement for the individual or for the institution. Resistance can also be lessened with three questions: Who brings the change? What kind of change? How will the change be instituted (Bryant 1991, 193–194)?

Change agents, the supervisors and other key individuals in the organization, need to spearhead the change, giving organizational full support to the change. Who introduces the change is crucial for its acceptance. The change cannot be seen as the agenda of one group or individual, even the top supervisor—or resistance will rise. Change projects must reduce rather increase work load, or at least appear to do so. The change must agree with the values and ideals, espoused by the individuals and groups of the organization. The change must interest participants enough to try it—while not threatening their security, work load, or autonomy (194–195).

Finally, individuals and groups need to participate in the diagnostic efforts that validate the need for change. They need to agree that there is a problem or a need and that it is important. Resistance is enhanced when individuals are left out of this crucial first stage. Proposals for change need to come from group discussions, rather than presented to groups for consensus. A series of meetings during the planning and implementing of the change builds support, trust, and confidence. Feedback on problems with the change is crucial. The change should be left open to revision and reconsideration if implementation shows need for changes in emphasis or direction (195).

Oshry's advice for middle managers and Bryant's advice for reducing resistance can help us deal with program development: especially pilots and other program proposals. Maybe other WC and WAC directors will not encounter the resistance that I have, although Hartzog's study showed that creating new programs was ranked as the most difficult to accomplish (1986, 57). As WPAs, our problems reside in the academic culture, in our middle management position, and in any attempt to create change in a bureaucracy. No wonder we experience such professional and personal burn-out. Perhaps that is why Hartzog shows many WPAs in their positions fewer than seven years (24).

The original WIC proposal was piloted in FS courses in the fall of 1996. The FS course requirement of three writing assignments that went through drafting and revision already fulfilled the WIC requirement. With the exception of increased writing assistant support for the FS courses, this pilot was basically a first-order change which improved what existed. That fall also saw new deans in all schools but one, and a new academic vice-president.

At this juncture, the new CAS dean called a meeting of the chair of the English Department who was in charge of the FYC program, the FS director, and myself (the IWP director). Several related problems needed to be solved. The present FS program did not provide all freshmen with these special courses, essential to attract and retain entering freshmen. The English Department's freshman writing program continued to be staffed by adjunct faculty and the IWP director. The IWP's successful FS pilot seemed ready to expand to other courses. This group began to brainstorm solutions. Perhaps we could pilot a program in which two WIC freshman courses substituted for the one freshman writing course. The FS program could be expanded to include courses called FYE courses that could be WIC courses, while introducing students to their major. Because both FS and IWP were to undergo program review next fall, the official approval of this proposal could be part of their combined program reviews. Such a programmatic combination would even free funds for the English Department to hire a position, recommended in its program review. All programs would benefit. This pilot would be evaluated at the end of the academic year and either be modified or scrapped if the results were not satisfactory. This initial diagnosis, problem-solving and planning stage, unlike the WC or the FS WIC pilot, involved only this group.

Next, a draft proposal was officially presented to the new Tops for their feedback. Several Tops saw this pilot WIC proposal as a way to eliminate the FYC issue; just implement WIC and get rid of the adjunct problem. With the adjunct salaries, the English Department would get a needed literature position. This proposal would be an opportunity to expand FS course offerings in a freshman year-WAC Program directed by the present WAC and WC administrator. For the Tops, or at least certain Tops, "three or even four birds would be killed with one stone." Here was a chance to make the university more cost-effective by unifying programs and expanding freshman course offerings.

The IWP Advisory Committee, most CAS departmental chairs, and other faculty were not involved in this initial brainstorming and planning. A change was needed before the recruitment and registration of the new freshman class for the fall of 1997. Consensus-building would slow this obviously logical move, approved by the Tops. Two WIC classes could substitute for English 107 solving the adjunct problem, the FS and IWP would be expanded under this new umbrella called Freshman Year Experience (FYE), and in a year of scant faculty resources, the English Department would get its Americanist position. The proposal, no longer a draft, was distributed to the campus as a whole. Resistance was immediate and intense.

An open forum was called to discuss the new FYE-WIC plan. Maurer explained that such a meeting was needed to "invite the storm." It came. In this case, even those who had supported the WIC pilot proposal were confused or threatened by the loss of the FYC program. Who would teach grammar? All the old misconceptions about writing surfaced. What would happen to the work load of those who taught WIC courses now that they replaced, rather than extended, FYC? Many CAS faculty, especially chairs, objected to the English department getting a new position, while their own faculty work loads would be increased by the proposed WIC assignments. The confluence of program agendas and terms like WIC, IWP, FS and FYE, the desire to implement this pilot immediately—all contributed to the demise of this proposal.

I experienced the powerlessness of the Middle to which Oshry referred. The Tops who modified the WIC proposal were perplexed by my perceived incompetence to win faculty acceptance: Didn't you and your program prepare faculty for this WIC proposal properly? What have you been doing with the WC and WAC for the last six years? The Bottoms, especially those who worked so hard on the piloted proposal, expressed dismay or frustration with the whole process: Why happened to the original proposal? Why did I allow it to be changed?

Although I was trapped in the Middle, I did not stay there. I knew from OD theory what had gone wrong, even though I lacked the authority to change or prevent it. Rather than risk any further the trust and consensus that created the

WAC-based Writing Center and WAC faculty development, I let the revised WIC proposal die, so the change cycle could resume.

The university lost the momentum of the original WIC proposal, carefully crafted by consensus. I had built the partnerships similar to those that had worked so well in developing the WAC-based WC, a program which continues to support and transform WAC. I even conducted action research. So what went wrong? Several things actually. A number of crucial Top partnerships were changed or lost. No significant change should have been attempted that year. The Tops who hired me and who knew the history of the IWP and the FS programs were gone. For the new Tops, all of this had become "a tempest in a teapot," a confusion to be calmed. The new Tops ideally should have had a year or more to learn the campus and its programs.

After the modifications, the proposal was no longer tied to a common vision. Past mistrust and rivalry for scant resources in CAS surfaced, when the proposal led to a new faculty position for another department. What began as a win-win proposal, formulated by consensus, ended in a battle of different agendas. OD theory does not assure WPAs of success in program development—but it does give us key strategies for our work as change agents in the complex social and cultural organizations of the academy.

As Kim Kipling and Richard Murphy concur:

> Academic change is not a matter of importing ideas or structures whole from outside the institution, or of imposing them. Academic change cannot be expected to be swift. Ideas need time to evolve, even in the minds of persons who think they understand them and to become familiar particularly to persons who are suspicious or afraid of them. Structures likewise need time to grow in response to the demands of the situation, and they need to be flexible enough to harmonize with the institution within which they are to do their work. (1992, xi)

Partnerships across academic cultures and power sources are essential for program development. These partnerships, however, can create resistance: if our common vision is lost, if coercion is used, or if trust is violated. WCs and WAC Programs need to nurture partnerships between themselves—and to reach out to other cross-disciplinary Middles like FS or FYE programs. For successful long-term program development and professional well-being, we need to enact OD-based partnerships that situate our agendas and our programs—powerfully "in the middle"—of our complex academic bureaucracies.

WORKS CITED

Bazerman, Charles, and David R. Russell, eds. *Landmarks Essays on Writing Across the Curriculum*. Davis, CA: Hermagoras Press, 1994.

Beer, Michael, Russell Eisenstat, and Bert Spector. "Why Change Programs Don't Produce Change." In *Managing Change: Cases and Concepts*, Todd Jick, ed. Homewood, IL: Irwin, 1993. 264–276.

Bergquist, William H. *The Four Cultures of the Academy.* San Francisco: Jossey-Bass, 1992.

Bryant, Don. "The Psychology of Resistance to Change." *Organizational Behavior: An Experiential Approach,* Fifth ed. Kolb, Rubin, and Osland, ed. Englewood Cliffs, NJ: Prentice, (1991). 193–195.

Bushe, Gervase R., and A. B. (Rami) Shani. *Parallel Learning Structures: Increasing Innovation in Bureaucracies.* New York: Addison, 1991.

Carter, Duncan, and Ben McClelland. "WPAs Assess the CCCC's 'Statement of Principles and Standards.'" *WPA: Writing Program Administration* 16.1–2 (1992): 71–87.

Dinitz, Susan, and Diane Howe. "Writing Centers and Writing Across the Curriculum: An Evolving Partnership." *Writing Center Journal* 10.1 (1989): 45–51.

Elbow, Peter. *What Is English?* New York: MLA, 1990.

Faery, Rebecca Blevins. "Teachers *and* Writers: The Faculty Writing Workshop and Writing Across the Curriculum." *WPA: Writing Program Administration* 17.1–2 (1993): 31–42.

French, Wendell L., and Cecil H. Bell, Jr. *Organization Development: Behavioral Science Interventions for Organization Improvement.* 4th ed. Englewood Cliffs, NJ: Prentice Hall, 1990.

French, Wendell L., Cecil H. Bell, Jr. and Robert A. Zawacki, eds. *Organizational Development and Transformation: Managing Effective Change*, 4th ed. Burr Ridge, Ill: Irwin, 1994.

Fulwiler, Toby, and Art Young, eds. *Programs That Work: Models and Methods of Writing Across the Curriculum.* Portsmouth, NH: Boyton/Cook, 1990.

Gill, Judy. "Another Look at WAC and the Writing Center." *Writing Center Journal* 16.2 (1996): 164–178.

Hall, Dennis R. *"Compost*: A Writing Program Newsletter and Its Rationale." *WPA: Writing Program Administration* 17.1–2 (1993): 75–82.

Haring-Smith, Tori, et al., eds. *A Guide to Writing Programs: Writing Centers, Peer Tutoring Programs, and Writing Across the Curriculum.* Glenview, IL: Scott, Foresman, 1984.

Harris, Muriel. "Talking in the Middle: Why Writers Need Writing Tutors." *College English* 57 (1995): 27–42.

———. *Teaching One-to-One: The Writing Conference.* Urbana, IL: NCTE, 1986.

Hartzog, Carol T. *Composition and the Academy: A Study of Writing Program Administration.* New York: MLA, 1986.

Hubbuch, Susan. "'Am I Understanding You Correctly?' Advantages of a Tutor's Ignorance." Pacific Coast Writing Centers Conference, University of Portland, Portland, OR, 2 Nov. 1996.

Hult, Christine, and The Portland Resolution Committee: David Jolliffe, Kathleen Kelly, Dana Mead, and Charles Schuster. "The Portland Resolution." *WPA: Writing Program Administration* 16.1–2 (1992): 88–94.

Jick, Todd, ed. *Managing Change: Cases and Concepts.* Homewood, IL: Irwin, 1993.

———. "The Vision Thing (A)." In *Managing Change: Cases and Concepts*, Todd Jick, ed. Homewood, IL: Irwin, 1993. 142–148.

———. "The Vision Thing (B)." In *Managing Change: Cases and Concepts*, Todd Jick, ed. Homewood, IL: Irwin, 1993. 149–151.

Jolliffe, David A., ed. *Advances in Writing Research. Volume 2. Writing in Academic Disciplines.* Norwood, NJ: Ablex, 1988.

Kelly, Kathleen. "Writing Across the Curriculum: What the Literature Tells Us." Information Analysis, 1985, ERIC ED274975.

Kiedaisch, Jean, and Sue Dinitz. "'Look Back and Say 'So What': The Limitations of the Generalist Tutor." *Writing Center Journal* 14.1 (1993): 63–74.

Kinkead, Joyce, and Jeanette Harris, eds. *Writing Centers in Context: Twelve Case Studies.* Urbana, IL: NCTE, 1993.

Kipling, Kim J., and Richard J. Murphy, Jr. *Symbiosis: Writing and an Academic Culture.* Portsmouth, NH: Boyton/Cook. 1992.

Kolb, David A., Joyce Osland, and Irwin M. Rubin, eds. *The Organizational Behavior Reader.* Englewood Cliffs, NJ: Prentice Hall, 1995.

———, Irwin M. Rubin, and Joyce Osland, eds. *Organizational Behavior: An Experiential Approach.* 5th ed. Englewood Cliffs, NJ: Prentice Hall, 1991.

Kuhn, Matthew, and Karen Vaught-Alexander. "A Context for Writing in the Engineering Curriculum." *The ASCE Journal of Professional and Educational Issues in Engineering Curriculum* 120.4 (1994): 392–400.

Maurer, Rick. *Beyond the Wall of Resistance: Unconventional Strategies That Build Support for Change.* Austin, TX: Bard Press, 1997.

McLeod, Susan, ed. *Strengthening Programs for Writing Across the Curriculum.* San Francisco: Jossey–Bass, 1988.

———, and Margot Soven, eds. *Writing Across the Curriculum: A Guide to Developing Programs.* Newbury Park, CA: Sage, 1992.

Mullin, Joan A., and Ray Wallace, eds. *Intersections: Theory-Practice in the Writing Center.* Urbana, IL: NCTE, 1994.

Olson, Gary A., ed. *Writing Centers: Theory and Administration.* Urbana, IL: NCTE, 1984.

Oshry, Barry. "Converting Middle Powerlessness to Middle Power: A Systems Approach." In *Organizational Behavior: An Experiential Approach* 5th ed., Kolb, Osland, and Rubin eds. Englewood Cliffs, NJ: Prentice Hall, 1991. 401–412.

Pemberton, Michael A. "Rethinking the WAC/Writing Center Connection." *Writing Center Journal* 15.2 (1995): 116–133.

Polanski, Virginia R. "We Are Autonomous: An Argument for a Separate Writing Department." 1990 WPA Conference, 26–28 July 1990.

Russell, David R. *Writing in the Academic Disciplines, 1870–1990, A Curricular History.* Carbondale, IL: Southern Illinois UP, 1991.

Senge, Peter. "The Leader's New Work: Building Learning Organizations." In *Managing Change: Cases and Concepts*, Todd Jick, ed. Homewood, IL: Irwin, 1993. 440–463.

Smith, Louise Z. "Independence and Collaboration; Why We Should Decentralize Writing Centers." *Writing Center Journal* 7.1 (1986): 3–10.

Smith, Steve, Brit Begley, and Leslea Goodwyn. "'What Do You Mean You're Not an English Major?': Tutors Across the Curriculum Confront Quibbling Concerns over Credentials." Pacific Coast Writing Centers Conference, University of Portland, Portland, OR, 2 Nov. 1996.

Soliday, Mary. "Shifting Roles in Classroom Tutoring: Cultivating the Art of Boundary Crossing." *Writing Center Journal* 16.1 (1995): 59–73.

Soven, Margot. "Curriculum-based Peer Tutoring Programs: A Survey." *WPA: Writing Program Administration* 17. 1–2 (1993): 58–74.

Swilky, Jody. "Reconsidering Faculty Resistance to Writing Reform," *WPA: Writing Program Administration* 16.1–2 (1992): 50–60.

Vaught-Alexander, Karen. "Integrating Writing into the Curriculum and the Academy: Organizational Change, Campus Politics, and the WPA." Paper presented at 1994 WPA-ADE Conference, University of Mississippi, Oxford, MS, 28–30 July 1994.

———. "'The New Kid at School': The Challenges of the Wyoming Resolution for a New WPA in a New WAC Program." Paper presented at 1990 WPA Conference, Portland State University, Portland, OR, 26–28 July 1990.

———. *A Practical Guide to Course Portfolios: Writing, Thinking, Learning Across the Curriculum.* Fairfield, NJ: Pencil Point Press, 1997.

———. "Using the Power and Politics of a Small University to Empower a WAC Program." Paper presented at 1991 WPA Conference, Saratoga Springs, NY, 13–16 June 1991.

———. "Why Not Let Faculty Write Across the Curriculum?" Paper presented at 1992 WPA Conference, University of Denver, Breckenridge, CO, 23–25 July 1992.

———, Travis Campbell, Jean Mulcahy, and Magdalena Visan. "'How Can I Help Your Students? May I Have a Copy of Your Writing Assignment?': Writing Assistants from the Disciplines Resituate Our Writing Center for Clients, Faculty, and Programs." Pacific Coast Writing Centers Conference, University of Portland, Portland, OR, 2 Nov. 1996.

Waldo, Mark. "The Last Best Place for WAC: The Writing Center." *WPA: Writing Program Administration* 16.3 (1993): 15–26.

Wallace, Ray. "The Writing Center's Role in the Writing Across the Curriculum Program: Theory and Practice." *Writing Center Journal* 8.2 (1988): 3–10.

Walvoord, Barbara Fassler. *Helping Students Write Well: A Guide for Teachers in All Disciplines.* 2nd ed. New York: MLA, 1986.

White, Edward M. "The Damage of Innovations Set Adrift: Change for the Worst." *American Association for Higher Education Journal* 43.3 (1990): 3–5.

———. "Use It or Lost It: Power and the WPA." *WPA: Writing Program Administration* 15.1–2 (1991): 3–12.

Young, Art, and Toby Fulwiler, eds. *Writing Across the Disciplines: Research into Practice.* Upper Montclair, NJ: Boyton/Cook, 1986.

Creating a Virtual Space:
The Role of the Web in Forging
Writing Center/WAC Connections

Irene L. Clark

For many faculty members, participating in a Writing Across the Curriculum program constitutes a first pedagogical venture outside of their own field of expertise; consequently, many "feel unqualified to judge anything but content . . . [and] are unaccustomed to responding to writing in progress" (Gill 1996, 167). Moreover, because faculty who have never taught writing before may never have worked with novice writers, have little experience with process pedagogy, and have not consciously articulated for themselves their expectations for student essays, they sometimes adopt what can be ironically characterized as the "assign and complain" method of teaching writing—that is, they present students with an often vaguely conceptualized writing assignment and then complain about the quality of the writing they receive.

To enable faculty to acquire strategies for working productively with inexperienced writers and to engage in actually teaching, not simply assigning, writing, it has been suggested that Writing Centers become a significant resource for WAC Programs. In "The Last Best Place for Writing Across the Curriculum: The Writing Center," Mark Waldo maintains that Writing Centers constitute "a definable space" for expertise in writing, because they encourage dialogue between diverse rhetorical communities, and offer a rhetorically neutral ground in that they do not privilege a discipline-specific "rhetorical agenda common to one discourse community" (1993, 17). Similarly, Judy Gill claims that Writing Centers can become a visible and instrumental force for changing faculty attitude toward writing, serving as "translators" for students who are not familiar with academic writing. However, although this concept of the Writing Center as "definable space" has important implications for WAC Programs (several excellent possibilities are discussed within this volume), it must also be recognized that many faculty members perceive the Writing Center as a place to which students are sent, rather than one in which faculty should become actively involved, and that it is by no means certain that faculty from various departments on campus will initiate a dialogic or collaborative relationship with the Writing Center, nor conceive of it as a resource for professional development.

This chapter will argue that the Writing Center can more effectively facilitate interdisciplinary dialogue in a Writing Across the Curriculum environment if it adheres to the old saying about Mohammed and the mountain— that is, if the mountain will not come to Mohammed, then, of course, Mohammed must come to the mountain. In the context of Writing Center/ WAC connections, the Mohammed principle suggests that the Writing Center should assume a proactive role in working with faculty, not only through frequent contact and classroom involvement, but by creating an interactive virtual space via the World Wide Web that faculty and students from a variety of disciplines can access and contribute to easily. The Web can serve as a dynamic mediating mechanism for this purpose in that it is not associated with a particular disciplinary agenda, is easily accessed from everywhere on campus, can establish connections between multiple disciplines, can facilitate dialogue between writing and content-area experts, and make a variety of writing resources available to both students and teachers. At the University of Southern California, as part of a new, writing-intensive undergraduate curriculum, the Writing Center is using the Web as a facilitative environment in which interdisciplinary dialogue, process pedagogy, and consciousness of genre expectations in various disciplines can be encouraged.

THE WEB AS FACILITATIVE SPACE IN A WAC CONTEXT

Central to the success of a Writing Across the Curriculum Program is the willingness of faculty to integrate writing into their courses both as writing-to-learn activities and as writing assignments that enable students to become acquainted with the assumptions, methods, and genre requirements of a particular discipline. Such integration, however, presumes faculty meta-knowledge of the interrelationship of discourse and information within their own discipline; moreover, it requires faculty to be actively conscious of how that interrelationship is manifested in text and concerned with making that interrelationship explicit to their students. However, what is often the case with a number of professors involved in Writing Across the Curriculum Programs is that they may know "a great deal about writing without having undergone much self-examination about . . . [their] own discipline-specific processes or discourse forms" (MacDonald 1987, 315). Consequently, many faculty will design a writing prompt without specifying what sort of writing they are expecting students to generate. We who work in Writing Centers know only too well that writing assignments are often poorly worded, unclear about what the professor is expecting. And because students are unacquainted with the genre requirements of college writing, they frequently fall back upon genres with which they are more familiar, such as exposition or narrative. Unaware that the professor is likely to expect a thesis-driven text that incorporates the conceptual and textual features of academic discourse, they write papers that consist of a linear sequencing of unprocessed material in the body of the essay, with evaluative comment, if it exists at all, postponed to the concluding paragraph.

Integrating writing into content area courses has been a concern of the Writing Across the Curriculum movement. However, as Fulwiler and Young point out, there are a number of faculty attitudes toward writing at the university that impede progress in this area, among them lack of respect for expertise in writing as a legitimate academic specialty, resistance or apathy toward the teaching of writing at the university, and entrenched notions about writing and the teaching of writing, for example, that students should have learned to write in high school, that learning to write means learning a set of discreet skills in isolation, that writing cannot be taught, and that writing can be taught by anyone with a college diploma (Fulwiler and Young 1990). Moreover, not surprisingly, the missionary model in which presumed writing "experts" bring the "word" to the unenlightened has frequently engendered faculty resistance, rather than co-operation. As Mike Rose points out, many departments associate writing with a literary tradition housed in the English Department, where it assumed a belletristic and then, later on, a basic skills orientation (Rose 1985), and both of these emphases have had the effect of isolating writing from other academic departments. Because writing is associated with the disciplinary agenda and textual conventions of the English Department, it is frequently perceived as occupying "its own intellectual domaine" (Anson 2), separate from the written discourse in other disciplines.

Recently, the University of Southern California (USC) has instituted a new writing-intensive undergraduate curriculum, and as a means of integrating writing across the disciplines, the Writing Center has developed a Web site that serves as a vehicle for disseminating the concept of process pedagogy through interactive resources that encourage students to scaffold their completion of writing assignments and receive online feedback. In addition, the Web site functions as a writing-oriented knowledge base focusing on the genre requirements of academic writing, thereby fostering interdisciplinary dialogue, and enabling the Writing Center to extend its influence beyond the confines of a physical location (the Mohammed to the mountain concept).

BACKGROUND: A NEW LINKED CURRICULUM AT USC

The undergraduate curriculum at the University of Southern California requires all students to complete two course categories that include writing during their freshman year. During the fall semester, the freshman class is divided in half for the purpose of fulfilling general education requirements, half the class (approximately 1,400 students) enrolling in writing courses linked to a variety of social science courses under the category "Social Issues"—bearing titles such as "Environmental Issues in Society," "Law, Politics, and Public Policy," "Stigma and Society," "Diversity and Race Conflict," and "Changing Family Forms." These courses are taught by social science faculty—Sociology, Political

Science, Economics, Geography, and International Relations, among others—
and when students choose a Social Issues course, they then co-register for a
linked writing course, which uses the content from the Issues course as material
for writing assignments.

The other half of the freshman class enroll in a curriculum category
labeled "Literature, Thought, and the Arts," which consists of courses from a
number of humanities departments—English, Russian, Art History, Philosophy—with titles such as "Masterpieces of the Russian Short Story," "British
Landscape and Pastoral Poetry of the 18th and 19th Centuries," "Baroque Art
and Culture," "Art and Text in Imperial Rome," "Philosophy in Fiction," and
"Free Will and Determinism." Although not linked directly to a writing course,
these courses are designated "writing intensive," which means that professors
are required to include a significant amount of writing in the course, although an
exact number of papers or page requirement has not been specified. During the
spring semester, students register for the category in which they were not enrolled during the fall—that is, students who took "Social Issues" in the fall take
"Literature, Thought, and the Arts" in the spring and vice versa.

THE ROLE OF ARGUMENT IN A WAC CONTEXT

In considering what sort of writing should be taught in the required
freshman writing course and the extent to which such a course should be viewed
as preparatory for writing in the disciplines, the writing program has focused
almost exclusively on academic argument. Although it is generally acknowledged that, at least to some extent, disciplines work in different ways to create
knowledge, that each discipline is characterized by particular structures and
modes of presenting knowledge, and that each discipline constitutes a distinct
culture in its concept of shared knowledge and presuppositions, the Writing
Program and the affiliated Writing Center views many of the approaches, strategies, and skills associated with argumentation as applicable to a variety of academic writing tasks and perceives academic argument as "more unified than is
commonly understood and far more unified than the fragmentation of academic
fields might imply" (Nelson, Megill, and McCloskey 1987, 4). In designing the
freshman course, the Writing Program thus maintains that many facets of academic argument—the privileging of discovering and supporting a thesis, the role
of problem definition (MacDonald 1987), the emphasis on reason and logic, the
use of evidentials (Barton 1993), strategies of research, the role of critical reading—as well as the meta-knowledge of argumentative discourse students acquire through writing, revising, and analyzing texts, will be useful to students in
many academic contexts.

This emphasis on argumentation as preparation for writing throughout
the disciplines is based on the idea that a great deal of the writing that students
are assigned at the university, the sort of writing that is frequently referred to as
"academic discourse" in a variety of disciplines, is really a form of argumentation, and that this is true whether or not the assignments are specifically labeled

as such or whether professors have thought of writing in this context. Most college writing assignments, from the freshman essay to the content area research paper, may be characterized as arguments to the extent that they require students to establish and support a clearly stated thesis or position concerned with a substantive and usually problematic topic which members of the discourse community have written about and consider important. Writing an effective argument means entering that community and indicating awareness of pertinent issues, concepts, and opinions—hence the importance of research and critical reading. Unfortunately, however, students often have a great deal of difficulty with argumentation, not only because they are unfamiliar with it, but also because professors often do not discuss the requirements of their assignments in an argumentative context.

THE ROLE OF THE WRITING CENTER IN THE LINKED CURRICULUM

As a means of assisting both students and faculty involved in the new linked curriculum, the Writing Center has assumed a central role, characterized by the following features:

1. A Web site developed by the Writing Center (http://www.usc.edu/dept/expo) is being used to encourage process pedagogy in the teaching of writing, to facilitate student/faculty communication, and to foster student awareness of the genre expectations of academic writing.
2. The Writing Center has been reconceptualized to include graduate student consultants from a variety of academic departments and has adopted a proactive role in the new program. Such proactivity involves initiating outreach to faculty in their home departments, participating in a limited way within the classroom, and developing workshops that focus on genre expectations of the writing in various disciplines.

FACILITATING PROCESS PEDAGOGY AND COMMUNICATION THROUGH THE WEB

The Web site serves as a vehicle for implementing process pedagogy by providing access to a great deal of information about the writing process that faculty and students can easily download. It also contains several interactive resources that encourage students to scaffold their completion of writing assignments and receive online feedback. These interactive online resources include the following:

Topic Idea List: A form that students can use to propose topics and ideas and mail their proposals to one another and to their instructors.
Thought Collectors: An interactive prewriting tool that enables students to generate ideas, develop a possible thesis for an argumentative essay, and summarize reading; they can then mail their work to themselves, to other students, or to their instructors.

Function Outline Worksheet: A form that initiates revision by focusing attention on thesis development and its contribution to other essay. Students analyze how each
paragraph functions within an essay in terms of its relationship to the thesis or
to one of the supporting points. The form can then be e-mailed anywhere.

Online Syllabi with E-Mail Capacity: Instructors in the Writing Program are encouraged
to post their syllabi on the Web and to encourage interactivity in presenting assignments and commenting on student papers.

These interactive resources are intended to create a process-oriented writing
environment, enabling faculty and students to become involved with essays
during development, drafting, and revision and to view teaching as a dialogic
enterprise. Although not every faculty member uses e-mail on a regular basis, a
great many of them welcome the opportunity of interacting with students electronically and appreciate resources that facilitate such interaction.

FOSTERING GENRE AWARENESS THROUGH THE WEB

The Web site also initiates dialogue about the generic requirements of
academic argument by providing several models with accompanying annotations that emphasize how the components of an essay contribute to its overall
purpose. Each article or essay is presented in two different versions, each of
which has pedagogical advantages and disadvantages. The *Side-by-side version*
has the annotations of the article running on the left side of the page with the
corresponding paragraphs running on the right side; this version enables both
annotations and article to be seen at the same time, although the running commentary on the left side of the page may be viewed by some as a distraction. *The
Hypertext version* presents the essay as a whole with highlighted links to corresponding annotations. In this way, the entire article can be viewed in one continuous page without distraction; however, moving from the article to the annotations may be viewed by some as disruptive.

Below are examples of both methods of presentation, using a student
essay written in response to the question, "Is the PC movement likely to be
beneficial or harmful to society?"

The Side-by-Side Version

Introduction

Introduction

**Opponents to the Political Correct-
ness movement often make the case
that any restriction on speech will
be harmful to society because it is a
violation of first amendment rights.**
*The introduction begins with the op-
posing viewpoint on the topic. Note
that Sarah does not define "PC," be-*

**Opponents to the Political Correct-
ness movement often make the case
that any restriction on speech will
be harmful to society because it is a
violation of first amendment rights.**
They are **concerned** that any prescribed limitation on speech will ultimately lead to a restriction on thought,

cause she assumes that her audience will already be familiar with the concept.

concerned
The second sentence elaborates on the concerns of the opposition.

speech can have powerful consequences on a society
This sentence cites a point that the opposition has overlooked.

if the PC movement can contribute to tolerance among diverse groups, it is likely to be beneficial to society
*Thesis statement.

a movement in the direction of an Orwellian "Big Brother" society. However, what is frequently overlooked in these arguments is that **speech can have powerful consequences on a society**, both the power to heal and the power to tear apart. In the interest of creating a harmonious society, then, it is necessary that some restrictions be placed on what people can and cannot say to one another, and **if the PC movement can contribute to tolerance among diverse groups, it is likely to be beneficial to society.**

Excerpt from the Body of the Paper

The need to establish some restrictions upon the First Amendment becomes urgent when the power and potential danger associated with speech
This is a supporting point that establishes the need to restrict speech under particular circumstances. Note the limitation and qualification of this statement.

Slanderous, racist speech
Establishes that racist speech can affect people and create disharmony, thus supporting the thesis.

detrimental speech under the same umbrella as all free speech
Clarifies the type of speech that should not be protected under the first amendment.

As Charles Lawrence States:
This quotation supports the point that intentionally harmful speech should

Excerpt from the Body of the Paper

The need to establish some restrictions upon the First Amendment becomes urgent when the power and potential danger associated with speech, especially speech of a racist and offensive nature is fully realized. **Slanderous, racist speech** can have an unfortunately rallying effect on ill informed citizens, who are always eager for a scapegoat. It is therefore unfair to protect this type of **detrimental speech under the same umbrella as all free speech.** Why should blatant and obvious lies, undocumented "facts," misinterpreted and manipulated statistics, as well as age old racial myths, stereotypes, and slurs, fall under the category of free speech at all? **As Charles Lawrence states:**

Racial insults are particularly undeserving of First Amendment protection because the perpetrators' intention is not to discover truth or initiate *not be protected.*

dialogue, but to injure the victim. . . . There can be no meaningful discussion of how we should recline our commitment to equality and commitment to free speech until it is acknowledged that there is real harm inflicted by racist speech and that the harm is far from trivial. (Lawrence, 394)

The Hypertext Version

The Hypertext version similarly highlights generic components of academic argument that students should understand in writing their own essays. Thus, the introduction appears as follows:

<u>**Opponents to the Political Correctness movement often make the case that any restriction on speech will be harmful to society because it is a violation of first amendment rights**</u>. They are *concerned* that any prescribed limitation on speech will ultimately lead to a restriction on thought, a movement in the direction of an Orwellian "Big Brother" society. However, what is frequently overlooked in these arguments is that <u>**speech can have powerful consequences on a society**</u>, both the power to heal and the power to tear apart. In the interest of creating a harmonious society, then, it is necessary that some restriction be placed on what people can and cannot say to one another, and <u>**if the PC movement can contribute to tolerance among diverse groups, it is likely to be beneficial to society**</u>.

Clicking on the underlined bolded areas enables students to access analytic commentary about their function within the text.

The Web and Genre Expectations

In developing the Web site, the Writing Center has incorporated insights from the recent reconceptualization of genre theory (Bazerman, Berkenkotter, Swales, Devitt) that views genre in terms of function rather than in terms of form and recognizes that text fulfills different functions within different disciplines. Although in the past, the word "genre," was associated with arbitrary notions of form and text classifications, in particular with describing the formal features of a literary work, current thinking about genre looks at these regularities in text form as representing "typical ways of engaging rhetorically with recurring situations" (Freedman and Medway 1994, 2), and suggests that similarities in textual form and feature derive from an effective response to situations that "writers encounter repeatedly. . . . Knowing the genre, therefore, means knowing such things as appropriate subject matter, level of detail, tone and approach, as well as the usual layout and organization" (Devitt 1993, 576). Because genres arise as a result of writers' responding in suitable ways to recurring rhetorical situations, the new concept of genre thus perceives generic conventions as deriving from suitability and appropriateness, both of which are extremely important for students to be aware of when they write in different disciplines. As Carol Berkenkotter and Thomas Huckin phrase it, "genres are the intellectual scaffolds on which community-based knowledge is constructed" (1995, 24).

To a great extent, this reconceptualized concept of genre builds on other theories of writing that have impacted the Writing Center, particularly those theories that emphasize the functionality of text and the role of context in determining text effectiveness. Genre theory is consistent with rhetorical approaches, which focus attention on context, audience, and occasion and which view writing as a way of responding to a specific reader (or readers) within a specific context on a specific occasion (Freeman and Medway 1994, 5). Genre theory is also compatible with social constructionist theory, which recognizes that the act of composing draws on previous interactions with others. As Carol Cooper and Michael Holzman point out, "asking students to write something based on their own ideas results in students writing what they have been told— by their parents, their peers, the media. Asking them to look into their souls results in their remembering conversations they have heard" (Cooper and Holzman 1989, ix). Genre theory is also consistent with speech act theory, which emphasizes the function of language as a way of acting in the world and the importance of context in creating meaning within specific communities.

In a WAC context, this focus on genre means encouraging dialogue about the generic features that characterize a particular discipline and generating discussion about the extent to which particular facets or features of and approaches to text, if any, can be utilized in a number of disciplines. For students, such an approach focuses on developing consciousness of what Janet Giltrow and Michele Valiquette refer to as "practical knowledge" (1994, 48)—that is, knowledge that "governs a writer's composing choices in a certain genre and maintains the genre's regularities over many instances" (48); this type of knowledge includes the disciplinary requirements of topic selection, purpose, audience, structure, support, style, and shared information. For faculty, such an approach aims to foster conscious or "discursive" knowledge (48)—that is, to facilitate faculty awareness of disciplinary expectations so that they can be made explicit to students.

THE EFFECTIVENESS OF MODELS AND THE EXPLICIT
TEACHING OF GENRE

The use of the Web to present models and analyses of suitable texts raises the ongoing debate concerning whether the explicit teaching of genre is necessary, desirable, or even possible and the extent to which writing skills from one venue can be transferred to another. In her article, "Show and Tell? The Role of Explicit Teaching in the Learning of New Genres," Aviva Freedman cautions against the explicit teaching of genre, using Krashen's distinction between acquisition and learning in second-language research to suggest that explicit teaching is not possible, since genre awareness is largely tacit and therefore can be learned only through membership in a discourse community (Freedman and Medway 1994). Freedman also notes that beyond broad generalizations, the rules governing the replication of text genres are too complex to be applied effectively and that any attempt to teach them explicitly can lead to meaningless memorization of formulae and rules.

Nevertheless, Freedman also acknowledges that at least some elements specifying genre expectations can be taught and, that in the case of novice writers, learning something about "the nature of genre as social action and of the role of genres in discourse communities can be useful " in raising consciousness. Moreover, she also points out in a note to this piece that "once we exempt explicit teaching of composing strategies such as brainstorming, revising, etc. . . most explicit teaching in the writing class is, in fact, genre based, and derived from recurring features of form and context, and focused on textual regularities and (or) underlying rules that tie form and substance to context" (248).

Arguing against Freedman's injunctions against the explicit teaching of genre, Joseph Williams and Gregory Colomb maintain that "explicit teaching is a necessary step in the process of empowering students to choose how they participate in the communities they encounter" (1993, 262) and that if teachers "avoid explicitly focusing their students' attention on the forms they are learning, they will ultimately hide from students—worse, from themselves—the ideological commitments and consequences of particular generic forms" (262). In this context, the models and textual analyses on the Writing Center Web site aim to focus student and faculty attention on genre expectations of which they may have been unaware, and more importantly to generate reflection and discussion about the topic. To use a metaphor noted by Richard Coe, genre analysis enables us to think of text structure the way archaeologists think in terms of artifacts—that is, to try to infer functions, and to resurrect the strategies implicit in the structure in order to relate them to the context of the situation. Form then can be perceived as "fossilized rhetorical processes" (Coe 1994, 160).

EXTENDING GENRE AWARENESS IN A WAC CONTEXT: THE WEB AS CATALYST AND FOCAL POINT

This approach of using model argumentative essays on the Web, accompanied by analyses of their conceptual and textual components, is intended for extension to other disciplines involved in the University of Southern California's undergraduate curriculum, those included in the category "Social Issues" as well as those in "Literature, Thought, and the Arts." The current plan is to develop a new Web site to which faculty from a variety of disciplines will contribute, the goal being to raise faculty consciousness about their own expectations for student writing and to stimulate dialogue about what it means to write in a particular discipline. As Berkenkotter and Huckin suggest, "Writing Across the Curriculum programs should try to sensitize faculty in the disciplines to the fact that, in contrast to the specialized rhetorics they routinely use in their professional writing, the genres of the undergraduate curricula are characterized by quite different textual features and conventions, given their classroom-based contexts and rhetorical functions" (1995, 13). In this context, it is expected that the Web will serve as a catalyst and focal point for interdisciplinary discussions crucial to the success of the new undergraduate program. Certainly, it will generate many meetings.

ADDITIONAL WRITING CENTER OUTREACH

The Web enables the Writing Center to reach out to faculty in a number of disciplines—the "Mountain to Mohammed" metaphor. But the Writing Center is also reaching out in other ways. Because consultants in the Writing Center are graduate students from a variety of departments, it is relatively easy for them to initiate and maintain ongoing dialogue with their home departments concerning the teaching of writing and the expectations of writing in a particular discipline. Such discussions foster a collaborative partnership between consultants and department faculty, enabling everyone involved to become both teachers and learners, and thereby preventing the Writing Center from assuming a "missionary" role of bringing the "word" to the unenlightened. Interdisciplinary consultants thus serve as a bridge between the Writing Center and faculty members teaching in the new program and foster productive relationships between various facets of the new program.

In addition to their role in fostering interdisciplinary interaction, consultants from different disciplines' departments are particularly well-equipped to tutor students working on papers in those disciplines and to develop workshops concerning genre expectations for papers written in particular disciplines. Bearing titles such as "How to Write a History Paper," "How to Write Essays about Literature," and "How to Write a Paper in Political Science," these workshops have immediate credibility with both students and faculty because they are created and conducted by graduate students who are actual participants in those disciplinary communities.

Writing Across the Curriculum Programs involve border crossings, which always entail the creation of new communities built on new relationships. The Writing Center constitutes a natural means of forging such relationships, and the use of the Web site to foster interdisciplinary dialogue, process pedagogy, and genre awareness enables the Writing Center to extend its influence beyond the confines of a physical location.

WORKS CITED

Anson, Chris M. "Toward a Multidimensional Model of Writing in the Academic Disciplines." *Writing in Academic Disciplines*, ed. David A. Jolliffe. Norwood, MA: Ablex, 1988. 1-33.

Barton, Ellen. "Evidentials, Argumentation, and Epistemological Stance." *College English* 55 (1993): 745–769.

Bazerman, Charles. *Shaping Written Knowledge: The Genre and Activity of the Experimental Article in Science*. Madison: University of Wisconsin Press, 1988.

Berkenkotter, Carol, and Thomas N. Huckin. *Genre Knowledge in Disciplinary Communication*. Hillsdale, NJ: Lawrence Erlbaum, 1995.

Coe, Richard M. "Teaching Genre as Process." *Learning and Teaching Genre,* eds. Aviva Freedman and Peter Medway. Portsmouth, NH: Boynton/Cook, 1994. 157–169.

Cooper, Marilyn, and Michael Holzman. *Writing as Social Action*. Portsmouth, NH: Boynton/Cook, 1989.

Devitt, Amy J. "Generalizing about Genre: New Conceptions of an Old Concept." *College Composition and Communication* 44 (1993): 573–586.

Freedman, Aviva, and Peter Medway, eds. *Learning and Teaching Genre*. Portsmouth, NH: Boynton/Cook, 1994.

Fulwiler, Toby, and Art Young. "Afterward: The Enemies of Writing Across the Curriculum." *Programs That Work: Models and Methods for Writing Across the Curriculum*, eds. Fulwiler, Toby and Art Young. Portsmouth, NH: Boynton/Cook, 1990. 287–294.

Gill, Judy. "Another Look at WAC and the Writing Center." *Writing Center Journal* 16.2 (1996): 164–178.

Giltrow, Janet, and Michele Valiquette. "Genres and Knowledge: Students Writing in the Disciplines." *Learning and Teaching Genre,* eds. Aviva Freedman and Peter Medway. Portsmouth, NH: Boynton/Cook, 1994. 47–62.

MacDonald, Susan Peck. "Problem Definition in Academic Writing." *College English* 49 (1987): 315–331.

Nelson, John, Allan Megill, and Donald McCloskey. "Rhetoric of Inquiry." *The Rhetoric of the Human Sciences: Language and Argument in Scholarship and Public Affairs*, eds. John Nelson, Allan Megill, and Donald McCloskey. Madison: University of Wisconsin Press, 1987. 3–18.

Rose, Mike. "The Language of Exclusion: Writing Instruction at the University." *College English* 47 (1985): 341–359.

Swales, John. *Genre Analysis*. Cambridge, MA: Cambridge University Press, 1990.

Waldo, Mark L. "The Last Best Place for Writing Across the Curriculum: The Writing Center." *WPA: Writing Program Administration* 16.3 (1993): 15–26.

Williams, Joseph, and Gregory G. Colomb. "The Case for Explicit Teaching: Why What You Don't Know Won't Help You." *Research in the Teaching of English* 27 (1993): 252–264.

Writing Centers/WAC in Pharmacy Education: A Changing Prescription

Eric Hobson and Neal Lerner

FUNDAMENTAL CHANGES IN AMERICAN HEALTH CARE

As a practice and an industry, American health care is experiencing its greatest period of change to date (Pew Commission 1995; Commission to Implement Change 1993). This observation should not be a surprise to anyone who has lived through the past decade. Although most academicians may not perceive that they have been directly affected by such macro/industry-wide events as hospital closings and consolidations, reductions in nursing and other support staff, or the introduction of strict capitation fees for most medical services, they have probably noticed the micro/local changes that have been wrought on how they receive their personal health care. Chances are they no longer enjoy the choice of providers or the flexibility in types and frequency of services once part of their health insurance package. These changes reflect fundamental shifts in the philosophy and practices driving American health care as it moves from largely autonomous specialized-care practices to a system based squarely on managed primary care. One aspect of this shift involves moving away from a reactive stance based on remediative care to a more proactive stance based on preventive care and demonstrable gains in patient outcomes (Pew Health Professions Commission 1995). Likewise, these shifts reflect an across-the-board move to a more intensely managed system of health care delivery with increasingly stiff competition for and close scrutiny of every health care dollar (Schafermeyer 1997).

As the delivery of health care changes in this country, so too do the roles of all health care providers. Responding to the effects that these changes have had on the pharmacy profession, the American Association of Colleges of Pharmacy (AACP) adopted sweeping curricular reforms in 1994 intended to prepare pharmacy practitioners to work in emerging and evolving practice situations. These developments have been enacted within the practice model of

"pharmaceutical care" (Hepler and Strand 1990), a model of health care pro-
vider/patient interaction that emphasizes pharmacists' active roles in recom-
mending, monitoring, and assuming more responsibility for all aspects of patients' drug therapies (Maddux et al. 1996). These disciplinary and professional
changes challenge fundamental and traditional curricular assumptions about
what information pharmacy students should learn and how best to enable that
learning (Commission to Implement Change). It is this set of complex concerns
and the daunting challenges that accompany them that offer opportunities to
academicians working in Writing Centers and Writing Across the Curriculum
(WAC) Programs.

    In this chapter, we focus on changes underway in pharmacy education,
changes in curricular structures, course content, delivery, and support services
that offer myriad opportunities for Writing Center and WAC colleagues. To
illustrate these changes and the opportunities that result from them, we recount
the process of educational revision underway in colleges of pharmacy generally,
then shift our attention to describe this change within the particular contexts of
the St. Louis College of Pharmacy (StLCOP) and Massachusetts College of
Pharmacy and Allied Health Sciences (MCP), institutions with which we have
worked to establish Writing Centers and WAC Programs as central components
in these school's curricular reform process. Finally, we provide suggestions and
advice for colleagues to consider in approaching and working with pharmacy
faculty and pharmacy curricula.

CATALYSTS FOR CHANGE IN PHARMACY EDUCATION

    Recent across-the-board developments (economic, managerial, techni-
cal, etc.) in the American health care industry have led to predictions that the
profession of pharmacy will not survive as a recognizable profession/industry if
it remains entrenched in a traditional, passive, drug-dispensing role (Pew Commission). Given such forecasts, AACP believes that if the profession is to survive as a meaningful contributor to the health care enterprise, pharmacy educators would be remiss to encourage passivity about knowledge and learning
among pharmacists in training. Put bluntly, because the profession is changing,
pharmacy education must change now. That change is not easy to accomplish,
however, for a number of reasons: a particularly perplexing issue, for instance,
resides in the mix of inaccurate, even naive, expectations about the nature of the
profession and the narrowly defined critical and communication abilities students bring to pharmacy school. The members of AACP's Commission to Implement Change in Pharmaceutical Education who authored the influential position paper, "Background Paper II: Entry-Level, Curricular Outcomes, Curricular
Content and Educational Process," note:

Most students enter health professional schools, including pharmacy schools, as depend-
ant learners; that is, they enter with the perception that it is the teachers' (sic) responsibility to teach students while deemphasizing, if not ignoring, the responsibility of stu-

dents to learn on their own. Students come to health professional schools adept at memo-
rizing facts, and the teaching methods at most professional schools readily focus on this
ability. In practice, the practitioner must rely on his or her ability to interpret data in
order to reach conclusions and solve problems. (1993, 19)

    To bridge this gap between teaching methods/expectations and practi-
tioner abilities, colleges of pharmacy are increasingly stressing the practitioner
model of "pharmaceutical care" as an essential guide in creating educational
outcomes. Underlying the concept of pharmaceutical care is the implicit assumption that all pharmacy practitioners are highly skilled diagnosticians, intermediaries, educators, as well as compendious data centers. And these precon-
ceptions hold true when assessed, using experienced pharmacy practitioners as
benchmarks; after all, twenty-to-thirty years of professional experience tends to
be a powerful form of continuing education. To a great extent, however, the
high level of critical and professional expertise expected of experienced clinical
and retail pharmacists extends (if unfairly) to entry-level pharmacists in these
areas of practice, even to those pharmacists on the first day of their first job after
they receive their pharmacy license. This scenario is especially true for pharmacists entering clinical practices where they are more likely than their colleagues
in retail pharmacy to be directly involved in collaborative decision-making and
planning with a team of health care providers (Pew Commission; Commission
to Implement Change; Maddux et al.). Even admitting the vast differences between practice sites, from day one of their professional practice, pharmacists are
expected to be professionals who are not only capable of, but inclined to independent learning and action. For that faith to be justified, however, pharmacy
educators must recast their teaching to enable students to rapidly develop
higher-order critical and decision-making skills, as well as the mature communication skills needed to put their extensive pharmaceutical and therapeutic
content bases into beneficial action (Commission to Implement Change).

RESPONDING TO CALLS FOR CHANGE

    Both the St. Louis College of Pharmacy's Writing Across the Curricu-
lum and the Massachusetts College of Pharmacy's Writing Center programs
were formed in direct response to the calls for curricular change as outlined in
AACP's "Background Paper II: Entry-Level, Curricular Outcomes, Curricular
Content and Educational Process." The charges contained in this document call
for, among other things, more classroom emphasis on communication and interpersonal skills—particularly critical thinking and writing skills—and more explicit descriptions of the collaborative interactions and interdependencies which
exist among health care providers. Beyond merely advocating giving more overt
attention to these skills within the pharmacy curriculum, AACP outlined the
need for these efforts to take place across the pharmacy curriculum so that students encounter instruction in these areas repeatedly and in a variety of disciplinary contexts. Throughout AACP's statement runs a strong advocacy of learn-

ing as a process-based activity taking place in academic and nonacademic settings. The commission argues repeatedly that this educational goal is probably best facilitated by instructional methods other than formal lectures and traditional didactic sessions. For instance, the authors note that:

A number of outcomes cannot be taught by discrete courses; many are inculcated into students across the curriculum through a variety of techniques. Professional pharmacy students must learn in school in the same manner in which they will learn throughout their careers; they will learn by solving patients' drug-related problems; they will learn facts as necessary for them to understand processes; and they will integrate material with information already known. (1993, 19)

That communication skills are paramount in all pharmacy practice sites is a claim that provokes little argument. And pharmacy educators have spent much time and energy helping students learn much needed face-to-face interpersonal skills. Given the economic realities the pharmacy professional faces in the near future, however, these skills will serve as only one of many needed communication skills. Pharmacists will increasingly communicate with a larger number of players in the health care system, expanding out from their traditional interaction with primary care givers to work closely with a broad spectrum of care givers and family members. In meeting the demand of creating positive patient outcomes, such interaction will involve a great deal of written communication via forms, letters, and electronic messaging and conferencing. The question that results from this picture is: Are pharmacy students prepared to write with the levels of skill and rhetorical sophistication they need to be able to work effectively in this environment?

Because writing is an extremely complicated process, one that is never mastered, the reductive answer is no. That outlook, however, is shortsighted and is one that pharmacy-practice faculty across the country are attempting to recast through their course structures and interactions with students. Instead of uncritically accepting the myopic view that pharmacy students are by definition somehow deficient as writers, pharmacy faculty with greater frequency are coming to realize that written communication is complex, requiring more than a strong vocabulary and an internalization of conventions of grammar and usage (Holiday-Goodman and Lively 1992; Hobson and Schafermeyer 1994; Maddux et al. 1996). Effective writers are aware that they continually grapple with issues related to the specific task, including audience, context, and purpose. For students to develop the levels of communicative maturity needed to allow them to function successfully, they must become confident in their abilities to write to achieve specific outcomes. That process, however, is neither easy nor quick.

As such, students need overt guidance about the many varied types of writing they will encounter as practicing pharmacy professionals. Additionally, they need frequent opportunities to practice producing these types of documents and to receive careful and meaningful feedback about their efforts. As with any athletic or artistic skill, practice and feedback are needed to develop increased agility.

SOME CONTEXTUAL, LOCAL HISTORY

The Writing Center and WAC Programs described in the following sections are both recent developments in their institution's histories. In fact, each institution's unique history is the major reason for their ability to develop the Writing Center-based WAC initiatives they have undertaken. StLCOP and MCP are two of five "free standing" AACP member colleges of pharmacy. Unlike the majority of pharmacy programs, these two schools are not part of a comprehensive private or state university from which students enter the pharmacy program after completing two years of traditional undergraduate work, during which they fulfill general program requirements in the humanities, social and basic sciences (these programs are generally referred to as "2-4 programs"). StLCOP and MCP have, from their founding, been self-contained private programs (commonly referred to as "0-6 programs"), offering their students the entire range of coursework necessary for the Bachelor of Science in Pharmacy or advanced degrees such as the terminal Doctor of Pharmacy (Pharm. D.) or Ph.D. programs in pharmaceutical sciences or pharmaceutical administrative sciences. Given this history, StLCOP and MCP resemble small four-year colleges more so than do most of their peer programs that function as departments/colleges within larger institutions. And, because both schools are relatively small and private, they are able to enact change much more rapidly and creatively than other programs constrained by federal and state funding, university curricular policy and program revision procedures, inter-unit scrambling for budgets, space, and services, and by boards of directors charged with oversight of sprawling, multimajor universities.

The upshot of these schools' independent, self-contained status, is that they can react more quickly and creatively than their peers to the recommendations for change put forth by AACP and others, such as the Pew Commission. What they have accomplished in the years since AACP first told its membership that change was more than just a suggestion—educational and curricular change is now codified by current accreditation guidelines—outpaces, to a great extent, the activity underway in the other seventy-eight colleges of pharmacy. The unique opportunity that StLCOP and MCP have enjoyed due to their free-standing status must be kept in mind, however, when one considers attempting to replicate the broad pattern and particulars of these two programs in colleges of pharmacy with fundamentally different institutional contexts.

STLCOP: A WRITING CENTER-BASED, WRITING ACROSS THE CURRICULUM PROGRAM

In an attempt to meet the communication goals outlined in AACP-endorsed calls for change and reflected in the college's educational outcomes adopted in 1994, especially in the area of written communication abilities, StLCOP decided that a coordinated cross-curricular effort involving the majority of courses in the college curriculum offered the greatest chance for longitudinal success, both in terms of student ability growth and program endurance. While other colleges of pharmacy had experimented with both writing-to-learn and writing- emphasis approaches in the classroom, often with the assistance of their university's Writing Center (Holiday-Goodman and Lively 1992), none had instituted an internal and consistent joining of both goals across the entire breadth of their students' educational experience. To lead this effort, the school hired an experienced educator with extensive training and experience in writing theory and writing program development to accomplish the following:

- shape the initial plans for a Writing Across the Curriculum Program housed in a Writing Center,
- train faculty to integrate writing into their courses and to support them in their efforts,
- collaborate with faculty to develop writing emphasis courses, and
- design, establish, and administer a Writing Center to act as the focus point for these activities.

The resulting WAC Program provides students with coordinated and ongoing writing instruction at every level of their education from first-year courses, including a first-year composition sequence, through every year of the students' highly demanding curricular experience, and extending even to their mandatory clinical rotations. This program incorporates three main components: a cross-curricular commitment to the concept of writing-to-learn and learning-to-write; specific Writing Emphasis courses; and the StLCOP Writing Center. In an attempt to strengthen students' critical thinking skills, self-learning strategies, and overall communicative agility, StLCOP's faculty continues to explore ways to incorporate writing-to-learn strategies in most courses within the required and elective curriculum. Additionally, formal writing instruction is a major focus in the first two years of the curriculum, most notably in the first-year composition sequence and the second-year Cultural Heritage sequence. Finally, students must also complete a two-course "writing emphasis" graduation requirement (one course a Professional Pharmacy Elective, one a General Elective).

WAC, as conceived of and implemented at StLCOP, rests on two interrelated principles: one cognitive, one persuasive. The cognitive layer echoes such composition theorists as Janet Emig in assuming that writing is more than just one way of demonstrating what one has learned. Rather, the complex cognitive processes that converge when we write create multiple opportunities for information to be recast in unique ways. The result, more often than not, is new knowledge. Therefore, when carefully linked to course goals, structure, and disciplinary content, writing can be a highly powerful mode of learning, hence its most common label "Writing to Learn." The rhetorical layer, which builds on and uses many strategies associated with writing-to-learn, focuses on using more formal assignments to teach writing as professional initiation, as a tool by which students can successfully enter into and master the social processes and discourse conventions which define and maintain a professional/academic community. Writing Emphasis courses provide one site on which these two tenets blend most obviously within the context of pharmacy.

The Writing Emphasis course is one model often employed to promote the development and maturation of students' higher-order thinking skills, which in turn enables them to better master course content. By having students actively engage course content through writing, Writing Emphasis courses involve students in coming to understand the information created by a discipline and the means through which that information is created, evaluated, and disseminated. Such a perspective is important to the training of future pharmacists for several reasons: Increasingly pharmacist/patient and pharmacist/caregiver interactions involve the pharmacist taking the role as bridge between divergent disciplinary specialties and audiences and as a watchdog in the process of prescribing and monitoring drug therapy. Roles such as these require pharmacists to analyze therapeutic and rhetorical problems, synthesize appropriate information and responses, and make effective evaluations to all participating stakeholders in the process. Writing Emphasis courses introduce students to thinking from within a profession where the body of knowledge that defines a professional community is understood to be dynamic and, thus, must be approached actively.

StLCOP currently offers twenty Writing Emphasis courses from which students can meet their two-course writing-emphasis graduation requirement (see Figure 1). These courses, and four other courses that are not currently offered due to changes in faculty expertise, have been developed through the collaboration of the Writing Center director, course masters, and the members of the college's Curriculum Committee. Other courses will be developed to meet an expanding need for WE courses as more students enter the six-year Pharm. D. curriculum as the five-year Bachelor of Science program is phased out. Although most of these efforts are less than five years old, they have had several marked effects, of which the following are representative:

- Exam structures within the Division of Pharmacy Practice have changed extensively: all recall-based questions had been replaced by higher-order questions that require written responses at varying degrees of complexity.
- New courses have been proposed and existing courses modified to intersect with these curricular efforts.
- Students are complaining about the "injustice" of having to study within a new paradigm (faculty consider this type of response a partial indicator of the program's vitality).

Figure 1
Current Writing Emphasis Course Offerings

St. Louis College of Pharmacy Writing Emphasis Courses

General Electives	Professional Electives
International Politics	Topics in Therapeutics: Primary Care
Science and the Media	Current Topics: Geriatrics/Neurology/Psychiatry
History of the Cold War	Introduction to Pharmacy Entrepreneurship
Psychology of Personality	Current Topics in Infectious Diseases
Abnormal Psychology	Topics in Pharmaceutical Care:
Shakespeare	Community Service
Social Psychology	Scientific Literature Evaluation
World Religions: African, Asian,	Geriatric Pharmacy
Native American	Introductory Clinical Clerkship
Culture Studies: Japan	Leadership: Coaching and Counseling
Basic Problems in Philosophy	Biomedical Ethics

Additionally, so far, thirty-eight students have been trained to serve as writing consultants in the Writing Center to help facilitate the development of a more collaborative approach to learning within the student culture, as well as to provide one-to-one assistance and support with regard to students' writing tasks. Overall the StLCOP WAC Program now performs many local and national functions:

- Models similar curricular change for other colleges of pharmacy.
- Educates pharmacy faculty about the theory and pedagogy needed to incorporate writing as a central learning tool within an extremely traditional curriculum and profession.
- Assists in the development of "Writing Emphasis" courses across the curriculum.
- Assists in the ongoing development and integration of writing activities within established courses.
- Participates in ongoing efforts to develop an outcomes assessment model based on ability for the school.

MCP: A WRITING CENTER'S INFANCY

Compared to StLCOP's efforts, current WAC/Writing Center initiatives at the Massachusetts College of Pharmacy and Allied Health Science (MCP) are just beginning: with the 1997–1998 academic year, the Writing Center began its second year of operation; the formal administrative position of Writing Programs Coordinator was created in the summer of 1997 to provide leadership; and a formal WAC initiative is an expected outcome of this post's creation.

Prior to the establishment of the Writing Center, one of the more visible mechanisms developed to address students' writing-related needs has been a Writing Proficiency Exam (WPE). According to George Humphrey, vice-president for Strategic Planning, this exam grew out of faculty frustration with students' writing skills. In particular, in the mid-1980s the college began attracting large numbers of transfer students—many of whom were non-native English speakers—into the middle years of the curriculum, and the number of first-year students dropped dramatically. Because of these new students' diverse experiences with composition, the WPE was instituted to ensure a minimum level of competency in writing, as well as to communicate to the faculty that "writing is an important activity to the college and to the profession" (Humphrey 1997).[1]

As writing-related initiatives move from primarily concern with competency testing to a focus on providing increased opportunities for class-based writing activities and outside-of-class support, the college's most recent Mission Statement provides an important foundation. This document, which was greatly influenced by the previously mentioned "Background Paper II," establishes several core values or goals for the college that invite the use of writing in all aspects of the curriculum. These goals include: 1) "innovative teaching which fosters student-centered learning," and 2) "integration of the liberal arts and basic sciences with professional studies." The statement notes that "the College reaches these goals by providing a state-of-the-art learning environment which facilitates critical thinking and problem-solving skills, research and scholarly inquiry." To fulfill this mission, the college's strategic plan states that "active learning will be fostered by innovative and creative teaching methods," and that "the College will graduate multidisciplinary, team-oriented practitioners who will be in high demand by health-care institutions seeking professionals with well-developed clinical, *communication, thinking*, technological and life-long learning skills" (emphasis added).

In many ways, this strategic plan can be read as a manifesto for using writing as a means of learning throughout the curriculum at Massachusetts College of Pharmacy (MCP). As indicated by the college's goals, writing can be essential to ensure "active" and "student-centered learning," "innovative and creative teaching," and the development of students' "communication," "critical thinking and problem-solving skills." The creation of the Writing Center in the fall of 1996 was an important step along the path to realizing writing's full potential as a centerpiece of a tightly constructed, closely assessed professional curriculum. An additional step in this process is that starting with the fall 1997 semester, the positions of Coordinators of the Writing Center, the Writing Proficiency Exam, and the First-Year Composition Program were combined into one role, Writing Programs Coordinator. Assigning these tasks to the current Writing Center Coordinator allows MCP to focus its WAC/Writing Center initiatives, presenting a coherent and responsive program to the entire college.

YEAR ONE: GETTING STARTED, ASSESSING NEEDS

In terms of its first year, Writing Center activity was primarily focused on outreach, establishing a toe hold in the institution, while attending to its originally articulated role of supporting the first-year composition program and providing tutorial assistance to ESL students. These efforts included publicizing Writing Center services through faculty memos, class orientations, bookmarks, semesterly newsletters, posters, flyers, and a World Wide Web page (http://www.mcp.edu/as/wc/wc.html). Comprehensive assessment was also essential to convince the administration of the Writing Center's efficacy. These efforts included many Writing Center standards: recording of student visits and presenting summaries of these records to the administration; surveying first-year students as to their satisfaction with Writing Center services; reporting to the Director of the Division of Arts and Sciences and the Academic Council (made up of division heads and the Provost) via a Fall Activities Report and an annual report. One of the more convincing pieces of data was a study comparing the first-year English grades of students who visited the Writing Center with the grades of those who did not (Lerner 1997). Results showed that students with the lowest SAT verbal scores—all of whom were ESL—benefited the most from coming to the Writing Center as compared to their cohorts who did not work with a tutor.

Other efforts in the first year were directed towards a decidedly WAC function—investigating the role of writing at MCP, particularly in the pharmacy-related curriculum. As part of this fact finding, during the spring 1997 semester, faculty across each division of MCP (Arts and Sciences, Pharmacy Practice, Pharmaceutical Sciences, Nursing, Allied Health Sciences) were surveyed about the uses of writing in their courses[2] (for the survey itself, see the Appendix to this chapter).

The intent of this survey was twofold: (1) to gain an understanding of the types of and purposes for assigned writing tasks and (2) to give faculty an opportunity to reflect upon the kinds of writing they assign and why. In terms of the purposes faculty identified for assigning writing, Table 1 shows that the most frequent purpose across the major divisions was to improve students' critical thinking/problem-solving skills, an explicit goal of the college's Mission Statement. The purpose of assessing students' content knowledge—perhaps the most traditional goal for assigning writing—was also cited frequently across divisions. It is interesting to note that the write-to-learn goals of providing aids to mastering content and for reading comprehension were most frequently cited in the Division of Arts and Sciences and much less so in the pharmacy-related divisions. This finding indicates a direction for future faculty consultations and workshops.

Faculty responses to the types of writing assigned in their classes show some interesting differences between divisions (see Table 2 for the most frequently cited responses). While the common analytical papers and in-class essay exams were frequently cited across divisions, a few tasks in the Division

Table 1
MCP Faculty Purposes for Assigning Writing—by Division

Purpose	Pharmaceutical Sciences (% of 8 total)	Pharmacy Practice (% of 9 total)	Arts & Sciences (% of 11 total)
Improve students' critical thinking/ Problem-solving skills	88%	100%	100%
Assess students' knowledge of content	88%	44%	73%
Improve students' creative thinking	75%	33%	73%
Provide an aid to mastering content	50%	44%	91%
Provide an opportunity for self expression	13%	33%	55%
Provide an aid for reading comprehension	0%	11%	64%

Pharmacy Practice stand out as representative of the kind of real-world writing students will need to do as professionals (e.g., drug information literature, drug consultations, and correspondence to care-givers). Also, the use of case study analysis is apparent in these results as this teaching method in the pharmacy-focused divisions has achieved widespread acceptance.

An additional purpose of the survey was to discover if differences exist in the criteria faculty in each division use to assess writing. As Table 3 shows, the greatest differences occur in the Pharmacy Practice faculty's perceived importance of appropriate format and an awareness of a reader's needs, not surprising considering again the real-world nature of the kinds of writing these faculty are assigning. While one might expect correct mechanics to be highly held by many faculty members—under the belief that correct writing is good writing—this assumption was not displayed in the survey responses. In fact, the Arts and Sciences faculty attached the greatest important to correct mechanics in assessing writing.

Table 2
MCP Faculty Types of Writing Tasks Assigned—by Division

Writing Task	Pharmaceutical Sciences (% of 8 total)	Pharmacy Practice (% of 9 total)	Arts & Sciences (% of 11 total)
Analytical papers	75%	56%	82%
In-class essay exams & quizzes	63%	22%	82%
Case-study analysis	63%	67%	18%
Debate outlines or reports	50%	0%	18%
Responses to reading	38%	11%	82%
Drug information literature	13%	89%	0%
Drug consultations	0%	89%	0%
Correspondence to care givers	0%	56%	0%

Table 3
MCP Faculty Ranking of Writing Assessment Criteria—by Division

Assessment Criteria (1 = extremely important; 4 = not important)	Pharmaceutical Sciences (avg. of 8 total)	Pharmacy Practice (avg. of 9 total)	Arts & Sciences (avg. of 11 total)
Accurate content	1.3	1.2	1.1
Logical structure/ organization	1.5	1.1	1.2
Concise & clear wording	1.5	1.1	1.4
Clarity of purpose	1.8	1.0	1.3
Correct mechanics	2.1	2.7	1.8
Appropriate format	2.4	1.3	1.8
Awareness of readers' needs	2.5	1.3	1.6
Unique style/strength of voice	2.6	2.7	2.5

Finally, one survey result that indicates a direction for faculty workshops is the most frequent response to the question, "What reasons prevent you from requiring writing in your course?" The response was: "Assessment is too time consuming," which is identical to that found by Hobson and Schafermeyer.

YEAR TWO: EXPANDING SERVICES, DEVELOPING FACULTY AND COURSES

As a result of this survey and the continuing integration of writing and the Writing Center into the curriculum of MCP, the following activities are planned for the upcoming academic year:

- Faculty workshops on writing assessment and assignment creation.
- Student workshops on using sources/paraphrasing/plagiarism and résumé/cover letter writing. These have been conducted during summer orientation for all fifth-year students undertaking a required clinical internship and will be repeated in the fall.
- One-to-one and small-group instruction of Division of Allied Health for students writing senior theses. These students will be taking a three-credit course in which instruction is supplied by Writing Center staff and supervision is coordinated between the Writing Center and students' divisional advisors.
- One-to-one instruction for graduate students writing dissertations and dissertation proposals. These consultations will initially be required by the students' graduate advisors.
- Writing Center administration and student preparation for the Writing Proficiency Exam. These activities will include publicizing the exam itself and the support the Writing Center can provide in preparing students for the exam, and running faculty practice-exam scoring sessions across divisions. The latter activity will allow the Writing Center to play a role in helping all faculty articulate their goals and criteria for writing and examining how best to communicate that information to students.
- The introduction of computer terminals in the Writing Center to allow an additional space for students to write using word-processing software and the potential for an online Writing Center to reach the majority of students who live off-campus.

Some less formal activities will include housing a book exchange area, where any member of the MCP community can contribute and borrow paperback books; and creating a writing group of interested faculty members, which can meet regularly to share work-in-progress for feedback and support. Overall, these initiatives are intended to communicate clearly that the Writing Center can truly be the center for writing-related activities at MCP.

AN ASSESSMENT

As the MCP Writing Center attempts to take on these challenges, its own institutional history provides an important reference point. The first mention of writing tutoring at MCP comes in the catalogue for the academic year 1975–1976, which describes a Learning Skills Center designed to help students who are having difficulty in reading, writing, or studying. Tutorial help, essentially on a one-to-one basis, is provided three days a week" (8). Moving from a model restricted to skills development to one focused on understanding and improving the curriculum and pedagogy of the college is an important Writing Center goal. Whether it is working with faculty on assignment creation or assessment, helping students to more successfully face their writing tasks, or contributing to the college's overall goals for student learning, the Writing Center can play an important role in ensuring that the college's graduates are well prepared to face the emerging challenges of a career in pharmacy. While the college's history shows varied attention to the importance of writing, the future will hopefully see writing as central to the education of all students at MCP.

OPPORTUNITES FOR WRITING CENTERS AND WAC HEALTH-CARE EDUCATION

StLCOP's and MCP's experiences with WAC/Writing Center initiatives dictate several key features to be attended to if future WAC initiatives are going to be successful and lasting. These features also provide important guidelines for other WAC Programs and Writing Centers hoping to make inroads with heath-care related or other professional programs on their campuses:

1. *WAC must be a grass-roots effort.* Top-down proclamations—whether from the highest administrator or the division director—will rarely succeed. At MCP, the administration has issued such proclamations that writing will be required in every course, but such top-down initiatives often lacked the support or means to be taken seriously (Humphrey 1997). While grass-roots thinking might seem common knowledge to most WAC/Writing Center practitioners, used to marshaling support though direct appeals to students and faculty members, it is worth reiterating. Funding sources for WAC efforts, if they are to be substantial and long-lasting, will necessarily come from influential administrators. However, if writing is to permeate the curriculum, conversations about curricular goals and standards, methods to achieve these goals, and sources of information to broaden those methods, will necessarily be institutionally specific *and* institution-wide.

2. *The Writing Center can lead this grass-roots effort by helping faculty examine the current role that writing and language plays in their intellectual and professional lives.* As we have noted, the size and scope of StLCOP and MCP can lend themselves to rapid implementation and curricular change. Nevertheless, we believe that WAC/Writing Center professionals in other institutions can effect change. Using their developed ethnographic skills—their abilities to help writers/reader/cultural members to have insight into their texts/cultures—Writing Center/WAC colleagues can begin conversations about the existing importance of writing/literacy in professional contexts.

3. *Once faculty are aware of the importance of writing in the intellectual life of their disciplines, we can begin to talk about the ways they can use writing in their courses to inculcate students into this disciplinary conversation.* These uses can include teaching written disciplinary conventions, utilizing writing as a means of assessing content knowledge, and capitalizing on the writing-to-learn potential of a variety of classroom activities.

4. *WAC's attractiveness to a professional curriculum lies in its efficiency.* Writing is a uniquely powerful education tool. It is one of the most flexible and broadly applicable teaching and learning tools in the active-learning toolbox and serves as a foundation for efforts to incorporate increased attention to critical thinking across the curriculum. All of these pedagogical issues are ones that professional programs face, often at the behest of such accreditation agencies as AACP; therefore, WAC offers teachers in professional programs a three-for-one bargain.

ISSUES FOR CONSIDERATION

Before attempting to collaborate with pharmacy and health-care-related faculty to integrate writing as a meaningful part of the professional curriculum, WAC/Writing Center personnel must educate themselves about disciplines and cultural contexts markedly different from their institutional homes, usually in the humanities. Although this type of warning is common in the WAC literature when discussing effective ways to work with faculty in such areas of the curriculum as the sciences, the disciplines that make up the health care community can be quite alien, and that unfamiliar terrain presents potential hurdles for WAC/Writing Center efforts despite the best intentions of everyone involved. As we have repeatedly discovered in our work with pharmacy and other health care faculty and non-faculty practitioners, it is easy to erroneously assume that, as when working with many educators in the Arts and Sciences, we can safely find such meeting points as a common lexicon and definition base, commensurate epistemological vantage points, and shared experience as educators working with undergraduate students in a general, preparatory curriculum. That desire is rarely met.

Our experience suggests that, as in many other areas of life, patience is a virtue when working with members of the medical education community. Because we, like the majority of our WAC/Writing Center colleagues, came to our collaboration with pharmacy educators out of the humanities, we chose to keep many of our great ideas about writing in check for an extended period—we kept our mouths shut—and opted instead to spend a great deal of time getting to know the pharmacy community from the inside. Although this approach may mean forestalling the introduction of many classroom initiatives, we highly recommend that, like ethnographers in the field, WAC/Writing Center practitioners take time to learn the many varieties of professional practice represented by a field such as pharmacy (e.g., retail pharmacy, mail order pharmacy, compounding pharmacy, nuclear pharmacy, clinical pharmacy, regulatory activities, etc.) because each of these represents different communities in and of themselves, with their own values, mores, and biases, and their own texts. For example, a text unique to clinical setting is the patient chart. This document is as rhetorically complex as any we know, posing a number of challenges to its author: in addition to the fact that pharmacy students receive little systematic training in how to effectively write in the medical record (Prosser, Burke, and Hobson 1997), the chart note in a mental health record may have over fifteen discrete audiences, many not involved in patient care (Reynolds 1995), and it serves therapeutic as well as legal purposes (Reynolds, Mair, and Fischer 1995). To gain this insight into what at first seemed a simple clerical task, we had to spend many days shadowing clinical pharmacists at their practice sites, talk to them about what they choose to record and the conventions they employ in that act of recording, consider who might read the contained information and how they might use that information, recognize the hierarchies among readers of the chart, and realize how little attention is given to formal instruction into how to carry out this everyday task.

Not only do everyday writing tasks offer complex rhetorical and disciplinary engagements, but the three traditional communities that make up most pharmacy programs—pharmaceutical sciences, pharmacy management and administration, clinical pharmacy—present unique challenges to any WAC initiative because they represent vastly divergent audiences. With their grounding in the hard sciences, faculty in the pharmaceutical sciences can be approached in much the same manner as faculty in chemistry, biology, or physics departments, using many of the same strategies for introducing WAC's foundational premises. Likewise, because most pharmaceutical management and administration faculty are trained, in part, as economists and upper-level managers, their introduction to WAC can borrow much from efforts to introduce WAC to faculty in any of the disciplines that comprise most business programs.

The situation differs, however, with clinical pharmacy faculty. The majority of these faculty are not traditional academicians in the same way as their pharmaceutical sciences or management/administration colleagues. Clinical faculty's training is usually professional; they teach as a sideline to their practice, providing a type of apprenticeship opportunity to initiates in the discipline. Most of these faculty spend the majority of their instructional contact time in an off-campus clinical setting, not in an on-campus classroom. Although their contract may state that they allot 50 percent of their time to their clinical practice and 50 percent to their teaching obligations, the reality is that they hold down two full-time appointments as they juggle their patient care responsibilities with their teaching responsibilities for in-class, clinical rotation, and clinical internship instruction and oversight. Given their tight schedules and their usual tendency to be extremely task oriented, clinical faculty often want the short version of the WAC Program: put simply, because most clinical faculty are not concerned about the theory behind the program or its philosophical or epistemological implications, WAC Programs and training sessions aimed at selling WAC to an audience of trained skeptics (what most academicians are, in essence) come off as a waste of these busy people's time. Instead, clinical pharmacy faculty are an audience that want the following questions answered: What do you want me to accomplish? How do you suggest I do it?

CONCLUSION

Like the industry to which it is affiliated, the education of health care providers is changing. Colleges of medicine (allopathic and osteopathic), nursing, dentistry, pharmacy, and allied health services are examining their curricula and teaching methods to ensure that their graduates are adequately prepared to enter quickly changing practice arenas (Pew Commission 1995; Commission to Implement Change 1993; Baum 1996). Perhaps the uniqueness of developing writing programs in pharmacy or health-care-related locales can be found in the intertwining of professional concerns and preparatory education. For example, professional organizations such as the AACP and the Pew Health Professions Commission are focused on the landscape of the future and offer important implications for current practice. Among the Pew Commission's third report, "Critical Challenges: Revitalizing the Health Professions for the Twenty-First Century," is the following:

The next generation of professionals must be prepared to practice in settings that are more intensively managed and integrated. Specifically, the clinicians of the future will be required to use the sophisticated information and communications technology, to promote health and preventing disease, to sharper their skills in areas ranging from clinical prevention, to health education to the effective use of political reforms to change the burden of disease, to be more customer and consumer focused and to be ready to move into new roles that ask them to strike an equitable balance between resources and needs. (1995, iii)

For those of us involved in the education of these health care professionals-to-be, this description and challenge offers an important rationale—and exciting opportunities—to integrate writing-to-learn and learning-to-write within the professional curriculum.

NOTES

1. For this two-hour written examination, given once per semester, students pick up a packet of three or four articles two weeks in advance of the test. These readings range from fairly technical to more general and will be focused on a particular topic in health care (recent topics include the use of Ritalin to treat ADHD and the development of antibiotic-resistant bacteria; see also Parkhurst). Students' essays are then graded holistically by pairs of faculty members across the college (after attending a "norming" session). Students who fail this examination are required to enroll in an additional three-credit course, where the focus is on effectively writing from source material.

2. Of ninety surveys distributed, thirty-one responses were received (a 34 percent return rate).

WORKS CITED

Baum, Bruce J. "The Dental Curriculum: What Should Be New in the 21st Century?" *Journal of Public Health Dentistry* 56 (1996): 286–290.

Commission to Implement Change in Pharmaceutical Education. "Background Paper II: Entry-level, Curricular Outcomes, Curricular Content and Educational Process." *American Journal of Pharmaceutical Education* 58 (1993): 377–385.

Hepler, C. D., and L.M. Strand. "Opportunities and Responsibilities in Pharmaceutical Care." *American Journal of Hospital Pharmacy* 47 (1990): 533–543.

Hobson, Eric H., and Kenneth W. Schafermeyer. "Writing and Critical Thinking: Writing to Learn in Large Classes." *American Journal of Pharmaceutical Education* 58 (1994): 423–427.

Holiday-Goodman, Monica, and Buford T. Lively, eds. *Writing Across the Curriculum in Colleges of Pharmacy: A Sourcebook.* Toledo, OH: The University of Toledo College of Pharmacy and American Association of Colleges of Pharmacy Grant Awards for Pharmacy Schools (GAPS), 1992.

Humphrey, George. Personal Interview. 13 May 1997.

Lerner, Neal. "Counting Beans and Making Beans Count." *The Writing Lab Newsletter* 22.1 (1997): 1.

Maddux, Michael S., Eric H. Hobson, Dimitra Vrahnos, Sheldon Holstad, Mary T. Roth, Thomas D. Zlatic. "Developing a Curriculum for Tomorrow's Pharmacy Practitioners." *Pharmguide to Hospital Medicine* 9.1 (1996): 1–4, 9–12.

Parkhurst, Christine. "A Writing Proficiency Examination for Pharmacy Students." *American Journal of Pharmacy Education* 61 (1997): 163–166.

Pew Health Professions Commission. "Critical Challenges: Revitalizing the Health Professions for the Twenty-First Century." The Third Report of the Pew Health Professions Commission. San Francisco: UCSF Center for the Health Professions, 1995.

Prosser, Theresa R., John M. Burke, and Eric H. Hobson. "Teaching Pharmacy Students to Write in the Medical Record." *American Journal of Pharmaceutical Education* 61 (1997): 136–140.

Reynolds, John F. "Preface to the Second Edition." John F. Reynolds, David C. Mair, and Pamela C. Fischer. *Writing and Reading Mental Health Records.* 2nd ed. Mahway, NJ: Lawrence Erlbaum, 1995: xi–xiii.

———, David C. Mair, and Pamela C. Fischer. *Writing and Reading Mental Health Records.* 2nd ed. Mahway, NJ: Lawrence Erlbaum, 1995.

Schafermeyer, Kenneth W. "Managed Prescription Drug Programs." *Managed Care Contracting: A Guide for Health Care Professionals*, ed. Wendy Knight. Gaithersburg, MD: Aspen, 1997: 229–242.

Appendix: MCP Faculty Survey on Their Uses of Writing

Massachusetts College of Pharmacy & Allied Health Sciences
Survey of Faculty Uses of Writing—March 1997

Your Division:

Courses Taught: (1)

        Required?   Elective?

                (2)

        Required?   Elective?

                (3)

        Required?   Elective?

PURPOSES FOR ASSIGNING WRITING

Please check which of the following reasons best describe your purposes for assigning writing (check all that apply):

____   to assess student knowledge of content
____   to provide an aid to mastering content
____   to provide an aid for reading comprehension
____   to provide an opportunity for self expression
____   to improve students' critical thinking/problem solving
____   to improve students' creative thinking
____   other (please describe)

WRITING TASKS

Please check which of the following writing tasks you assign to your students:

___in-class essay exams & quizzes	____ · drug consultations
___journals	____ case-study analysis
___responses to reading	____ chart notes
___patient education materials	____ patient evaluation
___correspondence to care givers	____ drug information literature
___collaborative research papers	____ individual research papers
___analytical papers	____ lab reports
(i.e., analyzing an issue or topic)	____ debate outlines or reports
___other (please describe)	

NON-LECTURE TECHNIQUES

What non-lecture techniques do you regularly use in your teaching (e.g., debates, group work, individual drill and practice, visual or drawing exercises)?

ASSESSMENT OF WRITING

Please rate the following text attributes according to their importance in the assessment of student writing:

Accurate Content

1	2	3	4
extremely important			not important

Unique Styles/Strengths of Voice

1	2	3	4
extremely important			not important

Correct Mechanics (Grammar/Usage/Spelling/Punctuation)

1	2	3	4
extremely important			not important

Appropriate Format

1	2	3	4
extremely important			not important

Logical Structure and Organization

1	2	3	4
extremely important			not important

Concise and Clear Wording

1	2	3	4
extremely important			not important

Clarity of Purpose

1	2	3	4
extremely important			not important

Awareness of Reader's Needs

1	2	3	4
extremely important			not important

What other attributes are important when assessing student writing?

Which of the following reasons best describe why you might not require writing in your courses:

_____   Assessment is too time consuming.

_____   Writing assignments are not appropriate for course content.

_____   Assigning and assessing writing are outside of my expertise.

_____   Other (please describe):

WORKSHOPS

I would be interested in attending workshops on (check all that apply):

_____   evaluating/assessing writing

_____   creating writing tasks

_____   integrating writing into my curriculum

_____   integrating the Writing Center into my curriculum

_____   familiarizing myself with ESL writing issues

_____   other (please describe):

ADDITIONAL COMMENTS:

Writing Center or Experimental Center for Faculty Research, Discovery, and Risk Taking?

Pamela B. Childers

The Caldwell Writing Center (CWC) and my role as director have changed in many ways since we first opened our doors in the fall of 1991. Yes, students, faculty and administration back then were eager to find out what a secondary school Writing Center was all about. Now, however, they are seeing that our paradigm of being student-centered has changed just as the administrative vision and faculty paradigms have shifted to more technology and new pedagogical approaches to writing, thinking, and learning. In 1991 faculty did not really understand the sign that said "The Writing Center is a low-risk environment where there is a reverence for writing" (Farrell-Childers 1994). In fact, they thought of it as a place where "they work on that touchy feely stuff." Some still do not understand that any more than they understand that when I am sitting at my desk or computer, I am responding to what I am reading (student and faculty writing), not napping or taking it easy. In 1991 teachers had trouble comprehending the idea of the computer as a tool to teach writing (not a glorified typewriter) because they did not have networked computers sitting in front of them in their offices (as they do now). Even with these advances some teachers still just bring their classes to the Writing Center to type drafts of their writing process (as if we all had the same writing process). In 1991 faculty, administrators, and students did not understand that Writing Across the Curriculum involved more than formal papers (Farrell-Childers, Gere, and Young 1994); writing-to-learn across disciplines meant little as did writing for real-life situations. Yes, our secondary school Writing Center and my role as director have metamorphosed more than I or my colleagues could have imagined in the last six years. My role focuses more now on how I can encourage my colleagues to grow as both teachers and learners, and I must model this belief by participating in their development. It is indeed a partnership.

In 1991 I began directing the CWC, as part of my position as endowed chair of composition at The McCallie School, an all boys' college preparatory day/boarding school in Chattanooga, Tennessee. This position included directing the Writing Across the Curriculum Program and developing a school-wide writing program. My role required me to physically occupy the facility from 8 a.m. to 4 p.m. each day. That part was not much different from being in the same room teaching and directing a secondary school Writing Center for approximately the same number of hours in a public school. I could only work with faculty by talking with them on the phone or by having them come to the CWC to plan their writing activities. The facility itself housed fifteen new Macintosh Classic computers networked to a Mac SE 30 fileserver with three HP Deskwriter printers. I had a Mac LC and Apple LaserWriter to use at my desk. We were the most advanced computer facility on campus at that time, and we attracted a group of ninth graders new to the upper school. These boys found the computers exciting, the CWC as a safe haven from the bigger boys, and me as someone who would listen to them and needed their volunteer service to help me learn the new equipment and programs. This kind of atmosphere, especially for boys, may be unique to secondary schools more than colleges, since students are still looking for their voice and style when writing. Also, in a male atmosphere there are not many places where students can safely write poems, discuss plays, and share their short stories and essays.

That first year we had mainly drop-ins, students who came to seek help with their writing or to use the computers. Initially, they thought I was this woman who would correct their essays so they could then turn in flawless papers. They thought they had discovered the ultimate "easy way" to get an A on a composition! After they heard me say that they could not afford me as an editor, they began realizing that they had to invest time into sitting down at a conference with me. And, that first year, the main focus was student writing conferences. I was trying to establish that low-risk environment that would make students feel comfortable trying to improve their thinking and writing. But teachers were also involved from the start. I invited the entire faculty to submit names for the fifteen computers, then the student volunteers selected the winners. Zeus was our file server. A few brave souls who were willing to try something new in their classrooms also walked through the door.

One must understand the unique situation of secondary schools and Writing Centers. First of all, faculty work long, hard days. In public schools that load includes usually five large classes, an extra duty, at least three different course preparations, and many after-school activities as class advisor, coach, or club sponsor. In private schools, especially ones with boarding students, faculty may have fewer students and classes to meet per week, but they are more committed to after-school assignments, dorm duties, and weekend activities with very little time to themselves. To even think about working with someone else on another project, secondary school teachers have to be convinced that their limited time will be productive. From the start, science teachers have been the innovative ones willing to try something new that might help their students learn. Maybe the science teachers were more willing because they knew I was also a certified biology teacher. Peter LaRochelle (LaRochelle and Farrell-Childers 1994) invited me to team teach one day a week with his honors biology class so that we could include year-long writing, thinking, and learning projects as part of the class. Immediately we began collaborating on ways that we could use writing to think and learn as part of his biology classes. Through the use of a book on tropical rain forests called *Tropical Nature* by Adrian Forsyth and Kenneth Miyata, we were able to create unique assignments that overlapped into literature, too. For instance, one chapter in the book, "Bugs and Drugs," discusses how various plants and insects emit poisons to protect themselves. I immediately thought of Nathaniel Hawthorne's short story, "Rappacini's Daughter," as a way for students to connect fiction and fact. Although the story is long and difficult, the students were able to read and connect it to the chapter in their biology book. LaRochelle and I also learned something important about ourselves. The next year we actually evaluated our own styles of working and teaching and shared those. We realized that we could actually complement each other in this partnership, so we began working on ways to help each other overcome our now-known weaknesses.

Cissy May (1994) began to try writing-to-learn activities to help her regular chemistry students discover how to apply knowledge they had been taught by writing letters to a classmate describing what they had difficulty understanding and having their partners respond to help them. May would then clarify any misunderstandings to make sure that all students had learned. A pragmatic teacher, May and I frequently "cut to the chase" when working together because we have understood the intentions of the other and only needed to ask questions, check work done, and revise what we discovered had not worked well.

As a young teacher eager to learn more, David Perkinson (1994) attended our Writing Across the Curriculum (WAC) retreat, then tried a variety of writing-to-learn activities in his math classes, including math histories and letters, and read as many articles and books as I could find on writing in mathematics. He asked me to help him as a participant on a public and private school consortium panel discussion of writing in mathematics. A more experienced art teacher and poet, Catherine Neuhardt-Minor (1994) asked her art students to critique what they were doing artistically in the language of visual arts so that they would comprehend the value of their visual art. She and I were also able to work on collaborative projects with my poetry class. Many of the teachers who initially came and attended our WAC retreat with Art Young realized some value in writing to learn as well as other writing in their subjects. These teachers of science, art, math, and English initiated our WAC Program and helped to establish the CWC as the hub of WAC. In secondary schools, many teachers feel isolated or forced to teach the way a domineering administrator has told them they must in order to keep their jobs. They found the CWC to be a low-risk environment in which to experiment with teaching and learning, and they felt safe trying new ideas with me, a kindred spirit, to support them.

As teachers joined the McCallie faculty, I gave them a short workshop on writing-to-learn at the new faculty retreat so that they knew me as a resource. With the addition of a part-time assistant, I was able to get out of the Writing Center itself to visit teachers, do workshops in their classrooms, and meet with groups of teachers (Farrell-Childers 1994). Being seen as both a resource and a partner in writing projects was okay, but also being able to get into their class-rooms or having their classes come to the CWC helped even more. In reality, I also had a chance to eat lunch, which afforded me an informal atmosphere for faculty interaction. Most college directors have assistants or a staff that permits them to have a more flexible schedule Also, secondary directors have to deal with such items as "insurance" concerns; that is, seeing that students are super-vised in all areas at all times; thus, we need coverage to leave a room for any reason.

The initial group of teachers continued to try new writing activities: we revised and expanded projects, and teachers discovered success with the learn-ing of their students. By my third year, teachers were also coming to the CWC for advice on research, grant proposals, and even job searches. Instead of direc-tor of WAC and the CWC, my role was changing into one of resource person, guide, and facilitator for faculty research. That is, teachers were coming to the CWC for books and articles on journal writing and research papers, asking for advice on creating and evaluating assignments, and suggesting possible class-room research projects that I could help facilitate. Teachers were also publishing (Farrell-Childers and Lowry 1994; Nickel 1994) and presenting (Childers and Lowry 1997; Childers and Lowry 1995; Farrell and Perkinson 1992; LaRo-chelle, Neuhardt-Minor, and Perkinson 1993) what they had learned about their students' learning through the use of writing activities. For example, science teacher Michael Lowry wanted to write about the research activity that he and I had developed for his eighth graders. Lance Nickel allowed me to sit in on an exercise he did to help math students learn the need for mathematical vocabu-lary to explain what they were doing with graphs so students could replicate a graph by following the written directions.

Another interesting development took place as part of teachers writing and presenting this information—they were rethinking pedagogical issues. Questions of learning styles, collaborative and cooperative learning, and stu-dent-centered learning entered the discussion of choosing appropriate writing activities. Yes, these questions were important in all aspects of our teaching at that time, but creating writing-to-learn activities as well as formal writing as-signments seemed to be a natural for study in these pedagogical areas. Finally, I was beginning to hear teachers say, "What if." New writing activities appeared, such as students showing their teachers how to research and use search engines on the computer for their writing assignments; teachers allowing their students to create writing activities, and teams of students competing against each other for the best class science booklet on plants in the Chattanooga area.

During the last three years, faculty have conducted research and dis-covered what happens with writing, technology, and the Internet. When David

Perkinson questioned whether his algebra students were learning more by using writing-to-learn activities, we did a year-long quasi-experimental research project to determine whether they actually were learning more over the sustained course of a year. To summarize the results of the project, Perkinson used experimental and control groups to test the effects of writing-to-learn activities on the learning of algebra in the two groups. Given the same final examination, the students in the experimental group had a mean score of 78.56 percent (5.66 percent higher than the mean score of the control group). The experimental group had no failures; whereas the control group had three. Also, Perkinson noticed major attitudinal differences in the experimental group who had a superior energy level and were "more focused in class, even in spring" (Farrell-Childers, "Effects of Writing to Learn," 1994).

Another interesting part of this faculty development through classroom research and writing is that teachers collaborated with colleagues and students to learn. For instance, as the technology in the CWC changed, we began to consider how it affected writing. Senior Jud Laughter and I (Laughter and Childers 1996) did our own project of working with his college application essays, using the computer as a means of conferencing when both of us were unavailable. We helped each other write and revise our sections of the article describing what we had done. Later that same year, Laughter and I added senior tutor Steve Trumpeter and science teacher Michael Lowry to a collaborative project. The four of us wrote a chapter for a book on collaborative writing in the Writing Center (Childers, Laughter, Lowry, and Trumpeter 1998). Through several months of revision, submission, and final draft for publication, the four of us learned more about our own collaboration, our thoughts on writing, and even about writing for another audience—editors and publishers. Now these two students are college sophomores, the book will finally be published, and they have a real sense of the world of publishing that they could not have learned without experiencing it.

This past year Michael Lowry wondered if portfolios would be effective as formative assessments of student learning and his teaching during the year in his conceptual physical science class of eighth graders. Not only did we do a study of the student progress, teacher growth, and the effects of portfolios as formative assessment during the year (Childers and Lowry 1997), but three senior peer tutors became involved in their own study and collaborated on an article for publication (Grant, Murphy and Stafford 1997). Computer science teacher Stephen Moody expressed the need for writing in his course when we were commuting down the mountain on our way to work, so I suggested he e-mail what he said (Moody 1995), and Dave Hall and I took the risk of using search engines on the Internet with a Bible class to discover whether there was a need for censorship on the Web (Childers and Hall 1995).

What is happening now is that teachers are taking more risks with writing, thinking, and learning across the disciplines. In 1996–1997 teachers of English, history, and science tried allowing their students to design the assessment tools for research papers, oral reports, and writing projects. They left their classes in the CWC and allowed students (with me as the facilitator) to create their own assessment tools. That is definitely trust in a partnership. Teachers new to McCallie have willingly tried activities in their classrooms. Don Obrecht used letter writing to peers on e-mail as a review of certain math processes that they had to explain to their partners, and he designed a math research activity that involved student collaboration and interaction to encourage students to become involved in their own learning. Jerry Ferrari, seventh-grade Bible teacher, assigned his students to write a letter to Isaac or Abraham voicing their opinions of his actions as a son or father. Partners responded as either Isaac or Abraham, and the teacher assessed their knowledge of the passages of Genesis that they have studied. No, these are not unique exercises to those of us who have been involved in WAC for decades, but they are exciting because the teachers have taken the risks of trying them. Both of these teachers were not afraid to e-mail me messages with their ideas, and we began the collaboration of creating the assignments and the means of responding to or assessing the writing through e-mail with attachments.

Over the years, I have encouraged teachers in workshops to give writing assignments for real audiences other than the teacher or for real situations. In science that has included reporting on discoveries as a scientist would do, using a scientific format. In history, we have talked about the value of letters to the editor or to Congressmen or CEOs of particular companies. In our keyboarding class, Karen Hulvey has invited me to help her students learn how to write their own business letters by creating real situations where they would write a business letter. They have complained about a cigarette machine in the entrance to a toy store, back-ordered athletic equipment for their teams, and even faulty merchandise they have ordered and received.

One project that has been of particular interest to me is the selection of essay prompts that teachers give for essay tests. Especially in science, we see many typical essays asking students to explain some major concept developed in the unit. Aware of the variety of learning styles of our students and of a particular interest I have in the relationship between writing and the visual arts, Michael Lowry and I decided to try offering students a choice of essay prompts that included creativity, independent thinking, critical thinking, and visual talent. Knowing that we have a great number of visual rather than verbal learners (Childers, Hobson and Mullin 1998), we wanted to give these students an opportunity to succeed. We used a choice of prompts for two different units. After each set of essays had been submitted and returned, I asked the students to tell me which choice they made, why they made it, and what grade they received. They were indeed partners in this study as much as Lowry and I. For both units, the typical science essay was selected by the fewest number of students in all three biology classes. Most interesting was the fact that all the students who chose other prompts said that they did not mind devoting more time to their choice because it was interesting, fun, and creative. Several liked the visual aspect and chose those prompts. As part of his final examination, Lowry gave students a take-home essay test with three choices. Students were allowed to

(1) select a typical science response; (2) use two visual creatures created by an artist; or (3) create their own creature. If they selected options 2 or 3, they had to give the accurate scientific information for the creature(s) just as they would have had to do with real animals in option 1. All but two students chose options 2 or 3. At the end of the year, we gave them one more questionnaire to indicate what they liked most and least about the course. From the three classes, all but two students said they loved using visuals with their writing to explain what they had learned; those two students said they liked someone telling them what to do so they would not have to make a decision for themselves. We are using this information to revise what we are doing this year and hope to develop the information we have gathered. We will be presenting this information at a workshop for the National Association of Independent Schools annual conference in 1998. What a great risk Lowry took in trying these new activities to help his students improve their writing, thinking, and learning.

Even though we have worked more with individual faculty members on faculty development and Writing Across the Disciplines, we still had over 800 individual conferences in 1996–1997, compared to 78 our first year. Also, I have been fortunate to have had two outstanding assistants during the past five years; both have worked well in individual conferences as well as with class groups. Since McCallie is an all-boys' school except for the last two periods each day when we exchange classes with Girls Preparatory School, I find it extremely important to offer students the opportunity to work with a male or female in conferences. Secondary students tend to relate to one gender more than another, so having a choice serves the individual needs of all. The importance of a full- or part-time assistant is more than the flexibility to get into the classrooms with teachers and students; it is having two points of view on writing theory and pedagogy, two responses to student writing, and positive support during the most difficult times. Peer tutors are rare indeed, since the course is an elective in a school loaded with required and elective options. At any one time I may have up to three tutors or none. I consider them an unexpected luxury. Many secondary schools use students in honors classes or create a special course; these options do not exist at McCallie because of the heavy schedule of courses and extracurricular commitments of our students.

What has happened since that first year? More students are using the CWC, so are more faculty and staff. Parents call with questions, admissions personnel ask us to check some of their letters to alumni, and we have become a school-wide resource for faculty development, teaching, and learning. No longer is WAC seen as just writing by those staff members who use our services. No longer is the Writing Center seen as a luxury that could easily be eliminated. Yes, we have a learning center where students with specific learning problems can pay to be tutored in specific subjects, but they do not learn to write there— the CWC offers that assistance for free to all our students. Since we know that writing, thinking, and learning are strongly connected, we are closer to the necessary pedagogical paradigm shifts of student-centered classrooms and collaborative learning. We also make students responsible learners; they must sit with us, ask and answer questions, and revise the work in their own words.

Another aspect of faculty risk taking, research, and discovery involves collaborative writing between students and among faculty. Teachers and students in several classes are now involved in e-mail exchanges with secondary students in Canada and the United States. Thanks to a dialogue with Sam Robinson, University of Saskatchewan, we were able to begin work with one of his classes three years ago. College students who were secondary education majors responded to students in Mike Lancaster's environmental science class. Last year Lancaster began a new dialogue with students in the classes of Glenn Blalock at Stephen F. Austin University. This year Blalock added a Web site for discussion groups among the secondary and college students and their teachers on readings by Aldo Leopold, Edward Abbey, and Wendell Berry, for instance. Out of the discussion groups, students and faculty are collaborating on reading, thinking, and writing activities that will help both groups of students improve their writing, thinking, and learning. In the process both teachers are discovering new ways of teaching and learning, too. Not all of these experiments with college teachers and technology have been successful, however, and that is also part of the learning experience for our faculty and students. For instance, one of the science teachers offered an essay for use in an exchange between his eighth graders and college English education majors. The college professor responded that she thought the essay was too "technical and scientific" for her English education majors to understand and respond to with the students. The science teacher and I were a little concerned that future English teachers could not read and comprehend what we have given to our eighth graders!

Finally, there is an air of professionalism associated with the CWC. We are not connected to one department, there's no hierarchical administrative connections here, we listen to teachers' concerns about their profession, we help them find grants and graduate programs for the summer, and we have resources. Over the years we have developed notebooks full of writing activities in different disciplines by saving copies of assignments our teachers have used. We keep current professional books and periodicals available, update our Web site with new information, send regular Writing Center updates to faculty through e-mail, share new ideas, and inform faculty of what their colleagues have found successful. Too often we see good, innovative teachers, who are continuous learners, lose faith in their own profession. If we can encourage them to publish, present, do some classroom research of their own, or apply for a grant; then maybe they will be "renourished" in their profession. Even more difficult for us but more important for our faculty is our role as buffer. We frequently take the brunt of secondary school administrative flack, rigidity on the part of misinformed or inflexible administrators, and sometimes verbal abuse for "stirring up trouble." As long as the teachers get to develop their ideas, we have learned to take that as part of our risk taking in a secondary school Writing Center.

This year we have started work with the faculty development program on a writing contest. We have asked all staff to write about their first years at

McCallie, and all who submit will receive a Barnes and Noble gift certificate. The authors of the two best pieces will get cash awards. All submissions in the form of letters, narratives, poems, or any other format will be published in a book entitled *My First Years at McCallie*. This book will be given to teachers at the new faculty retreat each fall. We think of it as another positive way of encouraging our faculty to develop as writers, thinkers, and learners.

Reflecting on my years in the Caldwell Writing Center, I recall some difficult, challenging, frustrating, and denigrating experiences that I would have encountered at most other secondary schools. It is impossible for me to deny that I often take the risks that put me in those situations. However, I get my delight from the student who walked in his senior year and said, "Doc, I know how to get an A on an essay, but I want to learn how to be a good writer." In the same way, my adrenaline surges when John and Kay Roth say at the beginning of my seventh year at McCallie, "We're ready to do some writing in our Latin classes. Can you help us?"; Mike Lancaster and Tommy Dillow trust us to hold individual conferences with each of their students doing research and give them progress grades in science and history; or Randy Odle says, "I want to do an e-mail exchange between my world history students and history majors at Sewanee. What do you think?" Isn't that the kind of partnership we need in a Writing Center?

WORKS CITED

Childers, Pamela. "A Few Thoughts on Writing Centers, WAC, and Faculty Development." *Radford* [University] *Writes: The Newsletter of Writing Across the Curriculum* (Nov. 1995): 4.

———. "Writing Centers and WAC: Connections for Faculty Growth." Guest Editorial. *Radford* [University] *Writes: The Newsletter of Writing Across the Curriculum* (Apr. 1995): 1+.

———, and David Hall. "What IS Safe Sex on the Internet?" The *ACE Newsletter* 10.1 (Summer 1995): 4–6.

———, Eric Hobson, and Joan Mullin. *ARTiculating: Teaching Writing in a Visual Culture*. Portsmouth, NH: Boynton/Cook, 1998.

———, Jud Laughter, Michael Lowry, and Steve Trumpeter. "Developing a Community in a Secondary School Writing Center." *Writing Centers in Collaboration Pedagogy*, eds. Carol Haviland et al. Emmitsburg, MD: NWCA Press, 1998.

———, and Michael Lowry. "Secondary School Collaborations for Faculty Development." Presentation at the National Writing Across the Curriculum Conference, Charleston, SC, Feb. 1997.

———. "WAC and Writing Centers in Secondary Schools: Beyond Institutional Assumptions." Presentation at the National Writing Across the Curriculum Conference, Charleston, SC, Feb. 1997.

———. "Writing Across the Disciplines for Faculty Growth." Presentation at the NAIS annual conference, New York, Feb. 1998.

———. "Writing Center as Center for Faculty Development." Presentation at the National Writing Centers Association National Conference, St. Louis, Sept. 1995.

Farrell, Pamela. "Effects of Writing to Learn." Unpublished paper, 1994.

———. *The High School Writing Center: Establishing and Maintaining One*. Urbana, IL: NCTE, 1989.

———. "Writing to Learn Math." Workshop presentation at the Tennessee Association of Independent Schools annual conference, Nashville, Nov. 1992.

———, and David Perkinson. "Ideas for Writing about Numbers." *Radford* [University] *Writes: The Newsletter of Writing Across the Curriculum* (Dec. 1993): 7.

Farrell-Childers, Pamela. "A Unique Learning Environment." *Intersections: Theory-Practice in the Writing Center*, eds. Joan A. Mullin and Ray Wallace. Urbana, IL: NCTE, 1994. 111–119.

———, Anne Gere, and Art Young, eds. *Programs and Practices: Writing Across the Secondary School Curriculum*. Portsmouth, NH: Boynton/Cook, 1994.

———, and Michael Lowry. "Science and Writing: Unexpected Bonuses." *Radford* [University] *Writes: The Newsletter of Writing Across the Curriculum* (Apr. 1994): 2+.

Forsyth, Adrian, and Kenneth Miyata. *Tropical Nature*. New York: Charles Scribner's Sons, 1984.

Grant, Tripp, Andrew Murphy, and Ben Stafford. "Peer Tutors and Students Work with Assessment." *The Clearinghouse* 71.2 (1997): 103-105.

Hawthorne, Nathaniel. "Rappacini's Daughter." *Elements of Literature*. 5th course. Chicago: Holt, Rinehart and Winston, 1992.

LaRochelle, Peter, and Pamela Farrell-Childers. "Honors Biology Writing Projects." *Programs and Practices: Writing Across the Secondary School Curriculum*, eds. Pamela Farrell-Childers, Anne Gere, and Art Young. Portsmouth, NH: Boynton/Cook, 1994. 205–207.

———, Catherine Neuhardt-Minor, and David Perkinson. "Writing Across the Curriculum." Presentation at the Virginia Association of Teachers of English annual conference, Roanoke, Oct. 1993.

Laughter, Jud, and Pamela Childers. "Collaboration and College Application Essays: Two Perspectives." *The Writing Lab Newsletter* (1996): 4–5.

May, Cissy. "Writing and Learning in Chemistry." *Programs and Practices: Writing Across the Secondary School Curriculum*, eds. Pamela Farrell-Childers, Anne Gere, and Art Young. Portsmouth, NH: Boynton/Cook, 1994. 198–200.

Moody, Stephen. "Writing in Computer Science." *Radford* [University]*Writes: The Newsletter of Writing Across the Curriculum* (Nov. 1995): 7.

Neuhardt-Minor, Catherine. "Words and Images." *Programs and Practices: Writing Across the Secondary School Curriculum*, eds. Pamela Farrell-Childers, Anne Gere, and Art Young. Portsmouth, NH: Boynton/Cook, 1994. 211–213.

Nickel, Lance. "Writing and Pre-Calculus." *Programs and Practices: Writing Across the Secondary School Curriculum*, eds. Pamela Farrell-Childers, Anne Gere, and Art Young. Portsmouth, NH: Boynton/Cook, 1994. 200–204.

Perkinson, David. "Writing in Math or Math in Writing?" *Programs and Practices: Writing Across the Secondary School Curriculum*, eds. Pamela Farrell-Childers, Anne Gere, and Art Young. Portsmouth, NH: Boynton/Cook, 1994. 207–210.

Writing Centers and WAC Programs as Infostructures: Relocating Practice within Futurist Theories of Social Change

Christina Murphy and Joe Law

Ellen Fremman always enjoys the surge of activity that comes with the beginning of a new school term, and academic year 2008–2009 promises to be especially busy. At the moment Fremman, a team leader with Campus Writing Programs (CWP), is consulting with Keith Johnson. Johnson is new to the faculty at Western Valley State University, where fall classes will begin in two weeks. While he was completing his doctorate at a much larger, research-oriented institution, his teaching experience was limited to grading exams for a large lecture section each semester and twice taking over his major professor's graduate seminar when she was away for a conference. Part of Johnson's teaching assignment for this fall is a section of Economics 200, a writing-intensive course in the general education sequence required of all students. He will have fifty students from all majors, and each will be expected to produce at least 2,000 words of writing, some of it revised in light of his response to it.

Working together in a synchronous chat mode, Johnson and Fremman are going over the drafts of a syllabus and writing assignments he has previously e-mailed to her. At their first meeting, Fremman had guided him through Western Valley State University's Institutional Research online profile of the students enrolled in his class and had shown him EC 200 assignments from WVSU and from similar courses at the other schools in the Campus Writing Programs' Online Archive. At the moment they are discussing ways to connect his writing assignments more explicitly to the instructional goals of the class and to accommodate the various learning styles identified in the student profiles. Before their meeting is over, they will have established an agenda for the training sessions that will be held for the WVSU Writing Center consultants who will be working with Johnson's students on campus. By the time classes begin, Johnson's syllabus and assignments will be posted on the CWP Web page, where they will be available to the students in his class, consultants in the Writing

Center, the rest of the campus community, and the other schools served by CWP. Because Johnson's materials for his writing-intensive courses will be archived indefinitely, they will also provide one means for the department to assess Johnson's progress as a teacher.

Fremman's next online appointment is with Anna Collier, who teaches chemistry at Middletown Community College. Fremman wants to enlist Collier for an interactive video conference at which Collier would demonstrate the project she worked out with CWP last year, online lab books with video simulations of several experiments. This conference will be joined by another CWP associate, Pat Lopardo, who will discuss upgrading the graphics in the program and increasing its speed. While that meeting is going on, other members of the CWP team may be working on any number of projects at the twenty schools where they have contracts: pairing instructors teaching their first writing-intensive courses with mentors in the same discipline, facilitating online alliances between businesses and technical writing classes, training local campus Writing Center consultants to work with specific classes and assignments, troubleshooting network problems, documenting changes in instructional practice and institutional culture, and designing assessment instruments to measure the effectiveness of those changes. Providing these customized services requires specialists in a number of fields, sometimes freelancers who are contracted for individual projects. More often, the core group of people employed by CWP work together on different aspects of a number of assignments, assuming more or less responsibility in the group according to their expertise. Though CWP has a central office with workstations and conference rooms available, many of the staff work from their homes, staying in constant contact electronically but seldom seeing each other.

For academicians used to the centrality of the classroom—and of the academy itself—in education, this scenario might seem an unlikely futuristic projection. Yet many aspects of this scenario are already in place, and three dominant trends indicate that Ellen Fremman's methods are more likely to be the future of educational delivery systems in writing instruction than will the traditional academic classroom buttressed by independent local Writing Centers and Writing Across the Curriculum Programs. Those three trends are technology, demographics, and the available funding sources for education. Because the history of education proves undeniably that social trends shape the educational process, it is crucial that writing program professionals understand how these trends will redefine educational systems in the twenty-first century. As social systems theorist Don Tapscott (1996) indicates, these trends offer both "promise and peril." The most important role for educators will be to configure these trends toward significant social and educational goals.

In the October 3, 1997, issue of *The Chronicle of Higher Education*, Jeffrey R. Young's "Rethinking the Role of the Professor in an Age of High-tech Tools" raises the question of how radically technology will change the roles of faculty members. Young states that "new technologies could take over many of the instructional duties that now define professors' jobs" and offers some striking possibilities:

- Courses could be designed in distant cities by teams of top faculty members and technology experts who could craft lessons that might mix online materials and face-to-face meetings with on-site instructors.
- Individual professors' lectures could be replaced by multimedia Web sites that could include video clips of famous scholars in the field.
- Tests could be selected from national test databases, or administered by outside organizations—eliminating even grading from the professor's portfolio. (A26)

As a result of the "unbundling" of their many duties, "professors could spend more time leading discussions that take place in classrooms and in online chat areas" (A26). "None of those ideas are science fiction," Young emphasizes. "Experiments in each of the areas are already under way, and seem certain to succeed eventually in one form or another" (A26).

For writing program professionals, it is vital to comprehend the immediacy and dramatic momentum of the technological change in educational settings that Young describes. Prior to the emergence of this technology, Writing Centers and Writing Across the Curriculum Programs, for example, had changed very little from their original concepts. Both Writing Centers and WAC Programs emphasized one-to-one contact or small group dynamics, both programs were relatively easy to situate within an institution in terms of the academic personnel shaping the program and the audience for whom the programs were intended, and the focus of both programs was consistently narrow in serving specific populations of students and faculty on a given campus. A person associated with early manifestations of such programs—such as the Writing Lab at the University of Iowa in the 1930s (Kelly 1980) or the university-wide Prose Improvement Committee at the University of California at Berkeley in the late 1940s (Russell 1992, 28)—would have had little difficulty taking over one of these programs in the late 1980s since so little had changed in the knowledge structures and day-to-day operations of either program. Even more significantly, hardly anything had changed in the paradigms that defined both programs because the controlling philosophies of education had not changed throughout most of the twentieth century.

The wide-scale introduction of new technology in the early 1990s, especially the development of multimedia applications and the extensive use of the Internet, generated the need to rethink many traditional components of education. This need to rethink philosophies and practices, Don Tapscott and Art Caston claim, is the central fact of contemporary society's transition into the twenty-first century. In *Paradigm Shift: The New Promise of Information Technology* (1993), they point out that social institutions responsive to this paradigm shift will survive; those that have "severe difficulties embracing the change" or that remain "constrained by traditional approaches" are in danger of elimination through irrelevance (xi). We find the concerns of Tapscott and Caston of particular importance to education because, as Michael D. McMaster claims in *The*

Intelligence Advantage: Organizing for Complexity, "politics, business, and education have managed to remain far behind in their integration of new thinking" (1996, x). Peter Drucker makes this point even more trenchantly: "Every few hundred years throughout Western history, a sharp transformation has occurred. In a matter of decades, society altogether rearranges itself, its world views, its basic values, its social and political structures, its arts, its key institutions. Fifty years later, a new world exists. And the people born into that world cannot even imagine the world in which their grandparents lived and into which their own parents were born" (qtd. in McMaster 1996, xv).

We would like to argue that the "new world" educational institutions are entering will have particular relevance for the shape of writing programs in the twenty-first century. Writing Centers, WAC Programs, and their offshoots in centers for academic excellence are the primary means through which students and faculty are introduced to technology in educational settings. Therefore, writing program professionals must be aware of major trends currently influencing electronic technologies as educational delivery systems. Like many social theorists, McMaster sees in the contemporary era a major paradigm shift in the transformation from machine-based to information-based economies and social realities. Describing this transformation as the move from the Industrial Age to the Age of Information or the Age of Knowledge, he claims that "to make the shift in thinking, we need the willingness to unlearn the old and the courage to grapple with the new and unfamiliar" (xviii). Tapscott describes this change in similar terms. In *The Digital Economy: Promise and Peril in the Age of Networked Intelligence*, he defines twelve themes as central to the new "digital economy" of the Information Age: knowledge, digitization, virtualization, molecularization, integration/internetworking, disintermediation, convergence, innovation, prosumption, immediacy, globalization, and discordance (1996, 43–72). We find that all twelve themes are relevant to the future of writing programs and to the influence writing programs will have upon educational practices in the twenty-first century.

With the theme of Knowledge, Tapscott claims that the "knowledge content" of products is increasing and will continue to be a central component of future products. Copy machines that can pinpoint the source of their dysfunction and can phone a central repair station to schedule repairs are but one instance of the ways in which machines will assume many of the functions previously carried out by humans. In writing programs, the theme of Knowledge will play an important role in the ways in which multimedia technology interacts with users by assuming many of the lower-level "cognitive" functions and by serving as "instructors" in some aspects of the learning process. That writing program professionals should be aware of this trend and participate in structuring the "knowledge content" of educational technology seems fundamental to the success—indeed, to the very survival—of writing programs in increasingly technological settings. At an even more fundamental level, learners who come to Writing Centers or who participate in WAC classes will come from a world in which the "knowledge content" of machines will be a given, and the cognitive processes of these learners already will have been shaped by this type of technological interaction. Thus, it is essential that writing program professionals understand the new ways in which learners will process, interpret, and apply knowledge via their continued interactions with technology in nearly all aspects of their lives.

Tapscott uses the term digitization to describe the movement from the physical transportation of information to the conversion of information into bits that are conveyed electronically at the speed of light. The advantages are not only speed but also capabilities to compress vast amounts of information and to merge many forms of information into multimedia documents. Digitization makes e-mail possible, in contrast to the earlier transportation of mail via physical delivery systems of trucks, planes, post offices, and mail carriers. While e-mail has speeded up the delivery process, it has also radically changed the way in which people can collaborate by eliminating all spatial and temporal restrictions and making collaboration immediate and global. That digitization will continue to be a component of how people will communicate and collaborate is a given of the Knowledge Age, and Writing Centers and WAC Programs must be aware that students will learn and communicate through virtual texts in the next century. The knowledge of how to teach students to create virtual texts, as well as to teach students via virtual texts, will be an essential component of Writing Center and WAC instruction.

Once information has been digitized, virtualization is possible. Tapscott uses the example of how numerous options are created when physical shelf space in a grocery store is transformed into virtual shelf space in a computer. Certainly, we already see similar virtualization when writing programs no longer need to be housed in physical spaces on campuses but can become, instead, virtual centers for interaction and instruction. Online Writing Centers (OWLS) are but one small application of virtualization to writing instruction, but they presage future trends in the movement away from the concept of a "center" or location toward a virtual "center" of global access.

Tapscott describes molecularization in this fashion: "The old corporation is being disaggregated, replaced by dynamic molecules and clusters of individuals and entities that form the basis of economic activity. The organization does not necessarily disappear, but it is transformed. 'Mass' becomes 'molecular' in all aspects of economic and social life" (51). In the transition from mass to molecular economic activity, the roles of consumer and producer can be merged—a development that digitization and other aspects of virtualization make possible. Tapscott illustrates with the manufacture of blue jeans. Previously, manufacturers would generate large runs of jeans for a mass market of "unindividualized" individuals. In the Knowledge Age, one consumer with technological access can customize the fit of the jeans, the color, the fabric, and so forth and can order one "molecularized" pair of jeans designed expressly for that one consumer. In time, the concept of "mass marketing" will be replaced by "molecularized marketing" as consumers play an increasingly active individual role in the creation, marketing, and production of merchandise that fits their own particular tastes and needs.

In the world of writing programs, as in the business world, molecularization will be the future of educational technology and instruction. The old industrial concept of "mass" instruction that has dominated classrooms and large lecture halls will be replaced by educational methods in which the individual is an active and interactive creator in the instructional process. While Writing Centers have tended to emphasize one-to-one instruction (as articulated, for example, by North 1984 or Harris 1986), the learning structure of the tutoring session still tends to follow broad principles or conceptual designs determined by the tutor. With molecularization, an increased emphasis upon individual learning will enhance one-to-one instruction in that the learner will have more control in conceptualizing, shaping, and assessing the tutoring process. The learner will be able to design tutoring sessions and approaches geared to his or her own highly individualized needs, whereas, currently, this responsibility rests largely with the tutor.

Likewise, molecularization will require that WAC professionals respond more dynamically and more extensively to the course design and pedagogical needs of individual faculty members. Workshops designed to emphasize commonalities among disciplines or among faculty members with similar pedagogical and assessment concerns will most likely yield to a more individualized approach drawn from an "archive" of knowledge that is "molecularized" for each instructor. Similarly, each instructor will also expect from WAC professionals the ability to participate in the "molecularization" of his or her own pedagogical needs and objectives—much as the consumer used Virtualization to create the physical product that best suits that consumer's immediate needs and objectives. High among the instructor's needs, moreover, will be accommodating the varying needs of the students who constitute each class. The customer "market of one" in business will become the instructor "market of one" for each pedagogical requirement associated with the instructor's educational objectives.

Integration/internetworking are central components of many Writing Centers and WAC Programs through the use of the Internet. What the future will offer will be the extension of Integration/Internetworking beyond individual campuses to broader, perhaps centralized, national databases—much in the fashion that Young suggests in *The Chronicle of Higher Education* (1997). At present the integration of Writing Center and WAC information is often conducted informally through conferences, meetings, and limited discussions on listservs and other online discussion groups. Internetworking is similarly informal. Though some groups have tried to establish clearing houses for Internet resources, individual writing program professionals continue to set up independent Web sites that may be linked to only a few others or none at all, and that often needlessly produce similar versions of existing materials. Extending integration/internetworking so that the knowledge base is broadened and made more accessible will be a central challenge for Writing Center and WAC professionals. It will also be an important component of how new professionals are introduced to the field and trained for future roles.

Integration/internetworking enhances the movement toward molecularization, convergence, innovation, prosumption, and immediacy. In a molecularized learning environment, the older roles of instructor (producer) and learner (consumer) are collapsed via Prosumption into one role in which the learner creates the instructor and the instructional means by which to learn. Like Tapscott's purchaser/producer of customized blue jeans, learners become involved in the actual production process of their knowledge; in this case, though, the product has greater consequences in that "human collaboration on the Net becomes a part of the international repository of knowledge" (Tapscott 70). In addition, prosumption and integration/internetworking demonstrate Tapscott's theme of convergence; in an educational setting, computing, communications, and content merge into something new that cannot be defined exclusively as either process or product. Immediacy is the most important aspect of learning and instruction via the Internet in that all learning becomes real-time learning that is constantly updated. Compare the process to the publication of data in print media. By the time a book or journal article is being printed, the information it contains often is outdated or could be enhanced by the inclusion of new information. With the Internet, the updating and immediacy of information can be made real for learners in a matter of seconds so that knowledge is current, dynamic, fluid, and interactive. The implications of this process invite—and necessitate—innovation in instructional methods and technology. Ultimately, globalization will be the largest outcome of the twelve themes Tapscott describes in that the global network will become the backbone of educational instruction with immediate access to increasingly broader bases of knowledge as well as to interaction in wider ranges of discourse communities supporting, sustaining, evaluating, and disseminating that knowledge. Again, these are important aspects of how future writing program professionals will be trained and will carry out their roles via electronic technologies.

Disintermediation involves the elimination of intermediaries in economic activity–in essence, the classic elimination of the middleman. Travel agents represent to Tapscott one group that faces imminent disintermediation through the introduction of online booking of airline tickets. Once a consumer has access to all flight and fare information and can book his or her tickets via the Internet, as is now possible, the travel agent no longer has a meaningful function and can be disintermediated from the process. We would like to argue that disintermediation is one of the key likelihoods facing writing programs. We can easily envision a scenario in which writing programs within the academy are disintermediated by the business and professional communities—a prospect we can also easily envision for many other aspects of educational systems. Nor are we alone in forecasting the possibility. Jeanne Simpson makes a similar argument in "Slippery Sylvans Sliding Sleekly into the Writing Center—Or Preparing for Professional Competition" (1996). In fact, her scenario is not a projection but an emerging educational reality. For example, a headline in the September 19, 1997, issue of *The Chronicle of Higher Education* announces, "Tutoring Companies Take Over Remedial Teaching at Some Colleges." In that story, Ben Gose states, "Remedial education is becoming big business. Kaplan [Education Centers] and another company, Sylvan Learning Systems, are designing, overseeing, and in some cases actually teaching remedial courses at a handful of colleges" (1997, A44). While, at present, the focus of Kaplan and Sylvan is upon remedial programs, it is not difficult to imagine the same approach applied to freshman composition, advanced writing courses, writing courses across the disciplines, the tutoring practices of Writing Centers, and the instruction of faculty members on the use of writing as a pedagogical tool.

Threats of disintermediation—together with the unfamiliarity of much of the technology and the bewildering speed of its development—lead to Tapscott's final theme: discordance. As he says, because of these developments, "unprecedented social issues are beginning to arise, potentially causing massive trauma and conflict" (66). Tapscott singles out traditional education as particularly vulnerable, noting its failure to meet the needs of the economy and predicting that learning will be provided increasingly by the private sector (67). Because learning can take place outside schools and because technology can take over many of the functions of teachers within schools, Tapscott sees teachers facing "a Catch-22 situation—become irrelevant by resisting change or possibly become irrelevant by leading it" (67).

If disintermediation alarms teachers, it is understandably attractive to academic administrators. Simply put, purchasing, maintaining, and updating computer, network, and software systems is expensive, and the cost can be disproportionate to other educational priorities and needs. Thus, it is not surprising that businesses offer attractive replacements or allies in this process of providing educational technology. Businesses generally have more capital to invest in technology and to keep systems current than do most public school systems, community colleges, colleges, and universities. This most important fact is an outgrowth of the two connected major trends that, in conjunction with technology, are currently shaping educational systems—demographics and available funding sources for education.

Demographics play an important role in education through their influence upon funding patterns. In America, the fastest growing segment of the population is individuals over the age of eighty-five. One consequence of this pattern is that a large proportion of the tax burden for education falls to people of retirement age and beyond. Often these individuals have paid taxes to support the schooling of one or two generations and, upon reaching retirement, no longer have the means for or interest in providing further funding for still another generation of students. The tight educational funding in Florida, Arizona, California, and Texas—states with large retirement populations and a high percentage of senior citizens—suggests the coming national trend in educational funding. Whereas education used to be state supported, it is now state assisted and may soon be merely state located. In a related vein, the public's trust in education is down as increased spending on education through the 1950s to the

1980s has not resulted in higher testing scores or in a better educated work force. In fact, scores have declined, and business and professional communities regularly question the quality of the education those entering the work force have received. As a consequence, educational funding generally can no longer depend upon the traditional nexus between the populace and the schools but must look instead to other sources for additional revenues. Ironically, as the need for educational technology increases to prepare each generation for the work force and social systems they will encounter, educational systems are increasingly unable to bear the cost.

In tight budget times, in which each expenditure for education must be examined carefully, it makes perfect sense that the high cost of technology would come under the greatest scrutiny. Thus, we see disintermediation for writing programs and other aspects of education as a strong possibility for the next century. That is why writing program professionals must be aware of this trend in order to shape the trend rather than be shaped by it. If social changes driven by economics and demographics lead to the "outsourcing" of writing programs, writing program professionals should help design the alliances education will create with the business and professional communities. Otherwise, we are only a few steps away from the disintermediation of many educational functions that will be taken over by businesses. Businesses, for example, can design Writing Centers of their own to train employees for the specific writing tasks and software systems they will encounter. Businesses have greater resources to set up and to maintain state-of-the-art Writing Centers than do many state universities struggling to survive with greatly reduced tax revenues. WAC Programs will not be immune to possible disintermediation by businesses in that corporations, knowing what types of training in writing and critical thinking skills their employees will need, can easily set up institutes for teachers and students that will do much of the work of WAC workshops and conferences, perhaps doing so with greater skill and efficiency because of their precisely developed emphasis.

Some academicians might view the scenarios of disintermediation we have described as alarming, but we see heartening possibilities if four important attitudes are embraced. First, we must be aware that the training for future writing program professionals will change and must change and that those of us currently at work in this field must have significant input into the training of our future Ellen Fremmans. The training of writing program professionals has gone through only two cycles in this century. In the earliest days, those drawn to this work generally were trained in traditional literature programs and found their way into Writing Centers or WAC Programs by chance more often than by design. In the second cycle, starting in the mid-1970s when universities began to offer Ph.D.s in rhetoric and composition, writing program professionals could study rhetorical theory and the application of cognitive psychology and composition theory to tutoring practices in the Writing Center and writing pedagogy in WAC Programs. In the next century, a third cycle will begin as people like Ellen Fremman come to writing program administration through different paths than a

Ph.D. in English. Such people will receive training in literacy issues and rhetorical theory as part of their studies in educational technology. In fact, many may receive multiple majors in computer science, neurolinguistics, cognitive psychology, business administration, systems theory, and so forth. Their degrees may represent true interdisciplinarity in assimilating, from many disciplines, the training and perspectives necessary for carrying out the complex demands of teaching writing and critical thinking via electronic literacy. We must give careful consideration to the types of courses, internships, and learning environments that will constitute this new preparation, and we must be active participants in designing new programs and philosophies.

Second, we must begin to direct attention away from the recurring micro-debates that have characterized Writing Center and WAC scholarship and onto the macro-debates that will engage a broader audience from many areas in the social and educational spectrum. Debates on whether Writing Centers are extensions of classroom pedagogy or exist in opposition to the classroom as the central learning structure in education will be meaningless when the concepts of "Writing Center" and "classroom" will themselves be redefined in the next century. We must move toward broader discussions of literacy in a technological age and ground our discussions in the social changes we are encountering now.

Third, we must look at what is actually happening in education and in systems theory in our social institutions and reduce the fear zone surrounding dynamic change so that we can be active participants in the process. We can no longer afford to idealize what used to be or to cling to the past because it is familiar. Instead, we must have a willingness to turn loose of the familiar in order to examine what constitutes value and quality within the new paradigm and the new realities it will create. As James C. Wetherbe argues, we must find the "points of leverage" through which we can have an effect on society and the broadest aspects of the educational process (1995, 12). Although it is uncertain what forms education will take in the next century, it is certain that education will always continue within social systems. Therefore, we must look to those systems so that we can assume roles of leadership in education. While we must be attuned to change, we must also seek continuities from which we can construct new roles and practices.

Fourth, we must be willing to learn from our students. They deal with and live in this emerging world, and their sensibilities will help orient us to the new landscape, the cognitive, affective, and behavioral backgrounds against which perspective and vision will develop. Their views of "text," for example, will necessarily differ from ours, and theirs is the view that will emerge as the leading one. For example, definitions of who "owns" the text are becoming increasingly problematic in the Internet era, and the eventual resolution of those issues will have important ramifications for tutoring and tutor training. From students familiar with the new ways of working with electronic texts, we need to learn to reconceptualize collaboration, for contemporary technologies are opening innovative possibilities that far exceed our current paper-bound practices. In fact, we need to be prepared to reconceptualize far more fundamental concerns about writing itself. Jay Bolter, a professor at Georgia Tech who studies the impact of technology upon language change, is concerned about the difficulties that will arise in teaching writing as computers become increasingly adept at transcribing speech. What will happen to the familiar conventional boundaries between speech and writing when we dictate everything? "The English community is totally unprepared for this," he says bluntly (qtd. in Hamilton and Rhodes 1997, 15). Such a statement constitutes a mandate for writing program professionals to find ways to take action now.

Learning is an action concept. It is not simply having a new idea or insight; instead, learning involves taking effective action (Argyris 1993). Certainly, there are compelling opportunities for us to act upon what we learn from the emerging digital economy, as two recent developments indicate. Since the fall of 1995, a design team commissioned by the Western Governors' Association has been at work on plans for a virtual university that will serve that entire region. The "Goals and Visions" statement for that university explicitly says that it is being developed in response to the constraints of "limited resources and the inflexibility and high costs of traditional educational practices and by outdated institutional and public policies." The new virtual university is committed to "shifting the focus of education to the actual competence of students and away from 'seat time' or other measures of instructional activity." Instead, instructional activity should be "focusing on needs of students and employers rather than instructional providers." That means, among other things, providing "flexible and responsive" delivery of instruction that is not "constrained by the fixed schedules and sequential structure typical of current educational delivery." In fact, this virtual university is identified as a "non-teaching" entity, one "not providing instruction directly, but drawing upon needed capacity whenever it exists, both in colleges and universities, and in the private sector and among individual experts as well" ("Western Governors" 1997). Similar to the Western Governors University plan is the Southern Regional Electronic Campus, an enterprise being organized by the Southern Regional Educational Board, a consortium of schools from a fifteen-state region. Drawing on existing resources at a dozen schools, the new electronic campus is scheduled to "open" in January 1998 (Blumenstyk 1997).

There is much to be gained by working in tandem with new enterprises like these. For many years, Writing Center and WAC practitioners have rightly opposed the standardized mass instruction created by traditional corporate structures. However, the digital economy provides the technical capability to create genuinely individualized instruction, and ventures like Western Governors University and the Southern Regional Electronic Campus demonstrate that society values and seeks innovation that responds to its needs. Because Writing Centers and WAC Programs have a consistent history of developing pedagogical strategies to meet the needs of the students and faculty with whom we work, we may be better positioned than more traditional forms of instruction to adapt to new conditions. Writing programs need to learn from businesses that have succeeded in the new digital economy, like those described by Richard J. Mahoney, former CEO of Monsanto. In "'Reinventing' the University," he notes that corporations learned to form alliances with other companies "to share expertise, cut costs, reduce risk, and increase profits." These partnerships "enabled companies to combine disparate skills and share the ultimate rewards" (1997, B5). As a source of funding and technological resources, private industry may well have much to offer educators; in turn, writing program professionals can offer their knowledge of learning theory, interpersonal skills, collaborative practices, rhetorical theory, cognitive theory, and assessment. This exchange will benefit all involved, particularly students, whose education would then be integrated into the world in which they are actually living. Mahoney's conclusions are just as relevant for writing programs as for corporations: "Redesign need not mean 'gulag' living standards or sacrificing programs that enrich the university experience for students and faculty members. But a university's failure to redesign itself may, by default, make straitened standards a reality" (B5).

While disintermediation seems a threat to what we know now, it may be an invitation for us to transform ourselves as we embrace and actually shape change. In discussing the "empowering nature" of the digital revolution, Nicholas Negroponte, Professor of Media Technology at Massachusetts Institute of Technology, writes, "The harmonizing effect of being digital is already apparent as previously partitioned disciplines and enterprises find themselves collaborating, not competing. . . . The access, the mobility, and the ability to effect change are what will make the future so different from the present" (1995, 230–31). If there is peril in the Digital Economy, there is promise as well.

WORKS CITED

Argyris, Chris. *Knowledge for Action: A Guide to Overcoming Barriers to Organizational Change*. San Francisco: Jossey-Bass, 1993.

Blumenstyk, Goldie. "Southern States Make Plans for Distance-education Program." *The Chronicle of Higher Education* (16 Oct. 1977): n. pag. Online. Internet. 17 Oct. 1997. Available at: http://chronicle.com/che-data/internet.dir/itdata/1997/10/t971016.htm.

Gose, Ben. "Tutoring Companies Take Over Remedial Teaching at Some Colleges." *The Chronicle of Higher Education* (19 Sept. 1997): A44–A45.

Hamilton, Kendall H., and Steve Rhodes. "So I'm Like, 'Who Needs This Grammar Stuff?'" *Newsweek* (20 Oct. 1997): 15.

Harris, Muriel. *Teaching One-to-One: The Writing Conference*. Urbana, IL: NCTE, 1986.

Kelly, Lou. "One-on-One, Iowa City Style: Fifty Years of Individualized Writing Instruction." *The Writing Center Journal* 1.1 (1980): 4–19.

Mahoney, Richard J. "'Reinventing' the University: Object Lessons from Big Business." *The Chronicle of Higher Education* (17 Oct. 1997): B4–B5.

McMaster, Michael D. *The Intelligence Advantage: Organizing for Complexity*. Boston: Butterworth-Heinemann, 1996.

Negroponte, Nicholas. *Being Digital*. New York: Random-Vintage, 1995.

North, Stephen M. "The Idea of a Writing Center." *College English* 46 (1984): 433–446.

Russell, David R. "American Origins of the Writing Across the Curriculum Movement." *Writing, Teaching and Learning Across the Curriculum*, eds. Anne Herrington and Charles Moran. New York: MLA, 1992. 22–42.

Simpson, Jeanne. "Slippery Sylvans Sliding Sleekly into the Writing Center—Or Preparing for Professional Competition." *The Writing Lab Newsletter* 21.1 (1996): 1–4.

Tapscott, Don. *The Digital Economy: Promise and Peril in the Age of Networked Intelligence*. New York: McGraw-Hill, 1996.

———, and Art Caston. *Paradigm Shift: The New Promise of Information Technology*. New York: McGraw-Hill, 1993.

"Western Governors University: Goals and Visions." WGU Home Page. Online. Internet. (17 Oct. 1997). Available at: http://www.westgov.org/smart/vu/vuvision .html.

Wetherbe, James C. "Principles of Cycle Time Reduction: You Can Have Your Cake and Eat It Too." *Cycle Time Research* 1.1 (1995): 1–24.

Young, Jeffrey R. "Rethinking the Role of the Professor in an Age of High-tech Tools." *The Chronicle of Higher Education* (3 Oct. 1997): A26–A28.

Selected Bibliography

Anderson, Chris. *Free/Style: A Direct Approach to Writing.* Boston: Houghton Mifflin, 1992.

Anson, Chris M. "Toward a Multidimensional Model of Writing in the Academic Disciplines." *Writing in Academic Disciplines*, ed. David A. Jolliffe. Norwood, MA: Ablex, 1988. 1–33.

Argyris, Chris. *Knowledge for Action: A Guide to Overcoming Barriers to Organizational Change.* San Francisco: Jossey-Bass, 1993.

Aristotle. *On Rhetoric.* Trans. George A. Kennedy. New York: Oxford, 1991.

Barnett, Robert W. "Redefining Our Existence: An Argument for Short- and Long-term Goals and Objectives." *Writing Center Journal* 17.2 (1997): 123–133.

Barton, Ellen. "Evidentials, Argumentation, and Epistemological Stance." *College English* 55 (1993): 745–769.

Baum, Bruce J. "The Dental Curriculum: What Should Be New in the 21st Century?" *Journal of Public Health Dentistry* 56 (1996): 286–290.

Bazerman, Charles. "From Cultural Criticism to Disciplinary Participation: Living with Powerful Words." In *Writing, Teaching, and Learning in the Disciplines*, eds. Anne Herrington and Charles Moran. New York: MLA, 1992. 61–68.

———. *Shaping Written Knowledge: The Genre and Activity of the Experimental Article in Science.* Madison: University of Wisconsin Press, 1988.

———, and David R. Russell, eds. *Landmarks Essays on Writing Across the Curriculum.* Davis, CA: Hermagoras Press, 1994.

Bean, John. *Engaging Ideas: The Professor's Guide to Integrating Writing, Critical Thinking, and Active Learning in the Classroom.* San Francisco: Jossey-Bass, 1996.

Becher, Tony. *Academic Tribes and Territories: Intellectual Enquiry and the Cultures of Disciplines.* Buckingham, England: The Society for Research into Education & Open University Press, 1993.

Beer, Michael, Russell Eisenstat, and Bert Spector. "Why Change Programs Don't Produce Change." In *Managing Change: Cases and Concepts*, Todd Jick, ed. Homewood, IL: Irwin, 1993. 264–276.

Benson, Thomas W., and Michael H. Prosser. *Readings in Classical Rhetoric.* Davis, CA: Hermagoras Press, 1988.

Bergquist, William H. *The Four Cultures of the Academy.* San Francisco: Jossey-Bass, 1992.

Berkenkotter, Carol, and Thomas N. Huckin. *Genre Knowledge in Disciplinary Communication.* Hillsdale, NJ: Lawrence Erlbaum, 1995.

————, Thomas N. Huckin, and John Ackerman. "Social Context and Socially Constructed Texts." In *Landmark Essays on Writing Across the Curriculum,* eds. Charles Bazerman and David Russell. Davis, CA: Hermagoras Press, 1994. 211–232.

Bizzell, Patricia. "Cognition, Convention and Certainty: What We Need to Know About Writing." *Pre/Text* 3 (1982): 213–243.

————. "What Can We Know, What Must We Do, What May We Hope: Writing Assessment." *College English* 49 (1987): 575–584.

Blair, Catherine Pastore. "Only One of the Voices: Dialogic Writing Across the Curriculum." *College English* 50 (1988): 383–389.

Blumenstyk, Goldie. "Southern States Make Plans for Distance-education Program." *The Chronicle of Higher Education* (16 Oct. 1977): n. pag. Online. Internet. 17 Oct. 1997. Available at: http://chronicle.com/che-data/internet.dir/itdata/1997/10/t971016.htm.

Braddock, R., R. Lloyd-Jones, and L. Schoer. *Research in Written Composition.* Champaign, IL: NCTE, 1963.

Bruffee, Kenneth. "Collaborative Learning and the 'Conversation of Mankind.'" *College English* 46 (1984): 635–652.

————. "Peer Tutoring and the 'Conversation of Mankind.'" *Writing Centers: Theory and Administration.* Ed. Gary A. Olson, Urbana, IL: NCTE, 1984.

Bryant, Don. "The Psychology of Resistance to Change." In *Organizational Behavior: An Experiential Approach,* 5th ed. David A. Kolb, Irwin M. Rubin, and Joyce Osland, ed. Englewood Cliffs, NJ: Prentice Hall, 1991. 193–195.

Bushe, Gervase R., and A. B. (Rami) Shani. *Parallel Learning Structures: Increasing Innovation in Bureaucracies.* New York: Addison, 1991.

Calabrese, Marylyn E. "I Don't Grade Papers Anymore." *English Journal* 71.1 (1982): 28–31.

Carter, Duncan, and Ben McClelland. "WPAs Assess the CCCC's Statement of Principles and Standards," *WPA: Writing Program Administration* 16.1–2 (1992): 71–87.

Childers, Pamela. "A Few Thoughts on Writing Centers, WAC, and Faculty Development." *Radford* [University] *Writes: The Newsletter of Writing Across the Curriculum* (Nov. 1995): 4.

————. "Writing Centers and WAC: Connections for Faculty Growth." Guest Editorial. *Radford* [University] *Writers: The Newsletter of Writing Across the Curriculum* (Apr. 1995): 1+.

————. "WAC and Writing Centers in Secondary Schools: Beyond Institutional Assumptions." Presentation at the National Writing Across the Curriculum Conference, Charleston, SC, Feb. 1997.

————. "Writing Across the Disciplines for Faculty Growth." Presentation at the NAIS annual conference, New York, Feb. 1998.

————. "Writing Center as Center for Faculty Development." Presentation at the National Writing Centers Association National Conference, St. Louis, Sept. 1995.

————, and David Hall. "What Is Safe Sex on the Internet?" *The ACE Newsletter* 10.1 (Summer 1995): 4–6.

———, Eric Hobson, and Joan Mullin. *ARTiculating: Teaching Writing in a Visual Culture*. Portsmouth, NH: Boynton/Cook, 1998.

———, Jud Laughter, Michael Lowry, and Steve Trumpeter. "Developing a Community in a Secondary School Writing Center." In *Writing Centers in Collaboration Pedagogy*, eds. Carol Haviland et al. Emmitsburg, MD: NWCA Press, 1998.

———, and Michael Lowry. "Secondary School Collaborations for Faculty Development." Presentation at the National Writing Across the Curriculum Conference, Charleston, SC, Feb. 1997.

Clark, Irene L. "Collaboration and Ethics in Writing Center Pedagogy." *Writing Center Journal* 9 (1988): 3–12.

———, and David Healy. "Are Writing Centers Ethical?" *WPA: Writing Program Administration* 20 (1996): 32–48.

Coe, Richard M. *Process, Form, and Substance*. 2nd ed. Englewood Cliffs, NJ: Prentice Hall, 1990.

———. "Teaching Genre as Process." In *Learning and Teaching Genre*, eds. Aviva Freedman and Peter Medway. Portsmouth, NH: Boynton/Cook, 1994. 157–169.

Commission to Implement Change in Pharmaceutical Education. "Background Paper II: Entry-level, Curricular Outcomes, Curricular Content and Educational Process." *American Journal of Pharmaceutical Education* 58 (1993): 377–385.

Cooper, Marilyn, and Michael Holzman. *Writing as Social Action*. Portsmouth, NH: Boynton/Cook, 1989.

Crossley, Gay Lynn. Workshop presentation for "Responding to Student Writing: Gearing Comments to Our Teaching Styles, Students, and Course Goals." Richard Straub, Chair. Conference on College Composition and Communication Convention. Phoenix Convention Center. 12 Mar. 1997.

Crowley, Sharon. *Ancient Rhetorics for Contemporary Students*. Boston: Allyn and Bacon, 1994.

Devitt, Amy J. "Generalizing about Genre: New Conceptions of an Old Concept." *College Composition and Communication* 44 (1993): 573–586.

Dickerson, Mary Jane, Toby Fulwiler, and Henry Steffens. "The University of Vermont." *Programs That Work: Models and Methods of Writing Across the Curriculum*, Toby Fulwiler and Art Young, eds. Portsmouth, NH: Boyton/Cook, 1990. 45–63.

Dillon, George. *Contending Rhetorics: Writing in the Academic Disciplines*. Bloomington: Indiana University Press, 1991.

Dinitz, Susan, and Diane Howe. "Writing Centers and Writing Across the Curriculum: An Evolving Partnership." *Writing Center Journal* 10.1 (1989): 45–51.

Duke, Charles R. "The Student-Centered Conference and the Writing Process." *English Journal* 64.9 (1975): 44–47.

Eagleton, Terry. *Literary Theory: An Introduction*. Minneapolis: University of Minnesota Press, 1996.

Ede, Lisa. "On Writing Reading and Reading Writing." In *Encountering Student Texts: Interpretive Issues in Reading Student Writing*, eds. Bruce Lawson, Susan Steer Ryan, and W. Ross Winterowd. Urbana, IL: NCTE, 1989. 147–157.

———. "Writing as a Social Process: A Theoretical Foundation for Writing Centers?" *Writing Center Journal* 9 (1989): 3–13.

Elbow, Peter. *What Is English?* New York: MLA, 1990.

———, and Pat Belanoff. *A Community of Writers*. 2nd ed. New York: McGraw-Hill, 1995.

Faery, Rebecca Blevins. "Teachers *and* Writers: The Faculty Writing Workshop and Writing Across the Curriculum." *WPA: Writing Program Administration* 17.1–2 (1993): 31–42.

Faires, Nora. "What Goes on Behind Closed Classroom Doors?" *UM–Flint WAC Newsletter* 5.1 (1998): 4.

Farrell, Pamela. "Effects of Writing to Learn." Unpublished paper, 1994.

———. *The High School Writing Center: Establishing and Maintaining One.* Urbana, IL: NCTE, 1989.

———. "Writing to Learn Math." Workshop presentation at the Tennessee Association of Independent Schools annual conference. Nashville, Nov. 1992.

———. "A Unique Learning Environment." In *Intersections: Theory-Practice in the Writing Center*, eds. Joan A. Mullin and Ray Wallace. Urbana, IL: NCTE, 1994. 111–119.

———, Anne Gere, and Art Young, eds. *Programs and Practices: Writing Across the Secondary School Curriculum.* Portsmouth, NH: Boynton/Cook, 1994.

———, and Michael Lowry. "Science and Writing: Unexpected Bonuses." *Radford* [University] *Writes: The Newsletter of Writing Across the Curriculum* (Apr. 1994): 2+.

———, and David Perkinson. "Ideas for Writing about Numbers." *Radford* [University] *Writes: The Newsletter of Writing Across the Curriculum* (Dec. 1993): 7.

Farris, Christine. "Giving Religion: Taking Gold: Disciplinary Cultures and the Claims of Writing Across the Curriculum." In *Cultural Studies in the English Classroom*, eds. James Berlin and Michael Vivion. Portsmouth, NH: Boynton/Cook, 1992.

Forsyth, Adrian, and Kenneth Miyata. *Tropical Nature.* New York: Charles Scribner's Sons, 1984.

Foucault, Michel. *The Archeology of Knowledge & the Discourse on Language.* Trans. A. M. Sheridan Smith. New York: Pantheon Books, 1972.

Freedman, Aviva, and Peter Medway, eds. *Learning and Teaching Genre.* Portsmouth, NH: Boynton/Cook, 1994.

Freire, Paulo. *Pedagogy of the Oppressed.* New York: Continuum, 1970.

French, Wendell L., and Cecil H. Bell, Jr., eds. *Organization Development: Behavioral Science Interventions for Organization Improvement.* 4th ed. Englewood Cliffs, NJ: Prentice Hall, 1990.

———, Cecil H. Bell, and Robert A. Zawacki, eds. *Organizational Development and Transformation: Managing Effective Change*, 4th ed. Burr Ridge, IL: Irwin, 1994.

Fulwiler, Toby, and Art Young. "Afterward: The Enemies of Writing Across the Curriculum." In *Programs That Work: Models and Methods for Writing Across the Curriculum*, eds. Toby Fulwiler and Art Young. Portsmouth, NH: Boynton/Cook, 1990. 287–294.

———, and Art Young, eds. *Programs That Work: Models and Methods of Writing Across the Curriculum.* Portsmouth, NH: Boyton/Cook, 1990.

Gabriel, Susan L. "Gender, Reading, and Writing: Assignments, Expectations, and Responses." In *Gender in the Classroom: Power and Pedagogy*, eds. Susan L. Gabriel and Isaiah Smithson. Urbana, IL: University of Illinois Press, 1990. 129–139.

Geertz, Clifford. *Local Knowledge: Further Essays in Interpretive Anthropology.* New York: Basic Books, 1983.

Gere, Anne Ruggles, and Eugene Smith. *Attitudes, Language, and Change.* Urbana, IL: NCTE, 1979.

Gill, Judy. "Another Look at WAC and the Writing Center." *Writing Center Journal* 16.2 (1996): 164–178.

Gillam, Alice M. "Collaborative Learning Theory and Peer Tutoring Practice." In *Intersections: Theory-Practice in the Writing Center*, eds. Joan A. Mullin and Ray Wallace. Urbana, IL: NCTE, 1994. 39–53.

Giltrow, Janet, and Michele Valiquette. "Genres and Knowledge: Students Writing in the Disciplines." In *Learning and Teaching Genre*, eds. Aviva Freedman and Peter Medway. Portsmouth, NH: Boynton/Cook, 1994. 47–62.

Gose, Ben. "Tutoring Companies Take Over Remedial Teaching at Some Colleges." *The Chronicle of Higher Education* (19 Sept. 1997): A44–A45.

Grant, Tripp, Andrew Murphy, and Ben Stafford. "Peer Tutors and Students Work with Assessment." *The Clearinghouse* 71.2 (1997): 103-105.

Greenhalgh, Anne M. "Voice in Response: A Postmodern Reading of Teacher Response." *College Composition and Communication* 43 (1992): 401–410.

Grimm, Nancy. "Rearticulating the Work of the Writing Center." *College Composition and Communication* 47 (1996): 523–548.

Hall, Dennis R. "*Compost*: A Writing Program Newsletter and Its Rationale." *WPA: Writing Program Administration* 17.1–2 (1993): 75–82.

Hamilton, Kendall H., and Steve Rhodes. "So I'm Like, 'Who Needs This Grammar Stuff?'" *Newsweek* (20 Oct. 1997): 15.

Haring-Smith, Tori. "Changing Students' Attitudes: Writing Fellows Programs." In *Writing Across the Curriculum: A Guide to Developing Programs*, eds. Susan H. McLeod and Margot Soven. Newbury Park, CA: Sage, 1992. 175–187.

———, et al., eds. *A Guide to Writing Programs: Writing Centers, Peer Tutoring Programs, and Writing Across the Curriculum.* Glenview, IL: Scott, Foresman, 1984.

Harris, Charles R., Jr. "I Know You Think You Know What I Said." *College English* 37 (1976): 661–662.

Harris, Muriel. "Collaboration Is Not Collaboration Is Not Collaboration: Writing Tutorials vs. Peer-response Groups." *College Composition and Communication* 43 (1992): 369–383.

———. "Talking in the Middle: Why Writers Need Writing Tutors." *College English* 57 (1995): 27–42.

———. *Teaching One-to-One: The Writing Conference.* Urbana, IL: NCTE, 1986.

Harris, Winifred Hall. "Teacher Response to Student Writing: A Study of the Response Patterns of High School English Teachers to Determine the Basis for Teacher Judgment of Student Writing." *Research in the Teaching of English* 11 (1977): 175–185.

Hartwell, Patrick. "A Writing Laboratory Model." In *Basic Writing: Essays for Teachers, Researchers, and Administrators*, eds. Lawrence N. Kasden and Daniel R. Hoeber. Urbana, IL: National Council of Teachers of English, 1980: 63–73.

Hartzog, Carol T. *Composition and the Academy: A Study of Writing Program Administration.* New York: MLA, 1986.

Hawthorne, Nathaniel. "Rappacini's Daughter." *Elements of Literature.* 5th course. Chicago: Holt, Rinehart and Winston, 1992.

Hepler, C. D., and L. M. Strand. "Opportunities and Responsibilities in Pharmaceutical Care." *American Journal of Hospital Pharmacy* 47 (1990): 533–543.

Hillocks, George, Jr. *Research on Written Composition.* Urbana, IL: NCTE, 1986.

Hirsch, E. D. "Remarks on Composition to the Yale English Department." In *The Rhetorical Tradition and Modern Writing*, ed. James J. Murphy. New York: MLA, 1982.

Hobson, Eric H., and Kenneth W. Schafermeyer. "Writing and Critical Thinking: Writing to Learn in Large Classes." *American Journal of Pharmaceutical Education* 58 (1994): 423–427.

Holiday-Goodman, Monica, and Buford T. Lively, eds. *Writing Across the Curriculum in Colleges of Pharmacy: A Sourcebook.* Toledo, OH: The University of Toledo College of Pharmacy and American Association of Colleges of Pharmacy Grant Awards for Pharmacy Schools (GAPS), 1992.

Horney, Karen. *Neuroses and Human Growth: The Struggle Toward Self-realization.* New York: W. W. Norton, 1950.

Hubbuch, Susan M. "'Am I Understanding You Correctly?' Advantages of a Tutor's Ignorance." Pacific Coast Writing Centers Conference, University of Portland, Portland, OR, 2 Nov. 1996.

———. "A Tutor Needs to Know the Subject Matter to Help a Student with a Paper: ___Agree ___Disagree ___Not Sure." *The Writing Center Journal* 8.2 (1988): 23–30.

Hult, Christine, and The Portland Resolution Committee: David Joliffe, Kathleen Kelly, Dana Mead, and Charles Schuster. "The Portland Resolution." *WPA: Writing Program Administration* 16.1–2 (1992): 88–94.

Humphrey, George. Personal Interview. 13 May 1997.

Jick, Todd, ed. *Managing Change: Cases and Concepts.* Homewood, IL: Irwin, 1993.

———. "The Vision Thing (A)." In *Managing Change: Cases and Concepts*, Todd Jick, ed. Homewood, IL: Irwin, 1993. 142–148.

———. "The Vision Thing (B)." In *Managing Change: Cases and Concepts*, Todd Jick, ed. Homewood, IL: Irwin, 1993. 149–151.

Johnston, Scott. "Basic Writers and Peer Tutoring." Dissertation, University of Nevada, Reno, 1996.

Jolliffe, David A., ed. *Advances in Writing Research. Vol. 2. Writing in Academic Disciplines.* Norwood, NJ: Ablex, 1988.

Kaufer, David, and Richard Young. "Writing in the Content Areas: Some Theoretical Complexities." In *Theory Into Practice in the Teaching of Writing: Rethinking the Discipline*, ed. Lee Odell. Carbondale: Southern Illinois University Press, 1993: 71–105.

Kelly, Kathleen. "Writing Across the Curriculum: What the Literature Tells Us." Information Analysis, 1985, ERIC ED274975.

Kelly, Lou. "One-on-One, Iowa City Style: Fifty Years of Individualized Writing Instruction." *The Writing Center Journal* 1.1 (1980): 4–19.

Kiedaisch, Jean, and Sue Dinitz. "Look Back and Say 'So What': The Limitations of the Generalist Tutor." *Writing Center Journal* 14.1 (1993): 63–74.

Kiniry, Malcolm, Ellen Strenski, and Mike Rose. "UCLA." In *Programs That Work: Models and Methods for Writing Across the Curriculum*, eds. Toby Fulwiler and Art Young. Portsmouth, NH: Boynton/Cook, 1990. 29–43.

Kinkead, Joyce, and Jeanette Harris, eds. *Writing Centers in Context: Twelve Case Studies.* Urbana, IL: NCTE, 1993.

Kipling, Kim J., and Richard J. Murphy, Jr. *Symbiosis: Writing and an Academic Culture.* Portsmouth, NH: Boyton/Cook, 1992.

Kline, Charles R., Jr. "I Know You Think You Know What I Said." *College English* 37 (1976): 661–662.

Knoblauch, C. H., and Lil Brannon. *Rhetorical Traditions and the Teaching of Writing.* Portsmouth, NH: Boynton/Cook, 1984.

Kolb, David A., Joyce Osland, and Irwin M. Rubin, eds. *The Organizational Behavior Reader.* Englewood Cliffs, NJ: Prentice Hall, 1995.

———, Irwin M. Rubin, and Joyce Osland, eds. *Organizational Behavior: An Experiential Approach.* 5th ed. Englewood Cliffs, NJ: Prentice Hall, 1991.

Kuhn, Matthew, and Karen Vaught-Alexander. "A Context for Writing in the Engineering Curriculum." *The ASCE Journal of Professional and Educational Issues in Engineering Curriculum* 120.4 (1994): 392–400.

Kuriloff, Peshe C. "What Discourses Have in Common: Teaching the Transaction Between Writer and Reader." *College Composition and Communication* 47 (1996): 485–501.

Langer, Judith A. "Speaking of Knowing: Conceptions of Understanding in Academic Disciplines." In *Writing, Teaching and Learning in the Disciplines,* eds. Anne Herrington and Charles Moran. New York: MLA, 1992. 69–85.

———., and Arthur N. Applebee. *How Writing Shapes Thinking: A Study of Teaching and Learning.* Urbana, IL: NCTE, 1987.

LaRochelle, Peter, and Pamela Farrell-Childers. "Honors Biology Writing Projects." In *Programs and Practices: Writing Across the Secondary School Curriculum,* eds. Pamela Farrell-Childers, Anne Gere, and Art Young. Portsmouth, NH: Boynton/Cook, 1994. 205–207.

———, Catherine Neuhardt-Minor, and David Perkinson. "Writing Across the Curriculum." Presentation at the Virginia Association of Teachers of English annual conference, Roanoke, Oct. 1993.

Laughter, Jud, and Pamela Childers. "Collaboration and College Application Essays: Two Perspectives." *The Writing Lab Newsletter* (1996): 4–5.

Lawson, Bruce, and Susan Steer Ryan. "Introduction: Interpretive Issues in Student Writing." In *Encountering Student Texts: Interpretive Issues in Reading Student Writing,* eds. Bruce Lawson, Susan Steer Ryan, and W. Ross Winterowd. Urbana, IL: NCTE, 1989. vii–xvii.

Leahy, Richard. "Rhetorical Analysis in Writing Assistant Training." *The Writing Lab Newsletter* 20 (1995): 1–4.

LeCourt, Donna. "WAC as Critical Pedagogy: The Third Stage?" *JAC: A Journal of Composition Theory* 16 (1996): 389–435.

Lerner, Neal. "Counting Beans and Making Beans Count." *The Writing Lab Newsletter* 22.1 (1997): 1.

Lindemann, Erika. *A Rhetoric for Writing Teachers.* 3rd ed. New York: Oxford, 1995.

Lunsford, Andrea. "Collaboration, Control, and the Idea of a Writing Center." In *The St. Martin's Sourcebook for Writing Tutors,* eds. Christina Murphy and Steve Sherwood. New York: St. Martin's Press, 1995. 36–42.

MacDonald, Susan Peck. "Problem Definition in Academic Writing." *College English* 49 (1987): 315–331.

Maddux, Michael S., Eric H. Hobson, Dimitra Vrahnos, Sheldon Holstad, Mary T. Roth, Thomas D. Zlatic. "Developing a Curriculum for Tomorrow's Pharmacy Practitioners." *Pharmguide to Hospital Medicine* 9.1 (1996): 1–4, 9–12.

Mahoney, Richard J. "'Reinventing' the University: Object Lessons from Big Business." *The Chronicle of Higher Education* (17 Oct. 1997): B4–B5.

Matsen, Patricia P., Philip Rollinson, and Marion Sousa. *Readings from Classical Rhetoric.* Carbondale: Southern Illinois University Press, 1990.

Maurer, Rick. *Beyond the Wall of Resistance: Unconventional Strategies That Build Support for Change.* Austin, TX: Bard Press, 1997.

May, Cissy. "Writing and Learning in Chemistry." In *Programs and Practices: Writing Across the Secondary School Curriculum*, eds. Pamela Farrell-Childers, Anne Gere, and Art Young. Portsmouth, NH: Boynton/Cook, 1994. 198–200.

McLeod, Susan. "The Foreigner: WAC Directors as Agents of Change." In *Resituating Writing*, eds. Joseph Jangelo and Kristen Hansen. Portsmouth, NH: Boynton, 1995: 108–116.

————, ed. *Strengthening Programs for Writing Across the Curriculum.* San Francisco: Jossey-Bass, 1988.

————, and Margot Soven, eds. *Writing Across the Curriculum: A Guide to Developing Programs.* Newbury Park, CA: Sage, 1992.

McMaster, Michael D. *The Intelligence Advantage: Organizing for Complexity.* Boston: Butterworth-Heinemann, 1996.

McQueeney, Pat. "Proposing a Writing Center: Experts' Advice." *Writing Lab Newsletter*, forthcoming.

Mellon, John C. "Round Two of the National Writing Assessment—Interpreting the Apparent Decline of Writing Ability: A Review." *Research in the Teaching of English* 10.1 (1976): 66–74.

Miller, Susan. "The Student's Reader Is Always a Fiction." *Journal of Advanced Composition* 5 (1984): 15–29.

Miraglia, Erica, and Susan McLeod. "Whither WAC? Interpreting the Stories/Histories of Enduring WAC Programs." *WPA: Writing Program Administration* 20 (1997): 46–65.

Moody, Stephen. "Writing in Computer Science." *Radford* [University] *Writes: The Newsletter of Writing Across the Curriculum* (Nov. 1995): 7.

Mortimer, K. P., A. W. Austin, J. H. Blake, H. R. Bowen, Z. F. Gamson, H. L. Hodgkinson, and B. Lee. "Text of a New Report on Excellence in Undergraduate Education." *The Chronicle of Higher Education.* (24 Oct. 1984): 35–39.

Mullin, Joan A., and Ray Wallace, eds. *Intersections: Theory-Practice in the Writing Center.* Urbana, IL: NCTE, 1994.

Murray, Heather. "Close Reading, Closed Writing." *College English* 53 (1991): 195–208.

Myers, Greg. *Writing Biology: Texts in the Social Construction of Scientific Knowledge.* Madison: University of Wisconsin Press, 1990.

Negroponte, Nicholas. *Being Digital.* New York: Random-Vintage, 1995.

Nelson, John, Allan Megill, and Donald McCloskey. "Rhetoric of Inquiry." In *The Rhetoric of the Human Sciences: Language and Argument in Scholarship and Public Affairs*, eds. John Nelson, Allan Megill, and Donald McCloskey. Madison: University of Wisconsin Press, 1987. 3–18.

Neuhardt-Minor, Catherine. "Words and Images." In *Programs and Practices: Writing Across the Secondary School Curriculum*, eds. Pamela Farrell-Childers, Anne Gere, and Art Young. Portsmouth, NH: Boynton/Cook, 1994. 211–213.

Nickel, Lance. "Writing and Pre-calculus." In *Programs and Practices: Writing Across the Secondary School Curriculum*, eds. Pamela Farrell-Childers, Anne Gere, and Art Young. Portsmouth, NH: Boynton/Cook, 1994. 200–204.

North, Stephen. "The Idea of a Writing Center." *College English* 46 (1984): 433–446.

————. "Revisiting 'The Idea of a Writing Center'" *Writing Center Journal* 15.1 (1994): 7–19.

Odell, Lee. "Context-specific Ways of Knowing and the Evaluation of Writing." In *Writing, Teaching, and Learning in the Disciplines*, eds. Anne Herrington and Charles Moran. New York: MLA, 1992. 86–98.

———, and Charles R. Cooper. "Procedures for Evaluating Writing: Assumptions and Needed Research." *College English* 42 (1980): 35–43.

Ohmann, Richard. *English in America: A Radical View of the Profession.* New York: Oxford University Press, 1979.

Olsen, Turee. "Grading Alternatives." *English Journal* 64 (1975): 106–108.

Olson, Gary A., ed. *Writing Centers: Theory and Administration.* Urbana, IL: NCTE, 1984.

Oshry, Barry. "Converting Middle Powerlessness to Middle Power: A Systems Approach." In *The Organizational Behavior Reader*, eds. David A. Kolb, Joyce Osland, and Irwin M. Rubin. Englewood Cliffs, NJ: Prentice Hall, 1995. 401–412.

Parker, William Riley. "Where Do English Departments Come From?" *College English* (1967): 339–351.

Parkhurst, Christine. "A Writing Proficiency Examination for Pharmacy Students." *American Journal of Pharmacy Education* 61 (1997): 163–166.

Pemberton, Michael A. "Rethinking the WAC/Writing Center Connection." *Writing Center Journal* 15.2 (1995): 116–133.

Perkinson, David. "Writing in Math or Math in Writing?" In *Programs and Practices: Writing Across the Secondary School Curriculum*, eds. Pamela Farrell-Childers, Anne Gere, and Art Young. Portsmouth, NH: Boynton/Cook, 1994. 207–210.

Pew Health Professions Commission. "Critical Challenges: Revitalizing the Health Professions for the Twenty-first Century." The Third Report of the Pew Health Professions Commission. San Francisco: UCSF Center for the Health Professions, 1995.

Pitts, Mary Ellen, David Sigsbee, and Bruce Speck. "The Vital Role of Writing Across the Curriculum Programs in Faculty Development." *Perspectives* 26.1 (1996): 53–80.

Podis, Leonard A., and Joanne M. Podis. "Improving Our Responses to Student Writing: A Process-oriented Approach." *Rhetoric Review* 5 (1986): 90–98.

Polanski, Virginia R. "We Are Autonomous: An Argument for a Separate Writing Department." 1990 WPA Conference, 26–28 July 1990.

Prosser, Theresa R., John M. Burke, and Eric H. Hobson. "Teaching Pharmacy Students to Write in the Medical Record." *American Journal of Pharmaceutical Education* 61 (1997): 136–140.

Purves, Alan C. "Reflections on Research and Assessment in Written Composition." *Research in the Teaching of English* 26.1 (1992): 108–122.

———, and Gail Hawisher. "Writers, Judges, and the Text Models." In *Developing Discourse Patterns in Adolescence and Adulthood*, eds. Richard Beach and Susan Hynds. Norwood, NJ: Ablex, 1990. 183–199.

Quellmalz, Edys S. "Toward Successful Large-Scale Writing Assessment: Where Are We Now? Where Do We Go From Here?" *Educational Measurement: Issues and Practice* 3.1 (1984): 29–32, 35.

———, Frank J. Capell, and Chih-Ping Chou. "Effects of Discourse and Response Mode on the Measurement of Writing Competence." *Journal of Educational Measurement* 19.4 (1982): 241–258.

Raimes, Ann. *Keys for Writers.* Boston: Houghton Mifflin, 1996.

Reiff, John D., and James E. Middleton. "A Model for Designing and Revising Assignments." In *Fforum*, ed. Patricia L. Stock. Montclair, NJ: Boynton/Cook, 1983. 263–268.

Reynolds, John F. "Preface to the Second Edition." John F. Reynolds, David C. Mair, and Pamela C. Fischer. *Writing and Reading Mental Health Records*. 2nd ed. Mahwah, NJ: Lawrence Erlbaum, 1995. xi–xiii.

———, David C. Mair, and Pamela C. Fischer. *Writing and Reading Mental Health Records*. 2nd ed. Mahwah, NJ: Lawrence Erlbaum, 1995.

———, ed. *Rhetorical Memory and Delivery: Classical Concepts for Contemporary Composition and Communication*. Hillsdale, NJ: Lawrence Erlbaum, 1993.

Rider, Janine. *The Writer's Book of Memory*. Hillsdale, NJ: Lawrence Erlbaum, 1995.

Ronald, Kate. "Style: The Hidden Agenda in Composition Classes or One Reader's Confession." In *The Subject Is Writing*, ed. Wendy Bishop. Portsmouth, NH: Boynton/Cook, 1993. 53–68.

Rorty, Richard. *Philosophy and the Mirror of Nature*. Princeton: Princeton University Press, 1979.

Rose, Mike. "The Language of Exclusion: Writing Instruction at the University." *College English* 47 (1985): 341–359.

Rose, Mike. *Lives on the Boundary*. New York: Free Press, 1989.

Russell, David R. "American Origins of the Writing Across the Curriculum Movement." In *Writing, Teaching, and Learning in the Disciplines*, eds. Anne Herrington and Charles Moran. New York: MLA, 1992. 22–42.

———. "The Triumph of Specialization." *Writing in the Academic Disciplines, 1870–1990*. Carbondale: Southern Illinois University Press, 1991.

———. "Writing Across the Curriculum in Historical Perspective: Toward a Social Interpretation." *College English* 52 (1990): 52–73.

———. *Writing in the Academic Disciplines, 1870–1990, A Curricular History*. Carbondale, IL: Southern Illinois University Press, 1991.

Ruth, Leo, and Sandra Murphy. "Designing Topics for Writing Assessment: Problems of Meaning." *College Composition and Communication* 35 (1984): 410–422.

Schafermeyer, Kenneth W. "Managed Prescription Drug Programs." In *Managed Care Contracting: A Guide for Health Care Professionals*, ed. Wendy Knight. Gaithersburg, MD: Aspen, 1997. 229–242.

Schwegler, Robert A. "The Politics of Reading Student Papers." In *The Politics of Writing Instruction: Postsecondary*, eds. Richard Bullock and John Trimbur. Portsmouth, NH: Heinemann, 1991. 203–205.

Senge, Peter. "The Leader's New Work: Building Learning Organizations." In *Managing Change: Cases and Concepts*, Todd Jick, ed. Homewood, IL: Irwin, 1993. 440–463.

Shamoon, Linda K., and Deborah H. Burns. "A Critique of Peer Tutoring," *Writing Center Journal* 15 (1995): 134–151.

Sigsbee, David L., Bruce W. Speck, and Bruce Maylath, eds. *Approaches to Teaching Non-native English Speakers Across the Curriculum*. No. 70, *New Directions for Teaching and Learning*. San Francisco: Jossey-Bass, 1997.

Simpson, Jeanne. "Slippery Sylvans Sliding Sleekly into the Writing Center—Or Preparing for Professional Competition." *The Writing Lab Newsletter* 21.1 (1996): 1–4.

Slamecka, N. J., and P. Graf. "The Generation Effect: Delineation of a Phenomenon." *Journal of Experimental Psychology, Human Learning and Memory* 4 (1978): 592–604.

Smith, Louise Z. "Independence and Collaboration; Why We Should Decentralize Writing Centers." *Writing Center Journal* 7.1 (1986): 3–10.

———. "Why English Departments Should 'House' Writing Across the Curriculum." *College English* 50 (1988): 390–395.

———. "Opinion: Why English Departments Should 'House' Writing Across the Curriculum." *College English* 50 (1988): 390–394.

Smith, Steve, Brit Begley, and Leslea Goodwyn. "'What Do You Mean You're Not an English Major?': Tutors Across the Curriculum Confront Quibbling Concerns over Credentials." Pacific Coast Writing Centers Conference, University of Portland, Portland, OR, 2 Nov. 1996.

Soliday, Mary. "Shifting Roles in Classroom Tutoring: Cultivating the Art of Boundary Crossing." *Writing Center Journal* 16.1 (1995): 59–73.

Sommers, Nancy. "Responding to Student Writing." *College Composition and Communication* 33 (1982): 148–156.

Soven, Margot. "Curriculum-based Peer Tutoring Programs: A Survey." *WPA: Writing Program Administration* 17.1–2 (1993): 58–74.

Straub, Richard. "The Concept of Control in Teacher Response: Defining the Varieties of 'Directive' and 'Facilitative' Commentary." *College Composition and Communication* 47 (1996): 223–251.

———, and Ronald Lunsford. *Twelve Readers Reading.* Cresskill, NJ: Hampton, 1995.

Swales, John. *Genre Analysis.* Cambridge, MA: Cambridge University Press, 1990.

Swilky, Jody. "Reconsidering Faculty Resistance to Writing Reform." *WPA: Writing Program Administration* 16.1–2 (1992): 50–60.

Tapscott, Don. *The Digital Economy: Promise and Peril in the Age of Networked Intelligence.* New York: McGraw-Hill, 1996.

———, and Art Caston. *Paradigm Shift: The New Promise of Information Technology.* New York: McGraw-Hill, 1993.

Throop, David P., and Daphne A. Jameson. "Behavioral Grading: An Approach Worth Trying." *The ABCA Bulletin* 39.3 (1976): 3–5.

Trimbur, John. "Peer Tutoring: A Contradiction in Terms." *Writing Center Journal* 7.2 (1987): 21–28.

Vaught-Alexander, Karen. "Integrating Writing into the Curriculum and the Academy: Organizational Change, Campus Politics, and the WPA." Paper presented at 1994 WPA-ADE Conference, University of Mississippi, Oxford, MS, 28–30 July 1994.

———. "'The New Kid at School' : The Challenges of the Wyoming Resolution for a New WPA in a New WAC Program." Paper presented at 1990 WPA Conference, Portland State University, Portland, OR, 26–28 July 1990.

———. *A Practical Guide to Course Portfolios: Writing, Thinking, Learning Across the Curriculum.* Fairfield, NJ: Pencil Point Press, 1997.

———. "Using the Power and Politics of a Small University to Empower a WAC Program." Paper presented at 1991 WPA Conference, Saratoga Springs, NY, 13–16 June 1991.

———. "Why Not Let Faculty Write Across the Curriculum?" Paper presented at 1992 WPA Conference, University of Denver, Breckenridge, CO, 23–25 July 1992.

———, Travis Campbell, Jean Mulcahy, and Magdalena Visan. "'How Can I Help Your Students? May I Have a Copy of Your Writing Assignment?': Writing Assistants from the Disciplines Resituate Our Writing Center for Clients, Faculty, and Programs." Pacific Coast Writing Centers Conference, University of Portland, Portland, OR, 2 Nov. 1996.

Vygotsky, L. S. *Mind in Society*, eds. Michael Cole et al. Cambridge: Harvard University Press, 1979.

Waldo, Mark L. "Inquiry as a Non-Invasive Approach to Cross-curricular Writing Consultancy." *Language and Learning Across the Disciplines* 1.3 (1996): 7–19.

———. "The Last Best Place for Writing Across the Curriculum: The Writing Center." *WPA: Writing Program Administration* 16.3 (1993): 15–27.

———, Jacob Blumner, and Mary Webb. "Writing Centers and Writing Assessment: A Discipline-based Approach." In *Writing Center Perspectives*, eds. Byron L. Stay, Christina Murphy, and Eric H. Hobson. Emmitsburgh, MD: NWCA Press, 1995. 38–47.

Wallace, Ray. "The Writing Center's Role in the Writing Across the Curriculum Program: Theory and Practice." *Writing Center Journal* 8.2 (1988): 3–10.

Walvoord, Barbara E. *Helping Students Write Well: A Guide for Teachers in All Disciplines.* 2nd ed. New York: MLA, 1986.

———. "The Future of WAC." *College English* 58 (1996): 58–79.

Welch, Kathleen. *The Contemporary Reception of Classical Rhetoric: Appropriations of Ancient Discourse.* Hillsdale, NJ: Lawrence Erlbaum, 1990.

"Western Governors University: Goals and Visions." WGU Home Page. Online. Internet. (17 Oct. 1997). Available at: http://www.westgov.org/smart/vu/vuvision.html.

Wetherbe, James C. "Principles of Cycle Time Reduction: You Can Have Your Cake and Eat It Too." *Cycle Time Research* 1.1 (1995): 1–24.

White, Edward M. "The Damage of Innovations Set Adrift: Change for the Worst." *American Association for Higher Education Journal* 43.3 (1990): 3–5.

———. "Use It or Lost It: Power and the WPA." *WPA: Writing Program Administration* 15.1–2 (1991): 3–12.

Williams, Joseph, and Gregory G. Colomb. "The Case for Explicit Teaching: Why What You Don't Know Won't Help You." *Research in the Teaching of English* 27 (1993): 252–264.

Young, Art, and Toby Fulwiler, eds. *Writing Across the Disciplines: Research into Practice.* Upper Montclair, NJ: Boyton/Cook, 1986.

Young, Jeffrey R. "Rethinking the Role of the Professor in an Age of High-tech Tools." *The Chronicle of Higher Education* (3 Oct. 1997): A26–A28.

Index

Topoi, 76–77
Training: future trends, 195–96; WAC
   center personnel, 111–12; writing
   fellows, 74–81
Transcience, myth of, 13–16, 20–23
TRIAC method of draft development, 77
Trimbur, John, 40
Trumpeter, Steve, 181
Tutors: graduate students as, 145, 151;
   peers as, 40–41; relationships with
   faculty, 49–56; services offered by,
   18–19. *See also* Writing fellows
Twenty questions, 76–77

Valiquette, Michele, 149
Vaught-Alexander, Karen, 119–40
Virtualization: of universities, 197; of
   Writing Centers, 191
Visibility: outreach activities, 4–6, 10,
   115, 130, 164; perceptions of Writing
   Center, 94–95
Visual arts, 179
Visual delivery, 80–81
Voice, 78–79
Vrahnos, Dimitra, 156, 158
Vygotsky, L. S., 18, 37

WAC programs. *See* Writing Across the
   Curriculum programs
Waldo, Mark L.: 59–69; on colonization,
   41; housing the WAC, 1, 27, 89; on
   impact of WAC workshops, 13; on
   WAC/Writing Center relationship, 7;
   on writing and learning, 2
Wallace, Ray, 121
Walvoord, Barbara E., 7, 91, 92, 117
Watterson, Nancy, 112
Webb, Mary, 43
Welch, Kathleen, 75
Western Governors' Association, 197
Wetherbe, James C., 196
White, Edward, 133
WID. *See* Writing in the Disciplines
Williams, Joseph, 150
Workshops, 17, 19–24, 74, 100; for
   requested topics, 130
World Wide Web, 99, 142, 145–49, 184
Writing: collaborative, 181; as learning
   tool, 2, 14–15, 22; outsourcing, 193–
   94
Writing Across the Curriculum programs:
   activities, 10, 162, 164–67;

characteristics, 67, 91–92, 106–7, 108,
   142, 160–61; colonialism, 46–48;
   compromise, 67–68; directors'
   responsibilities, 53, 54–55, 59–69; and
   discipline-specific language, 41, 109–
   10, 142–43, 149; distinguished from
   Writing Centers, 17; future trends,
   187–99, 198; genre focus in, 149, 151;
   goals, 163; ownership, 1, 17, 27, 46,
   48, 59, 66, 107; in pharmacy schools,
   159–67; relationship with Writing
   Center, 9–11, 20–27, 90–91, 116–17;
   as resource center, 113–14; staffing,
   112. *See also* Training; Visibility
Writing assistants. *See* Writing fellows
Writing Centers: as ambassador for WAC,
   16–17, 19–29; assistant to Director's
   role, 183; as de facto WAC center, 89–
   103, 109–17; and discipline-specific
   language, 39–43, 67 (*see also* Writing
   in the Disciplines); future trends, 187–
   99; operating principles, 107–8;
   perceptions of, 94–95; priorities, 93–
   94; relationship with WAC program,
   7–9, 11, 20–27, 90–91, 106; in
   secondary school, 177–86; working
   with faculty members, 24–26, 85–86.
   See also Online services;
   Virtualization; Writing fellows
Writing Emphasis courses, 161–62
Writing environment, 1–2
Writing fellows: assumptions of, 83–84;
   misconceptions about, 82–83; selection
   process, 130; training, 74–81
Writing-intensive courses, 2–3
Writing in the Disciplines (WID), 45, 47,
   71

Young, Art, 121, 143, 177
Young, Jeffrey R., 188–89, 192
Young, Richard, 46, 48–49, 56, 100

Zawacki, Robert A., 122
Zlatic, Thomas D., 156, 158

About the Editors and Contributors

ROBERT W. BARNETT is Assistant Professor of Composition and Rhetoric at the University of Michigan–Flint. He also directs the University Writing Center and co-directs the Writing Across the Curriculum Program. He currently serves as Chair of the Michigan Writing Center Association. Barnett has published articles in such journals as *The Writing Center Journal, The Writing Lab Newsletter, The Language Arts Journal of Michigan,* and *Exercise Exchange: A Journal for Writing Teachers.*

JACOB S BLUMNER is Assistant Professor of Composition and Rhetoric and co-director of the Writing Across the Curriculum Program at the University of Michigan–Flint. He serves as vice-president of the ECWCA Executive Board and publishes work on Writing Centers and WAC. His work has appeared in *Writing Center Perspectives* and *Alternatives to Grading Student Writing.*

PAMELA B. CHILDERS is Caldwell Chair of Composition at The McCallie School, where she directs the Writing Center and the WAC Program. She previously taught English and created a WAC-based Writing Center in Red Bank Regional High School (NJ). Past president of NWCA, she has published numerous professional articles and chapters, as well as *ARTiculating: Teaching Writing in a Visual World* (with Eric Hobson and Joan Mullin), *Programs and Practices: Writing Across the Secondary Curriculum* (with Anne Ruggles Gere and Art Young), and the award-winning *The High School Writing Center: Establishing and Maintaining One* (NCTE).

IRENE L. CLARK is Co-director of the Writing Program and Director of the Writing Center at the University of Southern California. Her publications include articles in *The Writing Center Journal, The Journal of Basic Writing, Teaching English in the Two Year College, College Composition and Communi-*

cation, and the *Writing Lab Newsletter*. Her book, *Writing in the Center*: *Teaching in a Writing Center Setting* (1985, 1992, 1998), received an award from the National Writing Centers Association (1987) as did her article, "Collaboration and Ethics in Writing Center Pedagogy" (1989). Dr. Clark's textbooks include *Taking a Stand* (1992, 1996), *Writing About Diversity* (1994, 1997), and *The Genre of Argument* (1998).

SHERRY GREEN is a graduate student in the M. A. in English Composition program at California State University, San Bernardino, where she has been a Writing Center tutor and teaching assistant. She also teaches part time at Chaffey Community College, Fontana, CA.

M. TODD HARPER is finishing a dissertation critiquing the role of English Studies in the Writing Across the Curriculum movement at the University of Louisville. In fall 1998, he will begin an appointment as Assistant Professor of English at Kennesaw State University.

MURIEL HARRIS, Professor of English and Director of the Writing Lab at Purdue University, edits the *Writing Lab Newsletter* and authored *The Prentice Hall Reference Guide to Grammar and Usage* (now in the 3rd edition) plus numerous book chapters and journal articles on Writing Center theory, pedagogy, and administration. She also coordinates the Purdue University OWL (Online Writing Lab): http://owl.english.purdue.edu. Her current research focuses on studying the effects of Writing Center tutorials, doing institutional research as part of Writing Center administration, and analyzing metaphors for Writing Centers.

CAROL PETERSON HAVILAND is Associate Professor of English, Writing Center Director, and Writing Across the Curriculum Co-director at California State University, San Bernardino. She teaches basic writing and graduate courses in rhetoric and composition and is particularly interested in collaboration, intellectual property, feminism, and pedagogy. She recently has co-edited *Weaving Knowledge Together: Writing Centers and Collaboration* as well as several book chapters on Writing Centers, intellectual property, and ethnography.

ERIC HOBSON is Assistant Professor of English at Eastern Illinois University. A long-standing member of the NWCA board of directors, he writes extensively about Writing Centers and consults with colleges of pharmacy and other health care disciplines about developing Writing Centers within medical education. His books include *ARTiculating: Teaching Writing in a Visual World* with Pamela Childers and Joan Mullin (1998), *Wiring the Writing Center* (1998), *Writing Center Perspectives* with Christina Murphy and Byron Stay (1995), and *Reading and Writing in High Schools* with R. Barid Shuman (1990).

SCOTT JOHNSTON is an Assistant Professor of English at the State University of New York at Fredonia where he teaches undergraduate and graduate courses in Secondary English Education and writing. He is the former director of the Writing Center at the University of Memphis.

PESHE C. KURILOFF, formerly Director of Writing Across the University, is currently Director of the Mello Project on Collaborative Writing Groups and Adjunct Associate Professor of English at the University of Pennsylvania. She is the author of *Rethinking Writing* (1989) and a number of articles and book chapters on issues related to discourse conventions and the implementation of Writing Across the Curriculum. She also does freelance writing and communications consulting.

JOE LAW is Coordinator of Writing Across the Curriculum and Associate Professor of English at Wright State University (Dayton). His publications include work on WAC, Writing Centers, writing pedagogy, Victorian literature, and connections among literature and the fine arts. With Christina Murphy, he edited *Landmark Essays on Writing Centers* (1995); with Christina Murphy and Steve Sherwood, he was one of the compilers of *Writing Centers: An Annotated Bibliography* (Greenwood, 1996).

RICHARD LEAHY is Professor of English and Director of the Writing Center and Writing in the Disciplines at Boise State University. He is managing editor and chief writer of *Word Works*, a series of publications on Writing in the Disciplines distributed to Boise State faculty and posted on the World Wide Web at http://www.idbsu.edu/wcenter/.

NEAL LERNER is Assistant Professor of English and Writing Programs Coordinator at the Massachusetts College of Pharmacy and Allied Health Sciences. He is the current treasurer of the National Writing Centers Association and is on the Steering Committee of the Northeast Writing Centers Association. His research interests include the history, theory, and pedagogy of Writing Center work.

MARIA MADRUGA is an English Instructor and Director of the Writing Center at Shasta Community College in northern California. She is the incoming president of the Northern California Writing Center Association, and she serves as a member of the Network for Professional Growth in Redding, California.

CHRISTINA MURPHY is Professor of English and Chair of the department at the University of Memphis. Dr. Murphy has published books on rhetorical theory and composition studies with St. Martin's, Greenwood, Hermagoras, Prentice Hall, and NWCA Press and has won the 1996 distinguished scholarship award from the National Writing Centers Association *Writing Centers: An Annotated Bibliography* (Greenwood, 1996), which she co-compiled with Joe Law and Steve Sherwood. During her career, Dr. Murphy has directed Writing Centers and writing programs and has worked extensively with educational technology, and her current work focuses upon the influence of technology on the changing shape of writing programs in the twenty-first century.

LOIS M. ROSEN is Professor of English at the University of Michigan–Flint where she is Director of the Writing Program and Co-director of the Writing Across the Curriculum Program with Robert Barnett. She teaches courses in writing, women and literature, and English education methods. Formerly Director of the Writing Center at University of Michigan–Flint and of the Flint Area Writing Project, she continues to give workshops on teaching writing and Writing Across the Curriculum for local schools and districts. She has published articles in *English Journal, Language Arts Journal of Michigan, The English Quarterly*, and others. Her reading methods text, *Multiple Voices, Multiple Texts*, co-authored with Reade Dornan and Marilyn Wilson, presents a psycholinguistic, whole language approach to secondary reading in the content areas and includes a chapter on theory and practice of writing-to-learn in all disciplines.

BARBARA KIME SHIELDS is a graduate student in the M. A. in English Composition program at California State University, San Bernardino, where she also tutors in the Writing Center and has been a teaching assistant. She has presented her work at several WAC and WC conferences as well as at the Conference on College Composition and Communication.

BRUCE W. SPECK is Professor of English and Acting Director of the Center for Academic Excellence at the University of Memphis, Memphis, Tennessee. He is also the Coordinator of the Writing Across the Curriculum Program.

KAREN VAUGHT-ALEXANDER is an Associate Professor of English and Director of the Integrated Writing Program and the University's Integrated Writing Program. Her work in cross-disciplinary Writing Center development and administration spans public university to high school to community college to private university settings. Her recent work in organizational change and culture has been instrumental for creating program innovation and understanding program stalemates. She teaches linguistics, Anglo-Saxon literature, and various writing and writing theory courses, in addition to coordinating freshman and ESL writing programs and providing faculty development workshops.

MARK L. WALDO is Writing Center Director and English Professor at the University of Nevada, Reno. He has directed Writing Centers with WAC Programs since 1983, first at Montana State University and then at UNR. His research interests include the relationship between Writing Centers and WAC, writing assessment, and Romantic rhetoric. His most recent publications have appeared in the *Journal of Criminal Justice Education* and *Language and Learning Across the Disciplines*.